What Can I Do Now?

Animal Careers

Books in the
What Can I Do Now? Series

What Can I Do Now?

Animal Careers

Ferguson Publishing
An imprint of Infobase Publishing

What Can I Do Now? Animal Careers

Copyright © 2010 by Infobase Publishing

Ferguson
An imprint of Infobase Publishing
132 West 31st Street
New York NY 10001

Library of Congress Cataloging-in-Publication Data

What can I do now? Animal careers. — 1st ed.
   p. cm. — (What can I do now?)
 Includes bibliographical references and index.
 ISBN-13: 978-0-8160-8075-5 (hardcover : alk. paper)
 ISBN-10: 0-8160-8075-5 (hardcover : alk. paper) 1. Animal specialists—Vocational guidance—United States. 2. Animal culture—Vocational guidance—United States. I. Ferguson Publishing. II. Title: Animal careers.
 SF80.W53 2010
 636.0023--dc22
         2009033932

Ferguson books are available at special discounts when purchased in bulk quantities for businesses, associations, institutions, or sales promotions. Please call our Special Sales Department in New York at (212) 967-8800 or (800) 322-8755.

You can find Ferguson on the World Wide Web at http://www.fergpubco.com

Text design by Kerry Casey
Composition by Mary Susan Ryan-Flynn
Cover printed by Sheridan Books, Ann Arbor, MI
Book printed and bound by Sheridan Books, Ann Arbor, MI
Date printed: March 2010
Printed in the United States of America

10 9 8 7 6 5 4 3 2 1

39009000829057

This book is printed on acid-free paper.

Contents

Introduction

There are many people just like you who want to get involved with animals—whether in a veterinary clinic, zoo, laboratory, college classroom, or other setting. You may see an animal-related career in your future and wonder how you can get started right away, while still in high school. There are countless areas of the animal field you can work in that you can match your skills and talents to. All you need is a general interest in the field to begin with. Although you will need a doctor of veterinary medicine degree before you can work as a veterinarian, there are other options in the field that require far less education. These include careers such as animal trainer and veterinary technician—both of which you can land by completing some postsecondary training or earning an associate's degree. And there are many jobs, such as pet sitter and pet groomer, that you can start with just a little on-the-job training.

There is absolutely no reason to wait until you get out of high school to "get serious" about a career. That doesn't mean you have to make a firm, undying commitment right now. Gasp! Indeed, one of the biggest fears most people face at some point (sometimes more than once) is choosing the right career. Frankly, many people don't "choose" at all. They take a job because they need one,

and all of a sudden 10 years have gone by and they wonder why they're stuck doing something they hate, like being an accountant rather than being a veterinarian (that may seem like a stretch, but it can happen!). Don't be one of those people! You have the opportunity right now, while you're still in high school and still relatively unencumbered with major adult responsibilities, to explore, to experience, to try out a work path. Or several paths if you're one of those overachieving types. Wouldn't you really rather find out sooner than later that you're not cut out to be a zookeeper after all, and that you'd actually prefer to be a wildlife biologist or a park ranger?

There are many ways to explore animal careers. What we've tried to do in this book is give you an idea of some of your options. Section 1, What Do I Need to Know?, will give you an overview of the field—a little history, where it's at today, and promises of the future; as well as a breakdown of its structure (how it's organized) and a glimpse of some of its many career options.

Section 2, Careers, includes 10 chapters, each describing in detail a specific animal-related career: animal shelter worker, animal trainer, aquarist, park worker, pet care worker, veterinarian, veterinary technician, zoo and aquarium curator or director, zookeeper, or zoologist. These chapters rely heavily on first-hand accounts from real people on the job. They'll tell you what skills you need, what personal qualities you need to have, what the ups and downs of the jobs are. You'll also find out about educational requirements—including specific high school and college classes—advancement possibilities, related jobs, salary ranges, and the employment outlook.

In keeping with the secondary theme of this book (the primary theme, for those of you who still don't get it, is "You can do something now"), Section 3, Do It Yourself, urges you to take charge and learn about animal-related careers on your own and start your own programs and activities where none exist—school, community, or the nation. Why not?

The real meat of the book is in Section 4, What Can I Do Right Now? This is where you get busy and *do something*. The chapter "Get Involved" will clue you in on the obvious volunteer and intern positions, the not-so-obvious summer camps and summer college study, and other opportunities.

"Read a Book" is an annotated bibliography of books (some new, some old) and periodicals. If you're even remotely considering an animal-related career, reading a few books and checking out a few magazines or professional journals is the easiest thing you can do. Don't stop with our list. Ask your librarian to point you to more materials. Keep reading!

While we think the best way to explore animal-related careers is to jump right in and start doing it, there are plenty of other ways to get into the animal mind-set. "Surf the Web" offers you a short annotated list of Web sites where you can explore everything from job listings (start getting an idea of what employers are looking for now), to educational requirements, to animal rights issues, to on-the-job accounts from those who care for and protect animals.

"Ask for Money" is a sampling of scholarships for people who are interested in working with animals. You need to be familiar with these because you're going to need money for school. You have to actively pursue scholarships; no one is going to come up to you one day and present you with a check because you're such a wonderful student. Applying for scholarships is work. It takes effort. And it must be done right and often as much as a year in advance of when you need the money.

"Look to the Pros" is the final chapter. It lists professional and advocacy organizations you can turn to for more information about accredited schools, education requirements, animal rights and environmental issues, career descriptions, salary information, job listings, scholarships, and more. Once you become a college student in an animal-related field, you'll be able to join many of these; others, such as The Nature Conservancy, can be joined by people of any age. Time after time, professionals say that membership and active participation in a professional organization is one of the best ways to network (make valuable contacts) and gain recognition in your field.

High school can be a lot of fun. There are dances and football games; maybe you're in band or play a sport. Great! Maybe you hate school and are just biding your time until you graduate. Too bad. Whoever you are, take a minute and try to imagine your life five years from now. Ten years from now. Where will you be? What will you be doing? Whether you realize it or not, how you choose to spend your time now—studying, playing, watching TV, working at a fast food restaurant, hanging out, whatever—will have an impact on your future. Take a look at how you're spending your time now and ask yourself, "Where is this getting me?" If you can't come up with an answer, it's probably "nowhere." The choice is yours. No one is going to take you by the hand and lead you in the "right" direction. It's up to you. It's your life. You can do something about it right now!

SECTION 1

What Do I Need to Know About Animal Careers?

When you think of animal careers, you probably think of veterinarians, dolphin trainers, and zookeepers. While these are exciting and rewarding professions, it might surprise you to learn that there are countless other careers available for those who want to work with animals. Did you know that pet sitters are needed to care for dogs, cats, and other pets while their owners are away? That zoologists study different types of animals in their habitats—from hot, dusty deserts to the deep, dark reaches of the ocean? That animal shelter workers care for animals that have been abused or are unwanted? That zoo curators manage exhibits and help educate zoo visitors, and that veterinary technicians assist veterinarians as they work to save the lives of sick or injured animals? And these examples really haven't even scratched the surface of the variety of jobs available to someone interested in this field. There are jobs for people of every educational background—from medical degrees (veterinarian) and bachelor degrees (zoologists), to those with some college training (dog trainers) or just a high school education (pet shop workers). There are opportunities in almost any work setting you can imagine, including veterinary clinics, laboratories, zoos, aquariums, college classrooms, the great outdoors, and many others.

GENERAL INFORMATION

Animal care involves the care and maintenance of animals, both wild and domestic. The animal care field includes the training and breeding of animals, as well as promoting their health and care. It also includes the entire range of actions taken by humans to protect and preserve wildlife and ensure its continued survival, such as the regulation of hunting and fishing and the establishment of zoos and sanctuaries. Another important part of animal care is educating people about animals and their needs; for example, naturalists educate the public in a general way while veterinarians educate pet owners about specific concerns.

The relationships between humans and other species are complicated and interdependent. Early humans hunted animals for food and killed animals that threatened their lives or their territory. Later, certain species were domesticated to ensure an available supply of food, clothing, and tools. Other species were domesticated as pets.

Through the centuries humans have found ways to use and control animals for their own benefit, which has contributed to changes in the genetics of some domesticated species, transplantation into new or man-made habitats for some, and even the extinction of some species. Since the 1600s nearly 200 species of birds and mammals are known to have become extinct, mostly as the direct result of human alteration of habitat (because of the development of industry and agriculture) or excessive hunting. Hundreds of other types of organisms have become extinct during this time, and hundreds of species are in danger of extinction right now.

An organized conservation movement didn't get started in the United States until the second half of the 19th century, when the government set up a commission to develop scientific management of fisheries, established the first national park (Yellowstone), and set aside the first forest reserves. Theodore Roosevelt's administration is noted for progress in saving natural resources, which included the establishment of the U.S. Forest Service and the appointment of a conservation commission. Progress in conservation was slow over the next 25 years until the 1930s, when many conservation programs were started under Franklin D. Roosevelt's administration. Conservation is now an established activity of the federal government, which takes responsibility for soil, forests, grasslands, water, fish and other wildlife, and federally owned recreation areas.

Since ancient times, many people, including the Greeks, Romans, Aztecs, and Incas, have kept collections of wild animals. Animals were collected for scientific study, and also for display, entertainment, and sport. Noblemen of the Middle Ages had private zoos.

One of the first zoos designed for public exhibition and scientific research was the Jardin des Plantes in Paris, which opened in 1793. By the end of the 19th century there were zoos open to the public in several large European cities and in the United States. Today, some animal species exist only in zoos, and animal scientists attempt to breed rare animals in captivity, usually with limited success, and sometimes to return animals to the wild.

The domestication of animals probably began as a herding process when early nomads moved from place to place according to the migrations of the animals that provided their food. Herders eventually developed ways to contain and control livestock production and then engaged in the bartering and selling of animals. Livestock farming and animal husbandry grew over the centuries to become the big business it is today, not just for the production of food, but also vaccines, antitoxins, hormones, and vitamins, as well as wool and hides.

Animals are also domesticated for sport, particularly horses and dogs, and as pets.

Lingo to Learn

animal husbandry The raising and breeding of animals. Also called animal science.

animal shelter A place where lost, abused, or unwanted pets are cared for. Animals are either eventually adopted or euthanized (if a home cannot be found for them).

animal welfare The responsibility of ensuring that an animal is well-fed, healthy, carefully handled, and otherwise content in its surroundings. If the animal is very sick or severely injured, the concept of animal welfare also involves humanely euthanizing it so that it does not suffer any longer.

aquarium A place where living aquatic plants and animals are studied and exhibited. Also, a tank, bowl, or other water-filled structure in which living aquatic plants and animals are exhibited.

domesticated animal An animal that has been kept and raised (and tamed) by humans. Examples would include pigs, cattle, and dogs.

Did You Know?

More than 1,315 plants and animals in the United States alone were considered endangered in 2008, according to the U.S. Fish and Wildlife Service.

Horses, once raised primarily for transportation and farm work, now are bred for leisure activities, including equestrian competition, racing, rodeo, and for show. Pets have been kept since ancient times. Originally they were tamed wild animals, but today most dogs and cats, the most popular pets, have been kept in captivity for generations and have been modified by selective breeding. People also keep other small mammals as pets, such as rabbits and hamsters, birds, amphibians and reptiles, fish, and insects.

STRUCTURE OF THE INDUSTRY

There is no single industry that employs people with an interest in animals. Instead, a vast, often interconnected web of organizations employ workers in a variety of industries. Generally speaking, people with a desire to work with animals can work in one of three areas, although there are many jobs common to all areas. These include animal conservation, the breeding and care of domesticated animals, and animal food supply inspection.

Many people find rewarding careers studying and caring for animals in the wild, which includes conservation, preservation of habitat, and research. Local, state, and federal agencies (such as the National Park Service, U.S. Bureau of Land Management, U.S. Forest Service, and U.S. Fish and Wildlife Service) are major employers of workers in this specialty. Zoos and aquariums also play an important role in wildlife conservation. In addition to displaying animals for educational and entertainment purposes to people who wouldn't otherwise get to see them, modern zoos and aquariums are research institutions where scientists can study the structure, habits, and diseases of animals for the purpose of improving our understanding of the animal world and thereby gaining insight into how to protect it. In addition, zoos play an important role in wildlife conservation by conducting breeding programs of endangered animals in captivity. These programs are sometimes the only hope of survival for animals facing extinction. Their ultimate goal is to be able to return animals to the wild in friendly habitats where their numbers can once again grow. Other wildlife management and conservation workers are employed by private environmental groups, such as the Sierra Club, Greenpeace, The Nature Conservancy, National Audubon Society, The Wilderness Society, and National Wildlife Federation, as well as many smaller state and local organizations. These groups together claim many millions of people as members, and membership support is used to hire staffs of scientific experts in the field and powerful lobbyists in Washington, D.C. Some of the groups also publish magazines and newsletters and organize wilderness outings.

The second area is the breeding and care of domesticated animals. A number of domesticated animals are raised for sport and leisure. Equestrian management is big business, with more than 9 million domesticated horses in the United States. Horses are raised for racing, showing, and riding. They are the only animals that participate in the Olympics, in events such as dressage, show jumping, and cross-country jumping. Horses are also bred and trained for polo, rodeo, and police work. Most types of domesticated animals are raised for show competition, including cows, pigs, chickens, horses, dogs, and cats. (Some domesticated animals as well as wild animals bred in captivity are used in circus and entertainment acts and in movies. These include horses, dogs, elephants, chimpanzees, bears, lions, and tigers.) Pet care is a rapidly developing industry in the United States, where new pet sitting and pet grooming businesses are opening all the time. It is estimated that more than 75 percent of American households have one or more pets and that Americans spend more than $43 billion a year on their pets, including food, veterinary care, animal purchases, grooming, boarding, and toys and supplies.

The last major employment area for people interested in animals is animal food supply inspection. The federal government, as well as local and state governments, is responsible for ensuring that our nation's food supply is safe from disease. Major employers of workers in this industry segment include the U.S. Department of Health and Human Services (U.S. Public Health Service, Food and Drug Administration, the National Institutes of Health, and the Centers for Disease Control and Prevention) and the U.S. Department of Agriculture (Animal and Plant Health Inspection Service and other subagencies).

CAREERS

Following are broad definitions of just some of the careers available for people interested in working with animals:

Animal breeders and technicians help breed, raise, and market a variety of farm animals—cattle, sheep, pigs, horses, mules, chickens, turkeys, geese, and ducks—and other more exotic animals, such as ostriches, alligators, and minks.

Animal caretakers feed, water, nurture, and exercise animals. They monitor the animals' general health, as well as clean and repair cages. Caretakers who work in zoos are responsible for transferring animals, if need be, as well as arranging exhibits and setting temperature controls to ensure that the animals are comfortable. Those who work with veterinarians may help treat animals for illness or disease, administer medications, or assist during surgery. Animal caretakers who work in veterinary research are involved in medical testing procedures.

Animal rights activists work to make sure that animals are well cared for and not mistreated in any way.

Animal shelter workers promote animal welfare and protect animals. Most shelter workers care for small domestic animals, such as dogs, cats, and rabbits. Employees at some shelters also work with horses, pigs, goats, and other larger domesticated animals.

Animal trainers teach animals to obey commands, to compete in shows or races, or to perform tricks to entertain audiences. They also may teach dogs to protect property, find bombs or illegal drugs, or to act as guides for the visually impaired. Animal trainers may work exclusively with one type of animal or with several types.

Aquarists feed fish, maintain exhibits, do research, oversee breeding programs, and participate in conservation and educational programs at aquariums, oceanariums, and marine research institutes. Their job duties are similar to zookeepers.

Biological technicians assist biologists, often working on teams in laboratory experiments. They may work with lab animals, record data, and use lab equipment such as microscopes and centrifuges.

Ecologists are both scientists and activists who advocate measures to protect wildlife and other components of the natural environment. As scientists, they study the distribution of organisms, their abundance, and their relationship and impact on their environment. Some work in basic research, while others apply the findings of basic research to develop new ways to protect an animal or plant.

Equestrian management workers work as farriers, horse breeders, horse trainers, judges, jockeys, stable managers, riding instructors, farm managers, racetrack managers, equine insurance adjusters, breed association managers, race associa-

tion managers, and in related business, sales, and marketing positions.

The care of domesticated animals requires a wide variety of workers. The agricultural industry involves the care and handling of beef and dairy cattle, hogs, poultry, sheep, goats, and fish and shellfish. The people who care for livestock and poultry on a daily basis are the *farmers, farm managers,* and *agricultural technicians* who feed the animals and keep barns, pens, coops, and other farm buildings clean and in good condition. They oversee breeding and marketing activities. *Aquaculture farmers* raise fish and shellfish in marine, brackish, or fresh water, usually in ponds, floating net pens, raceways, or re-circulating systems. They stock, feed, protect, and otherwise manage aquatic life sold for consumption or used for recreational fishing.

Fish and game wardens protect wildlife and manage natural resources. They are also called *wildlife inspectors, wildlife conservationists, refuge rangers,* and *refuge officers.*

Food inspectors are empowered by state and federal law to inspect meat, poultry, and their by-products to verify that they are safe for public consumption.

Foresters manage trees and monitor ecosystems in which many species of animals live. This means taking inventory of the kinds of trees, their amount, and their location on a given piece of land. Foresters choose sites where new trees should be planted or where a tract of land needs to be thinned of trees. Determining how wildlife habitats and ecosystems are affected by the loss of trees and other damage are part of the forester's duties. They work on protecting forests from fires, insects, and diseases, and maintaining water and soil quality. Many foresters work for the federal and state governments and logging companies.

Forestry technicians assist foresters. They may raise and transport tree seedlings, apply pesticides to combat insects and diseases, or employ techniques to control erosion. They help foresters follow through with whatever plans are necessary for properly managing a forest. This may involve knowing how to operate logging equipment and taking surveys of the land.

Genetic scientists study how characteristics of parents are passed along to their offspring. Some genetic scientists are also zoologists who specialize in hereditary traits in animals.

Jockeys train and ride thoroughbred horses in professional competitions. They exercise the horses by galloping and working them throughout the day. Along with the horse's owner and trainer, the jockey prepares his or her horse for competition by improving the horse's specific racing strengths and, if possible, reducing or eliminating its weaknesses.

Naturalists observe patterns in nature and study the history of nature. Naturalists are particularly concerned with plants and animals, and many are also *botanists* (plant scientists) or zoologists. Many naturalists have written books that are widely appreciated by the general public.

Park rangers are responsible for ensuring the safety of visitors to national and state parks. They wear uniforms and enforce rules and regulations. In addition, they collect fees, help with the study of wildlife behavior, issue backcountry permits, provide information, lead tours, and help maintain the parks.

Pet groomers care for animals' overall appearance to help make them look good and help them stay healthy.

Pet shop workers sell pets and pet supplies; answer customers' questions and provide animal care advice; keep the store, aquariums, and animal cages clean; care for animals at the store; stock shelves; order products from distributors; and keep records on the animals and products they sell.

Pet sitters visit clients' homes to care for their pets. They feed the animals, give them fresh water, and play with them. They also clean up after them, give them medications when needed, and let them in and out of the house for exercise. *Dog walkers* may be responsible only for taking their customers' dogs out for exercise.

Range managers, also called *range conservationists*, *range scientists*, or *range ecologists*, manage rangeland. They determine how much livestock grazing the land can safely support without robbing the natural wildlife in the area of the grass, shrubs, or other forage it needs. Range managers determine how to conserve soil, how to restore areas damaged by fire, how to irrigate an area, and how fences should be erected. In short, they are responsible for seeing that the land used by wildlife as well as domesticated animals remains healthy and useful.

Veterinarians diagnose illness and disease in animals and prescribe treatment.

They also perform surgery on animals, inoculate them against diseases, set broken bones, and advise caretakers on proper care and feeding. All large zoos employ their own full-time veterinarian to oversee the health care of the entire animal population. Most veterinarians are in private group practices or self-employed.

Veterinary technicians are the most skilled assistants employed by a veterinarian. Although they do not diagnose illnesses, prescribe medication, or perform surgery, technicians do assist in these procedures. They keep records, take specimens and X rays, perform lab tests, dress wounds, and prepare animals for surgery.

Wildlife photographers take photographs and make films of animals in their natural environments.

Zoo and aquarium curators are assigned to the overall care of one or more species in the institution's collection. Large facilities may have a general curator who oversees the entire animal collection and several others who specialize in one area. Curators keep track of animals, prepare budgets, and supervise other workers.

Zoo and aquarium directors are responsible for the business management of the facility and are as such administrators responsible for the entire operation, including budgets, fund-raising, and public relations, just as the head of a company would be in a private business.

Zookeepers take care of the animals on an around-the-clock basis, preparing their food, cleaning their living areas, and observing their behavior for signs of anything unusual that might indicate an illness. They may also assist in research

---

More Lingo to Learn

ecosystem A community of various species that interact with one another and with the chemical and physical factors making up its nonliving environment.

endangered species A species having so few individual survivors left that it may become extinct over all or most of its natural range.

euthanize To kill an animal in a humane manner.

global warming The combined result of human-caused emissions of greenhouse gases and changes in the radiance of the sun. Nearly all of the world's leading scientists believe that global warming is causing major detrimental climate change.

inventory of species Counting the number of different types of plants or animals in a given area.

species A group of related organisms that are capable of breeding.

wild animal An animal that has not been tamed by humans. Examples would include bears, gorillas, or mountain lions.

---

projects and in training animals. Zookeepers also interact with the public, answering questions about the animals and making sure that visitors do not interfere with them.

Zoologists study the origins, behavior, diseases, and life processes of animals, usually further specializing in one type of animal, such as birds (*ornithologists*), mammals (*mammalogists*), reptiles (*herpetologists*), and fish (*ichthyologists*). *Ethologists* are zoologists who study animal behavior and how patterns of behavior occur in specific natural environments. Zoologists may work in both controlled, laboratory settings and out in the field. *Marine biologists* study animals living in salt water, and *limnologists* study animals living in fresh water.

EMPLOYMENT OPPORTUNITIES

The U.S. Department of Labor reports that animal care and service workers (including animal caretakers, animal trainers, aquarists, equestrian care workers, kennel attendants, pet groomers, and zookeepers) held approximately 200,000 jobs in 2006.

A variety of employers hire people who are interested in working with animals, including animal hospitals, animal humane societies, boarding kennels, animal shelters, circuses, dog and horse racetrack operators, laboratories, stables, grooming shops, pet stores, racing stables, theme parks, veterinary offices, and zoos and aquariums.

State and local governments, as well as the federal government, also employ many workers. Major federal government employers include the U.S. Departments of Agriculture, Health and Human Services, Interior, and Homeland Security and the armed forces.

People who are interested in animals also can find employment at colleges and universities, at professional care and welfare associations and organizations, and as writers, editors, and photographers for media companies and other organizations that present information on animals and environmental issues.

INDUSTRY OUTLOOK

The U.S. Department of Labor predicts that employment of animal care and service workers will grow faster than the average for all careers through 2016. Those occu-

Facts About Chimpanzees

- Chimpanzees are the closest relatives of humans. Humans and chimpanzees share more than 98 percent of the same genes.

- Their average height ranges from four to 5.5 feet.

- Chimpanzees can live to be up to 45 years old in the wild.

- They usually walk on all fours (known as knuckle-walking), but can walk upright like humans, too.

- Chimpanzees eat hundreds of types of food, including many kinds of fruits and plants, insects, meat, and eggs.

- They are one of the few animals that use tools. Until the 1960s, it was thought that humans were the only animals that used tools. Chimpanzees also can be taught human sign language.

- Chimpanzees are endangered— primarily as a result of the destruction of their habitat and because they are overhunted for food.

Source: National Geographic

pations related to pets have an especially promising outlook because pet ownership is on the rise and many owners are willing to invest substantial amounts of money in the care and grooming of their pets.

Employment for veterinarians is expected to grow much faster than the average for all careers through 2016. Employment for biological scientists and agricultural scientists is expected to grow about as fast as the average during this same time period.

The outlook for occupations related to the care of wild animals is less cer-tain. Popular concern for wildlife is high, but public funding for park rangers and other wildlife caretakers is limited. Fur-thermore, competition for such jobs is very high and turnover is low, resulting in comparatively low salaries and few job openings.

As in all fields, animal-related jobs can always be found by people with the right combination of education, experience, and determination; unlike many other fields, animal lovers can often create their own jobs (such as pet sitting, pet therapy, and pet taxi services).

SECTION 2

Careers

Animal Shelter Workers

SUMMARY

Definition
Animal shelter workers protect and care for animals that are lost, have been abused, or are unwanted.

Alternative Job Titles
(Note: The following jobs are a small sampling of career opportunities available at animal shelters.)
Adoption counselors
Humane investigators
Kennel attendants
Shelter managers

Salary Range
$14,520 to $35,000 to $150,000

Educational Requirements
Varies by position

Certification or Licensing
Voluntary (managers)
Required by certain states (euthanasia technicians, humane investigators)

Employment Outlook
Faster than the average

High School Subjects
Biology
Mathematics
Speech

Personal Interests
Animals
Science

Janel Biglin, the behavior coordinator at the Capital Area Humane Society, says that one of her most rewarding experiences in the field was when she was able to help a dog that was rescued from inhumane conditions find a great home with people who were thrilled to have her. "We had a group of dogs brought in by our cruelty investigators," she recalls, "from a home with too many dogs that had been living in filthy conditions. The dogs had never been walked on a leash before and were timid with strangers. Over the course of their time with us, I got to know them and became attached to them. A couple with their dog was looking at one of the dogs named Pokey, but they didn't look too interested in her, and she was acting shy and uninterested in them. I came into the room, and Pokey instantly became animated and her sweet personality came out. I showed them how she knew 'Sit,' and they became very interested in her. I provided them with some behavior and training advice to help her be successful in their home. They ended up adopting her. I followed up with them, and they told me she now gets along great with their dog. They think they are lucky to have such a wonderful dog who has become a fantastic part of their family."

WHAT DOES AN ANIMAL SHELTER WORKER DO?

Animal shelter workers are employed by nonprofit organizations. Their duties are similar to those performed in animal control agencies, which are run by government entities—city, county, state, or federal. Animal shelters and animal control agencies differ in their purpose and philosophy. Animal shelters, also called humane shelters, are usually dedicated to the protection of animals and the promotion of animal welfare. Animal control agencies exist to ensure that the safety and welfare of people and property are not compromised by animals. In recent years, animal shelters and animal control organizations have increasingly been working together. Some animal control organizations maintain shelter facilities or take animals to shelters for care and adoption.

Animal shelter workers perform a variety of jobs related to the welfare and protection of domestic animals. Most shelter workers care for small domestic animals, such as cats, dogs, and rabbits, but employees at some shelters may also work with horses, goats, pigs, and other larger domestic animals. Sick and injured wild animals are usually cared for by wildlife refuges and wildlife rehabilitation centers, not animal shelters.

The duties of shelter employees range from cleaning cages and grooming animals to education, fund-raising, and business management. The functions a specific worker performs frequently depend on the size of the animal shelter. In a large shelter, duties are more specialized, and there may be a large staff to accomplish them. In a small shelter, a few individuals may be responsible for nearly all of the functions that are performed. Whatever the specific duties of an animal shelter worker may be, the goal is always to promote the welfare of animals.

Kennel attendants (also called *kennel workers*) are generally responsible for the animals' physical needs, such as exercising, feeding, and cleaning of living quarters. Of all shelter staff, the kennel attendants work most closely with the shelter animals, and an important part of their job is nurturing the animals through caring handling. In some shelters, kennel attendants receive animals that are brought in by their owners or by a humane investigator. The *receiving attendant* may be responsible for checking the general health of the new animal, finding an appropriate habitat for it in the shelter, and referring it for medical treatment when necessary. Kennel attendants maintain records, such as the identification of the animal and its weight, size, and general condition. More experienced or skilled kennel attendants may be trained to give some inoculations and perform euthanasia under the supervision of a veterinarian. (In larger shelters, a worker with special training called a *euthanasia technician* may perform euthanization procedures.) Kennel attendants sometimes act as adoption counselors.

Adoption counselors screen applicants who wish to adopt animals from the shelter. They interview applicants to determine if they will provide a good, caring home for an animal. They ask questions, listen carefully, and judge the character of potential adoptees. If the counselor decides that the applicant would make a good pet owner, he or she must try to match the qualified owner with an appropriate animal. If the adoption counselor believes that a proposed adoption would not be in the animal's interest, the application is denied. A skilled counselor may be able to suggest a different animal that would be a better match for the applicant's situation. The adoption counselor puts the animal's welfare first, but also promotes the public image of the shelter.

Humane investigators (also known as *cruelty investigators* or *animal treatment investigators*) follow up on reports of animal neglect and abuse. They interview witnesses as well as animal owners who are accused of mistreatment. If the cruelty investigator determines that abuse or neglect exists, he or she may issue a warning, call the police to arrest the individual, or confiscate the animal. Humane investigators respond to reports of abandoned, stray, or injured animals, and they free trapped animals. They transport rescued animals to the shelter.

Humane educators work at the shelter and in the community teaching about humane treatment of animals and other animal-related issues. They travel to grade schools, high schools, clubs, and other community organizations. They lecture about animal rights, animal care and treatment, the overpopulation problem and potential solutions, the relationship between violence to animals and violence to people, and the roles of the individual and the community in effecting change. Humane educators arrange tours of the animal shelter for interested groups, distribute printed educational materials, and inform people about other resources for humane education.

Shelter managers (also called *kennel managers* or *kennel supervisors*) oversee the daily operations of the shelter itself. They hire and train kennel attendants, create schedules for staff and volunteers, evaluate work performance, and provide continuing education opportunities to improve job performance. Shelter managers supervise and/or perform the maintenance of the property, buildings, vehicles, and euthanasia equipment. In some shelters, the manager is responsible for operating the euthanasia equipment when animals must be destroyed. Some larger shelters may have specialized managers, such as *animal care managers*, who are responsible for any staff or department that deals directly with animal management.

Shelter administrators are responsible for the overall operation of the shelter, its departments, and its programs. They select and hire shelter managers, humane educators, humane investigators, and department heads, and they may be in charge of personnel. Administrators advocate for the shelter by holding interviews with the media, fund-raising, attending community events, and recruiting new members. Shelter administrators must work well with people, and they must be good business managers. According to the American Humane Association (AHA), the majority of animal shelters that fail in the United States are forced to close because they were not run like businesses. Some larger organizations have both an *executive director* and an *administrative director* who divide the administrative duties.

To Be a Successful Animal Shelter Worker, You Should...

- love animals

- be able to work well with others

- be able to work independently, when necessary

- have patience

- have compassion

- be organized

- have a strong work ethic

- have excellent communication skills

Other career options at animal shelters include veterinarian, veterinary technician, customer care manager, behavior coordinator, human resources manager, secretary, and receptionist.

Animal shelter employees have the moral satisfaction of promoting the welfare of animals. They feel joy and pride because they make a difference in the lives of animals and people. They may also experience sadness and anger at the suffering they witness among the animals that are sick, injured, or abused. In some shelters, suffering or unadoptable animals are euthanized. Animal shelter employees may be upset when this is necessary. Individuals who are philosophically or emotionally opposed to euthanasia can choose to work in no-kill shelters where the animals are kept until they are adopted.

Schedules and hours of work vary for animal shelter employees. In smaller shelters, and even in some larger ones, everyone—including the executive director—may be involved in the care and feeding of the animals. If the work is not done at the end of an eight-hour day, it must be completed. Most shelters are staffed 24-hours-a-day every day of the year. Animal shelter employees must often work on weekends, evenings, and holidays.

WHAT IS IT LIKE TO BE AN ANIMAL SHELTER WORKER?

It takes a team of workers with a variety of educational backgrounds and skills to make an animal shelter successful. The following paragraphs feature profiles of four workers (Jodi Buckman, executive director; Scott Baxter, animal care manager; Sarah Tayse, customer care manager; and Janel Biglin, behavior coordinator) who are employed at the Capital Area Humane Society in Hilliard, Ohio. Jodi Buckman provides an overview of the organization: "The Capital Area Humane Society is a wonderful organization that serves the pets and people of central Ohio. It is our mission to fight animal cruelty, help animals in need, and advocate for their well-being. Our two primary services to the community are adoptions and cruelty investigations. We shelter more than 14,000 animals each year—the majority of those animals are cats. Here in Ohio, animal control services are only available for dogs; although we are a nonprofit organization funded almost exclusively by donations, we shelter thousands of stray cats

Lingo to Learn

animal shelter A place where lost, abused, or unwanted pets are cared for. Animals are either eventually adopted or euthanized if a home cannot be found for them.

euthanasia The act of causing death painlessly. Also known as "putting an animal down" or "putting an animal to sleep."

no-kill shelter An animal shelter where it is forbidden to euthanize animals.

spay/neuter Medical procedures that prevent animals from reproducing. Males are neutered (castrated) and females are spayed (ovaries removed).

(generally more than 8,000 each year). Our adoption rate for dogs is very high; our adoption rate for cats is tragically low. Our very best opportunity to save the lives of cats is to prevent births, so we have begun to focus much of our outreach effort on spay and neuter programs for cats in central Ohio. The responsibility for investigating cruelty to animals in Ohio (every state is different) falls to county humane societies. We are the humane society for Franklin County, so in addition to sheltering pets who need us, our Cruelty Investigations Department investigates reports of cruelty and neglect. Our agents are law enforcement officials—they wear bulletproof vests, carry police radios, and have the authority to make arrests."

The Capital Area Humane Society is a fairly large animal sheltering organization. It has nearly 50 full- and part-time employees and more than 1,600 active volunteers.

"As the executive director," says Jodi, "I am the chief executive and report to a 15-member board of directors (exceptional business leaders and professionals from our community). My primary responsibilities include providing leadership and support for our staff and volunteers, ensuring they have the resources and programs necessary to support our mission-oriented work. This means I spend time raising money, managing people resources, managing the business of our nonprofit (reporting, financials, administration), and ensuring that our work is strategic—and advances the mission of our organization. Secondarily, I am responsible for everything else. I believe that good managers are always prepared to do what is necessary to support their colleagues, so when a challenge or opportunity presents itself I am always ready to roll up my sleeves and figure how to help. This might mean cleaning cat cages, helping evaluate a dog's behavior, managing media at the site of a large-scale animal cruelty case, or ordering pizza for our hard-working staff on a snow day when few of them could get to work. I love this work. It is difficult, demanding, challenging, dynamic, and incredibly rewarding. Every day, there is an opportunity to impact the lives of people and pets in a way that is profound. I think that's very cool."

Scott Baxter is an animal care manager at the Capital Area Humane Society. He has worked for nonprofit humane societies for more than 12 years. "What I like most about shelter work," he says, "are the variety of situations that are encountered related to an animal's health and temperament, and the continuing opportunities to learn and improve my skills in solving problems related to these situations. I am direct supervisor for the animal care staff and our behavior coordinator, and I am supported by one assistant manager. I have managerial responsibility for day-to-day animal care and shelter activities that pertain directly to animal management. Flow of animals through the shelter is a primary responsibility. I manage and oversee our canine behavior assessment program. I work closely with our admissions, medical, cruelty investigations, and adoptions departments on a daily basis to ensure proper care and enrichment for our sheltered animals."

Scott is also a certified euthanasia technician. "As odd as it may sound," he says, "participation in the euthanization of animals has been very rewarding to me, on a professional and personal level. I support a philosophy of 'good death' for suffering or unwanted domestic animals, and I'm proud of my ability to provide this service with skill and dignity. This activity has given me a great deal of self-discipline, and has also helped me to become a person that others look to for support and guidance during difficult emotional times. It is a fundamental and important part of our organization, and is so often misunderstood and demonized. But those who understand and support its role in our fight to eliminate animal cruelty and neglect are the people I respect the most."

Sarah Tayse is the customer care manager at the Capital Area Humane Society. She has worked in the field for more than six years. "I started as a veterinary assistant, and moved to adoptions, admissions, and cruelty investigations departments before becoming the assistant shelter manager three years ago and finally the customer care manager four months ago," she says. "I always loved animals, and had worked at a veterinary clinic prior to the humane society. Once I started working at the humane society, I realized how much the animals in the community needed advocates and decided that this career path was the right choice."

Sarah is responsible for supervising the adoptions and admissions staff and resolving any customer-related concerns in both areas. She is also responsible for managing the facility's on-site retail store. "We value teamwork here at the shelter," she says, "so I cross-train customer service staff to assist in our animal care and veterinary services departments as necessary. I also collect much of the statistical data on the number of animals our organization serves and track the different services we provide. I am involved in population management in the shelter and making euthanasia decisions, as well as performing the euthanasia itself. I also evaluate dogs' behavior for adoptability using the Safety Assessment For Evaluating Rehoming (SAFER) tool developed specifically for shelter dogs by Dr. Emily Weiss at the American Society for the Prevention of Cruelty to Animals."

Sarah says that the she loves her job primarily because it allows her to help animals and people in her community. "Additionally," she says, "the situations that we face are different every day, which allows me to think and be creative in ways to solve problems that arise. The people I work with are fantastic as well. We are all here for similar reasons, and are all willing to pitch in and help other departments and other animal welfare organizations that reach out to us for help." Sarah says that there are obvious downsides to working in animal welfare—mainly the issues leading to compassion fatigue. "Making eutha-

nasia decisions can be very difficult," she explains, "especially if you're dealing with an animal that has significant attachment from staff members or volunteers. The goal is to make the best decisions possible as quickly as possible."

Moving Moments

● ● ● ● ● ● ● ● ●

The editors of *What Can I Do Now? Animal Careers* asked Jodi Buckman, executive director of The Capital Area Humane Society, to detail some of her most moving experiences in the field:

The moments that are most important to me in my work are the moments that were the most challenging. I remember being changed forever at my very core the first time I euthanized—they were kittens. I remember holding a fawn in my arms on the side of the road—she'd been hit by a car—as a colleague administered an injection that ended her suffering, and again I was changed as I understood what a gift euthanasia can be when it ends suffering. The police officer who would have had to shoot her otherwise thanked us as a tear crept down his cheek.

And more recently, there was Stranger. In September 2006 our humane agents were executing a routine search warrant for the seizure of a dog named Stranger. She was an old chow whose owners refused to provide her with proper medical care (she had a melon-sized tumor hanging from her chin) and housing (they kept her in the basement and never let her outside) despite multiple visits and warnings from our agents.

On this day, our agents and the Columbus Police (who provided our agents with escort and protection) were

greeted at the door by a gentleman with a ski mask pulled over his face and automatic shotgun cradled in his arms. Our agents and the police dove for cover, called the SWAT team, and blocked off the street. After a brief standoff, the owner surrendered, and our agents were able to get to Stranger and bring her here to the Capital Area Humane Society.

We removed her tumor, put her on a quality diet, and our volunteers began working with her. Her response to our staff and volunteers was extraordinary. It was almost as though you could see and understand in her eyes her gratitude for the care and love she received—perhaps for the first time in her life. She lived with us here at Capital Area while her case very slowly worked its way through the courts. But seven months after her seizure she lost her battle with the cancer that had caused the tumor. She died here in my arms after one last walk out in the sun. Several weeks later, we won her case. Though working and winning the case is our job, it is improving the life of a dog like Stranger that is our passion. Just over one year later, I sat in the Ohio House of Representatives as House Bill 71 became law—law that today ensures that the next Stranger in my life will likely only live with us here at the Humane Society for a couple of weeks, rather than months, and will then be off to find that permanent home that every amazing dog and cat deserves.

Janel Biglin is the behavior coordinator at the Capital Area Humane Society. She also operates a dog behavior and training consulting business. She has worked in the field of dog behavior and training for nine years. "I lived with pets almost my whole life and have really enjoyed caring for them and learning about them," she says. "I had been an executive assistant and decided to make a career change. When I looked back over the experiences I enjoyed the most, the ones that stood out all involved animals. I had volunteered at two different humane societies and really enjoyed training the dogs. I took a veterinary assisting course to learn more about animal medicine and apprenticed for a year with the behavior and training department of a shelter. Through them, I learned current methods of positive reinforcement training. So when a position opened up as a behavior trainer in that department, I was hired for the job. I have since moved back to Ohio, and this position was created at the Capital Area Humane Society."

Janel's primary job duty is to perform timely behavior assessments of all dogs surrendered to the shelter by their owners or brought in by cruelty investigators. "I perform a SAFER behavior assessment on the dogs to screen them for aggression before they are placed for adoption," she explains. "This involves handling the dog's collar, paws, and body; testing them for food and toy aggression; and observing how they act around other dogs. I then provide information about their behavior—based on their assessment and the information the previous owners provide—to help place them in the most suitable home, whether that is through our adoption programs or a rescue organization. My secondary job duty is coordinating with the medical department to get the dog medically processed, on the adoption floor, and with the adoptions department to provide the information they need to help find the best home for the dog.

"The advantages of my job," she continues, "are getting to spend all day working around dogs and cats and with people who also love pets. It is also very rewarding to be able to help the dogs move quicker through the system, to get them into new, loving homes. The disadvantages are that the pay is low and it often doesn't smell nice, due to the animal urine and feces. Another is having to cope with the daily reality of working with animals that may need to be euthanized, due to reasons such as aggression or medical issues."

DO I HAVE WHAT IT TAKES TO BE AN ANIMAL SHELTER WORKER?

Two of the most important traits of animal shelter workers are a respect for people and a love of animals. They must work well with people in order to effectively promote the welfare of animals. "People often think that they would succeed at an animal shelter because they love animals, but that's not enough," says Sarah Tayse. "To work in this field, you have to be passionate about animals, but you also have to love people. The public are your adopters, your donors, and your admissions clients. The only way to improve animals' lives in the community is to educate the public, and every person who walks in the doors of an animal shelter can be moved to support the cause by our actions." Sarah also believes that it is important to have a supportive group of friends and family members. "Working in animal welfare can be an incredibly difficult job sometimes," she says, "and you need to be able to go home and have your friends and family understand that your job is challenging, both emotionally and physically."

"To do this job," says Janel Biglin, "you really need to love dogs and cats and realize that not all the animals we deal with are friendly. It's also important to know how to act around dogs and cats and know how to handle them—for your own safety and to minimize the stress on the animal. Working in a shelter, you need to be able to accept the fact that some of the pets that come into the shelter will need to be humanely euthanized for various reasons. You can't let yourself get too attached to most of the animals you work with or it becomes too difficult to be objective, do your job, and to have to say goodbye to an animal."

Animal shelter workers must be able to be good team players, but at the same time they need to be self-motivated in order to work independently. They must be dedicated, organized, patient, compassionate, and hard working. Animal shelter workers must have excellent communication skills and be effective decision makers.

Successful animal shelter managers need to have "empathy and compassion— but not so much that we lose sight of the big picture," says Jodi Buckman. "When in a leadership position in animal welfare, I believe it is crucial (and very difficult) to maintain a proper balance between the importance of the individual and the greater good. The lives of animals and the passion of the people who care about

them are in your hands—and while never losing sight of that incredible responsibility, you must also be able to make difficult decisions in the interest of the greater good and the mission of your agency."

HOW DO I BECOME AN ANIMAL SHELTER WORKER?
Education
High School
Kennel attendants and adoption counselors usually need a high school diploma or GED certificate. Some shelters hire high school students who are of legal age to work and who show an aptitude for working with animals and with the public. High school classes in biology and other sciences will help prepare you to work with shelter animals. Classes such as English, speech, debate, and drama will help you develop self-confidence and the verbal skills needed to successfully interact with the public and interview adoption candidates. Business, mathematics, and computer-science classes will be especially useful for aspiring managers, but they will also be of value to any type of shelter worker. Volunteering at a local shelter, kennel, or veterinary hospital is an excellent way to gain experience in this field while still in high school. Owning and caring for a pet and reading about animals, their care, and related topics can also be helpful.

Postsecondary Training
Many animal shelter workers learn their skills via on-the-job training and through short courses that are offered by professional associations and other providers.

"Training in shelters, in my experience, is often a matter of 'shadowing' more experienced employees," says Scott Baxter. "I had no professional animal welfare experience before I started working in a shelter, and I learned animal care and handling through observing others, self-education, some formal training, and admittedly some trial-and-error (particularly related to animal handling). I have been lucky in that the shelters that I have worked for have occasionally been able to offer me training through nationally-sponsored certification training courses, but for the most part I am a product of hands-on experience working directly with animals and people."

College-level courses in law enforcement, psychology, animal science, animal behavior, and veterinary technology could be useful for humane investigators. Humane investigators must be nominated by a humane organization for the special training required for certification.

Humane educators are often teachers. Although there are presently no degree requirements for this position, shelters are beginning to look for humane educators who have degrees in education and related fields. In addition to the high school courses recommended for kennel workers, college or continuing education courses in psychology, public relations, and environmental education would be helpful to humane educators.

Shelter managers are frequently required to have a college degree, but experienced kennel workers who do not have degrees can be promoted to this position. Veterinary technicians or managers of other types of kennels might also be considered for a shelter manager posi-

tion. An individual who hopes to become a shelter manager would be well advised to take college or continuing education courses in business management, veterinary technology, animal management, or animal husbandry.

Shelter administrators generally need a bachelor's degree or strong experience in business management or shelter management. Some executive director positions may even require a master's degree. Helpful areas of study include business administration and management, finance, public relations, fund-raising, grant writing, negotiations, and personnel development. Jodi Buckman advises aspiring executive directors and other managers to learn how to lead and manage while in school. "Many of the most amazing leaders in our field today went to school to learn about leadership, management, nonprofit administration, marketing, and development," she says. "The animal portion will come, but if you want to lead an organization, learn how to do so in college."

Educational requirements for other shelter workers vary by position. For example, veterinarians need a medical degree, while veterinary technicians must have a minimum of an associate's degree in veterinary technology. Customer care managers may need some postsecondary training or prior experience in customer service, but many learn their skills on the job. Behavior coordinators learn their skills by attending community colleges and vocational schools that offer courses and workshops in animal training. Human resources managers often have associate's or bachelor's degrees in human resources management or business.

Certification or Licensing

A variety of certifications are available for animal shelter workers. The Society of Animal Welfare Administrators offers the voluntary certified animal welfare administrator designation. Other applicable certifications are available from the Animal Behavior Society, the American College of Veterinary Behaviorists, the Certification Council for Professional Dog Trainers, the International Association for the Study of Animal Behavior, the International Association of Animal Behavior Consultants, the International Association of Canine Professionals, and the National Association of Dog Obedience Instructors. Additionally, the positions of humane investigator and euthanasia technician require certification or licensing by some states.

Internships and Volunteerships

Internships are available to those interested in shelter positions, such as executive director, that typically require a college degree. Internships are an excellent way to learn more about the demands of a career in the field while you are still in school. Colleges and universities usually have established internship programs with animal shelters, humane organizations, and other employers.

Volunteering at a shelter is probably the best way to learn how you would like a career at an animal shelter. Animal shelters welcome volunteers who are considering a career in the field. Sarah Tayse advises young people to volunteer at their local humane society or animal shelter. "Many shelters have opportunities for volunteers of any age," she says. "I would also advise them to learn as much as possible about animal behavior. Animal behavior has a huge part in animal sheltering—it can help you to make a great match with an adopter, counsel an admissions client on how to keep the animal in their home, and keep you safe while handling potentially dangerous animals."

WHO WILL HIRE ME?

Animal shelters are located throughout the United States. Smaller shelters may depend on a few workers to handle a variety of job responsibilities, whereas larger shelters may have very specialized job categories for workers.

The best way to break into this field is by volunteering. Shelters rely heavily on volunteers, and loyal volunteers are often the first to receive an opportunity when a paid position becomes available. Most volunteers, like most animal shelter workers, start out as kennel workers and/or adoption counselors. The skills learned in those positions provide the basis for advancement. A helpful aspect of beginning a career as an animal shelter employee is that it is possible to enter the field from many backgrounds. A teacher might become a humane educator. A public health official could become a humane investigator. Business professionals and accountants could become shelter managers, administrators, or executive directors. It takes many skills to successfully run an animal shelter, and each individual can apply his or her expertise to improve the shelter and enhance the welfare of the shelter animals.

Local animal shelters and newspaper listings are good places to look for local job openings. The national associations are good sources of information on job

Combating Black Dog Syndrome

Million of dogs are placed in shelters each year. While dogs are adopted more quickly than cats, ZooToo.com reports that black dogs—especially black Labrador retrievers and mixes—languish in shelters sometimes for years because of their color. Shelter workers cite the following reasons why black dogs are not adopted as quickly as lighter ones:

Fear. The facial features of black dogs are sometimes harder to read, and their eyes may not be as bright and shiny as lighter-colored canines. These qualities in combination with a flash of white teeth—especially by large dogs—can make them appear menacing or angry.

Superstition. Some people equate the color black with death or the devil.

Preference. Some people simply want dogs that are lighter colored.

This may not sound like a serious problem, but shelter employees report that backlogs of black-colored dogs take up spots that can be used for other dogs, cats, and animals. And black dogs that are not adopted are eventually euthanized if they are not housed at a no-kill shelter.

Shelter employees have developed several strategies to encourage people to adopt black dogs. They place them with lighter-colored blankets or sheets to provide a contrast that makes them appear more attractive. Others try to interact closely with the animals in front of potential adoptees to show that they are friendly. They also feature them prominently on their Web sites to encourage interest.

openings throughout the country. Visit their Web sites for more information (see "Look to the Pros").

WHERE CAN I GO FROM HERE?

Most advancement opportunities for animal shelter employees come from within. As animal shelter workers learn more and become more skilled, they are often promoted from one position to another. A good kennel attendant might be given the opportunity to study to become a humane investigator. An experienced kennel attendant, adoption counselor, humane investigator, or humane educator could eventually become a shelter manager. A shelter manager might become a shelter administrator. A shelter administrator may eventually become executive director of an organization. Any animal shelter employee who is interested in gaining a different position can study to acquire the skills needed for that position and work to acquire the experience.

In some instances, advancement may depend on the size of the shelter. Small shelters offer opportunities for employees to learn a variety of skills, but they may not offer many avenues for advancement. Large shelters have more positions and more opportunities for advancement, but they may not provide the opportunity to learn as many skills at one time. Workers may need to be willing to relocate to find a better chance for advancement.

WHAT ARE THE SALARY RANGES?

Animal shelter workers receive a wide range of salaries and benefits depending on their job duties and on the size and location of the shelter. Large shelters in metropolitan areas generally offer higher pay and more benefits. Small shelters and those in rural areas may offer lower salaries, and some may only provide part-time employment.

Salaries for middle managers range from $20,000 to $50,000 or more. Senior managers can earn from $25,000 to $100,000, while executive directors make between $25,000 and $150,000.

Salaries for nonfarm animal caretakers (a career category that includes animal shelter workers) ranged from less than $15,140 to $31,590 or more in 2008, according to the U.S. Department of Labor. The median salary for nonfarm animal caretakers was $19,360. Animal control workers who worked for social advocacy organizations had mean annual earnings of $29,550 in 2008.

New kennel workers and adoption counselors often start at minimum wage. Their salaries increase as they gain experience and training.

Most shelters provide a minimum of health insurance benefit, though some may not. Some shelters offer retirement plans. Some of the larger shelters and associations have very attractive benefits packages.

WHAT IS THE JOB OUTLOOK?

According to the Humane Society of the United States and the American Humane Association, the United States is in a pet-overpopulation crisis. According to the American Pet Products Association, there were 74.8 million dogs and 88.3 million cats in the United States in 2008. Despite early spay/neuter programs and the dedicated efforts of shelters and veterinarians to reduce the problem, overpopulation is expected to continue for the next decade. The U.S. Department of Labor predicts that the pet population will continue to increase, and that employment of animal caretakers in kennels and animal shelters should remain strong. Turnover is often high among kennel workers due to the strenuous physical work and generally low pay. As a result, the there will be many jobs available in animal shelters.

Animal Trainers

SUMMARY

Definition
Animal trainers teach animals to obey commands in order to be family companions, to perform tricks to entertain audiences, to compete in shows or races, to protect property, or to work as service dogs for people with disabilities.

Alternative Job Titles
Obedience instructors

Salary Range
$16,700 to $27,270 to $51,400+

Educational Requirements
Varies by specialty; some postsecondary or on-the-job training is required for dog and horse trainers, while a bachelor's degree is required for marine mammal trainers.

Certification or Licensing
Voluntary (certification)
Required by certain states (licensing)

Employment Outlook
Much faster than the average (dog trainers)
More slowly than the average (horse trainers, marine mammal trainers)

High School Subjects
Biology
Psychology

Personal Interests
Animals
Science
Wildlife

"A couple years ago, the local humane society called me in on a tragic case," recalls Teoti Anderson, the owner of Pawsitive Results, LLC. "They had confiscated several German shepherds in a cruelty and neglect case. The director asked me to evaluate one of the dogs, Rocky. He was approximately four years old and only weighed 25 pounds. Rocky was completely emaciated—just skin tightly wrapped over protruding bones. His legs splayed out, and he was hunched over due to muscle atrophy. Rocky's fur was coarse and he reeked—he had been living in a small outdoor pen, full of his own waste. He had open sores and ear infections. Rocky also had the warmest chocolate eyes, and he greeted me with kisses."

The humane society was hoping to rehabilitate Rocky and wanted to use him as an example to encourage support for the prevention of animal cruelty in the community. "I proceeded with my temperament evaluation," Teoti recalls, "but I was so afraid that even the slightest touch would hurt him! I worked hard to keep my objectivity, as a lot was riding on this evaluation. While I was calm and collected on the outside, inside my heart was just breaking.

"He passed with flying colors. Rocky was a sweet, loving dog. Even though he had been treated terribly, he still loved people.

"Rocky recovered with the help of dedicated veterinarians and a great foster family. He came through my dog training classes and excelled. He always was a bit hunched over due to his early lack of nutrition, but he ended up being a healthy, happy dog, and was adopted into the kind of home he should have always had. Through community promotion, Rocky also helped raise thousands of dollars to help other animals who were suffering. Rocky proved to me that even when things look terrible and forsaken, there is always hope. It was a challenging case, and very difficult to see the result of such cruelty. But it taught me a lot as a trainer, and I was glad I was able to help Rocky find his forever home."

WHAT DOES AN ANIMAL TRAINER DO?

Many animals are capable of being trained. The techniques used to train them are basically the same, regardless of the type of animal. *Animal trainers* conduct programs consisting primarily of repetition and reward to teach animals to behave in a particular manner and to do it consistently.

First, trainers evaluate an animal's temperament, ability, and aptitude to determine its trainability. Animals vary in personality, just as people do. Some animals are more challenging or easily distracted and can only be taught by trainers with advanced education and skills. All animals can be trained at some level, but certain animals are more receptive to training; these animals are chosen for programs that demand great skill.

One of the most familiar examples is the seeing-eye dog, now usually called a companion animal for the blind. These dogs are trained with several hundred verbal commands to assist their human and to recognize potentially dangerous situations. The dog must be able to, without any command, walk his or her companion around obstacles on the sidewalk. The companion dog must be able to read streetlights and know to cross at the green, and only after traffic has cleared. The dog must also not be tempted to run to greet other dogs, grab food, or behave as most pet dogs do. Very few dogs make it through the rigorous training program. The successful dogs have proved to be such aids to the visually impaired that similar programs have been developed to train dogs for people who are confined to a wheelchair, or are hearing impaired, or incapable of executing some aspect of a day-to-day routine where a dog can assist.

Animal trainers teach an animal to obey or perform on command or, in certain situations, without command, by painstakingly repeating routines many times and rewarding the animal when it does what is expected. In addition, animal trainers feed, exercise, groom, and generally care for the animals, either handling the duties themselves or supervising other workers. In some training programs, trainers come in and work with the animals; in other programs, such as the companion animal program, the animal lives with the trainer for the duration of the program.

Trainers usually specialize in one type of animal and are identified by this type of animal. Dogs, partly because of the variety of breeds available and partly because of their nature to work for approval, have countless roles for which they are trained. *Pet dog trainers* work with owners to teach their dogs family manners and to help fix destructive or dangerous habits. *Police dog trainers* work with police dogs, training them to search for drugs or missing people. The programs to train drug-detecting dogs use different detection responses, but each dog is trained in only one response system. Some dogs are trained to behave passively when the scent is detected, with a quiet signal given to the accompanying police officer that drugs have been detected. The signal can be sitting next to the scent, pointing, or following. Other dogs are trained to dig, tear, and destroy containers that have the drug in them. As one animal trainer from the U.S. Customs & Border Protection office pointed out, these dogs may be nightmare pets because they can destroy a couch in seconds, but they make great drug-detecting dogs. The common breeds for companion dogs and police dogs are German shepherds, rottweilers, and Labrador retrievers.

Some trainers teach guard dogs to protect private property; others train dogs for performance, where the dog may learn numerous stunts or movements with hand commands so that the dog can perform on a stage or in film without the audience hearing the commands spoken from off-stage. Shepherding dogs are also trained with whistle or hand commands because commands may have to be given from some distance away from where the dog is working.

Horse trainers specialize in training horses for riding or for harness. They talk to and handle a horse gently to accustom it to human contact, and then gradually get it to accept a harness, bridle, saddle, and other riding gear. Trainers teach horses to respond to commands that are either spoken or given by use of the reins and legs. Draft horses are conditioned to draw equipment either alone or as part of a team. Show horses are given special training to qualify them to perform in competitions. Horse trainers sometimes have to retrain animals that have developed bad habits, such as biting or bucking. Besides feeding, exercising, and grooming, these trainers may make arrangements for breeding the horses and help mares deliver their foals.

A highly specialized occupation in the horse-training field is that of *racehorse trainers*, who must create individualized training plans for every horse in their care. By studying the animal's performance record and becoming familiar with its behavior during workouts, trainers can adapt their training methods to take advantage of each animal's peculiarities. Like other animal trainers, racehorse trainers oversee the exercising, grooming, and feeding of their charges. They also clock their running time during workouts to determine when a horse is ready for competitive racing. Racehorse trainers coach jockeys on how best to handle a particular horse during a race and may give owners advice on purchasing horses.

Police horse trainers work with police horses to keep them from startling in crowds or responding to other animals in their presence. These animals require a very stable, calm personality that remains the same no matter what the situation the animal works in. Police officers who work with animals on a routine basis develop strong attachments to the animals.

Other animal trainers work with more exotic animals for performance or for health reasons. The *marine mammal trainers* at the Shedd Aquarium in Chicago teach dolphins and whales to roll over, lift fins and tails, and open their mouths on command, so that much veterinary work can be done without anesthesia, which is always dangerous for animals. These skills are demonstrated for the public every day, so they function as a show for people, but the overriding reason for training the dolphins is to keep them healthy. Other training elements include teaching dolphins to retrieve items from the bottom of their pool, so that if any visitor throws or loses something in the pool, divers are not required to invade the dolphins' space.

Animal trainers also work with hunting birds, training them to fly after an injury, or to hunt if the bird was found as a hatchling before a parent had trained it. Birds that are successfully trained to fly and hunt can be released into the wild; the others may remain in educational programs where they will perform for audiences. It is, however, illegal to keep any releasable hunting bird for more than one year in the United States.

Each species of animal is trained by using the instincts and reward systems that are appropriate to that species. Hunt-ing birds are rewarded with food; they don't enjoy petting and do not respond warmly to human touch, unless they were hand-raised from hatching by humans. Some dogs respond immediately to petting and gentle handling, while others may respond very well to food rewards. Some prefer toys. Sea mammals respond to both food and physical contact.

Some animal species are generally difficult to train. Sea otters are extremely destructive naturally and do not train easily. African elephants are much more difficult to train than Asian elephants, and females are much more predictable and trainable than the larger males. Most circus elephants are Asian because they are much easier to handle. Captive elephants, though, kill more handlers and keepers than every other species combined.

Animal trainers' working hours vary widely, depending on the type of animal, performance schedule, and whether travel is involved. For some trainers, such as those who work with show horses, educational programs with hunting birds, or new animals being brought into zoos and aquariums, the hours can be long and quite irregular. Travel is common and will probably include responsibility for seeing to the animals' needs while on the road. This can include feeding, creative housing, and transporting the animal. For one program director of a rescue center that works with injured hawks, it means traveling frequently for educational shows with a suitcase full of frozen rats and chicks for food.

Trainers conduct much of their work outdoors. In winter, trainers may work indoors, but depending on the animal, they may continue outdoor training year-round.

If the animal is expected to work or perform outdoors in winter, it has to be trained in winter as well. Companion animals have to cope with every type of weather, so the trainer is responsible for training and testing the animal accordingly.

WHAT IS IT LIKE TO BE AN ANIMAL TRAINER?

Teoti Anderson is the owner of Pawsitive Results, LLC, which offers reward-based group dog training classes in Lexington and West Columbia, South Carolina. She is also the author of several dog training books (including *Your Outta Control Puppy, The Super Simple Guide to House-training)*, a columnist for *Modern Dog* magazine, and a public speaker. "I decided to become a dog trainer because of one very special dog," she recalls. "More than 15 years ago, I adopted a three-legged Labrador retriever puppy and named him Cody. He was so sweet and loving, I thought he would make a good candidate for a therapy dog. I didn't know how to go about training him for therapy work, so I enrolled us in some local classes. I ended up taking several classes and found I had a knack for it. I became an assistant, then an instructor, and then it all blossomed from there. As for the writing and public speaking part, that's my background. My degree was in broadcast journalism. I started out writing advertising and now, for my day job, I write and edit Web sites for a large corporation. I've been very lucky in that I've found a way to combine my love of writing with my love of dogs!

"My favorite part about being a professional dog trainer is that light bulb moment for a team—when an owner learns how to communicate with her dog and the dog responds. It's wonderful to know that I'm helping improve that relationship and helping a dog stay in that home, rather than possibly being given up to a shelter."

Teoti says that one of the challenges that dog trainers face is similar to that faced by anyone working in a customer service profession. "There are bound to be times when you get a difficult student in class," she says. "And I'm talking about the people, not the dogs! Perhaps the student has unrealistic expectations for his or her dog, or maybe you get someone who wants to wave a magic wand and have a trained dog, rather than understanding that it takes work. These folks can be a challenge to work with at times, but they motivate me to become a better communicator."

Kellyann Payne has been a dog trainer for more than 20 years. She is past-president of the Association of Pet Dog Trainers and also served on its board. "Deciding to be a dog trainer full time was simply a natural progression," she says. "While it was mostly a hobby at first, I quickly realized that I truly enjoyed working with and helping people and their dogs. I also saw that dog training was a viable way for me to make a living. Every client (human and canine) provides me with new challenges to grow and learn—and a challenge is something that I need in order to enjoy my work. I work mostly from home now, though I have owned two training centers in the past. I do a good deal of work at my local animal shelters as well."

A typical day for Kellyann begins with her reviewing the day's appointments and confirming any for the next. "Before leav-

To Be a Successful Animal Trainer, You Should...

- like and respect animals
- enjoy working with people, as well as animals
- be attentive to detail
- have excellent communication skills
- have physical strength (if working with large animals)
- be in good physical shape
- have patience
- be calm under pressure
- be willing to continue to learn throughout your career
- have strong business skills (if you own your own business)

ing for my first appointment I review my notes from my last session with the client and print out materials that they could need for this session. Immediately following my session I verbally record notes from the session that I will transcribe later into the client file. If my appointment was with a local animal shelter or rescue group I will submit a copy of my notes to the organization for their records as well. Once I return to my home office I log in any payments and receipts for the day, answer phone messages, and try to get a jump-start on e-mail consultations. It's often a full day's work."

Most of Kellyann's appointments are at animal shelters. "If you haven't visited one lately, you should go," she says. "There has been a revolution over the last decade or so. Fewer and fewer animal shelters are the dungeons of the past. More and more are focusing on the enrichment of the animals' surroundings. They take into account the mental/behavioral well-being of the animals in addition to the medical needs. If I am working with a breed-specific rescue group I will often be in someone's home, just as I would be for a typical private client."

DO I HAVE WHAT IT TAKES TO BE AN ANIMAL TRAINER?

To be a successful animal trainer, you should like and respect animals and have a genuine interest in working with them. Animal trainers, especially those who specialize in training dogs, must have excellent communication skills. "Many people make the mistake of thinking dog trainers just work with dogs," says Teoti Anderson. "I've heard from people who wanted to get into this field because they don't like people, or are not good at working with people. To be a successful dog trainer, you have to be an excellent communicator, with dogs *and* people. If you can't reach the people, you can't help their dogs. You must also have patience, compassion, and a thirst for knowledge."

Trainers should also be prepared to work intensely with an animal and then have that animal go on to work somewhere else. The relationship with the trained animal may not be permanent, so separation is part of the trainer's job.

It takes physical strength to work with certain types of animals. It takes arm strength, for example, to control an 80-pound dog that doesn't want to heel or to hold a falcon on your wrist for an hour. You may also have to lift animals, bend, or spend extended periods standing or swimming. Trainers of aquatic mammals, such as dolphins and seals, work in water and must feel comfortable in aquatic environments.

It is also important to have patience. Just as people do, animals have bad days where they won't work well and respond to commands. Even the best trainers encounter days of frustration where nothing seems to go well. As an animal trainer, you will spend long hours repeating routines and rewarding your pupils for performing well, while being careful never to get angry with them or punish them when they fail to do what is expected. You also must be able to exhibit the authority to keep animals under control without raising your voice or using physical force. Calmness under stress is particularly important when dealing with wild animals.

HOW DO I BECOME AN ANIMAL TRAINER?

Education

High School

High school students interested in entering this field should take courses in anatomy, physiology, biology, and psychology. Understanding how the body and mind work helps a trainer understand the best methods for training.

The Benefits of Association Membership

Mychelle Blake, communications director of the Association of Pet Dog Trainers (APDT), discusses the benefits of membership in professional associations:

Association membership is extremely important and, while one can certainly go into business as a trainer without being a member of an association such as the Association of Pet Dog Trainers, the road to becoming a professional, successful trainer can be greatly enhanced through association membership. Being a part of an association such as the APDT gives you access to thousands of other trainers, both new to the field and experienced experts, who can give you advice on everything from how to start your business to working with your individual client cases. This networking can also provide critical emotional support in a field that can be often difficult when one deals with issues such as severe behavior cases. Association membership also provides ongoing educational opportunities, such as publications like the APDT's award-winning *The APDT Chronicle of the Dog* magazine, and our annual educational conference and trade show. Members of the APDT also have access to important benefits such as discounts from pet supply vendors and on insurance policies, and the ability to showcase the APDT logo on your Web site and marketing materials. The benefits of belonging to an association such as APDT will only continue to grow in the years ahead.

Knowledge of psychology will help the trainer recognize behaviors in the animals they train as well as in the people to whom the animals belong.

Postsecondary Training

There are no formal education requirements to enter this field, although some positions do require a college degree. Animal trainers in circuses and the entertainment field may be required to have some coursework in animal psychology in addition to their caretaking experience. Zoo and aquarium animal trainers usually must have a bachelor's degree

in a field related to animal management or animal physiology. Trainers of companion dogs prepare for their work in a three-year course of study at schools that train dogs and instruct the disabled owner-companion.

Many community colleges and vocational schools offer courses and workshops for aspiring dog trainers. "When I started out, there were not as many schools or associations available to dog trainers as there are now," says Teoti Anderson. "For those interested in this field, I would recommend attending a school that focuses on modern, scientific,

---

Advice For Young People

Mychelle Blake, communications director of the Association of Pet Dog Trainers, offers the following advice to young people who are interested in becoming dog trainers:

- Get as much experience as possible with dogs in a variety of ways. Volunteer at your local shelter to walk and groom dogs and show them for adoption. Attend dog sports and obedience shows to watch trainers at work. Take your dog, or even a shelter dog, through a training class and ask trainers if you can watch them teach and if you can help out during class. Many trainers apprenticed with experienced trainers, so this is a common way to start.

- Read as much as possible about dogs and watch DVDs about dog behavior and training, as well as training of other types of animals.

- Find out if there are local trainer networking groups that you can join or if conferences/seminars will be held locally. There are also many resources and groups on the Internet that you can join to learn from other trainers.

- The other critical component that you should address is working with people. Often I hear people say that they want to become a trainer because they love dogs and don't like people. If that's the case, this is not the career for you! Dog trainers work hand-in-hand with people, including dog owners, veterinarians, breeders, groomers, shelter workers, and volunteers, and having good people skills is critical to success in the field. Make sure you engage in activities and learning opportunities that allow you to develop your abilities to work with people!

reward-based techniques. There are still schools out there promoting outdated methods of training. I would also recommend that any dog trainer or aspiring dog trainer join the Association of Pet Dog Trainers (APDT). It's a tremendous resource for education."

Most trainers begin their careers as animal keepers. This allows them the chance to obtain on-the-job experience in evaluating the disposition, intelligence, and "trainability" of the animals they look after. At the same time, they learn to make friends with their charges, develop a rapport with them, and gain their confidence. The caretaking experience is an important building block in the education and success of an animal trainer. Although previous training experience may give job applicants an advantage in being hired, they will still be expected to spend time caring for the animals before advancing to a trainer position.

Establishments that hire trainers often require previous animal-keeping or equestrian experience, as proper care and feeding of animals is an essential part of a trainer's responsibilities. These positions serve as informal apprenticeships. The assistant may get to help an animal trainer on certain tasks but will be able to watch and learn from other tasks being performed around him or her. For example, racehorse trainers often begin as jockeys or grooms in training stables.

Certification or Licensing

The Certification Council for Professional Dog Trainers offers the voluntary certified pet dog trainer designation to dog trainers who have "at least 300 hours experience in dog training within the last five years; a high school diploma or equivalent; and one reference each from a veterinarian, a client, and a professional colleague." Teoti is a certified pet dog trainer. "I've attended 13 APDT conferences and numerous other conferences and seminars," she says. "I also graduated with honors from the San Francisco Society for the Prevention of Cruelty to Animals Academy for Dog Trainers and earned my counseling certificate with that program. I believe that there is always something new to learn about canine behavior and becoming a better instructor."

Other certifications for animal trainers are provided by the Animal Behavior Society, the American College of Veterinary Behaviorists, the International Association for the Study of Animal Behavior, the International Association of Animal Behavior Consultants, the International Association of Canine Professionals, and the National Association of Dog Obedience Instructors.

"Certification is becoming more and more important as we work toward professionalizing and strengthening the field of dog training," says Mychelle Blake, communications director of the Association of Pet Dog Trainers and editor-in-chief of *The APDT Chronicle of the Dog*. "Certification will set you apart from other trainers and will demonstrate that you have dedicated yourself to your craft and to rigorous educational and professional standards. What's important to understand is that there are many different types of 'certification' available in dog training today, and you should fully investigate all options before making a decision. There are many schools that will 'certify' you after attending an online series of courses; this is not the same as becoming certified by an independent organization such as the Certification Council for Professional Dog Trainers that tests applicants based on their knowledge and experience against a standard set of criteria from the most up-to-date, science-based training techniques and knowledge in the field, and that requires one to acquire continuing education in order to maintain your certification."

Kellyann Payne is a certified animal behavior consultant, a certification designation that is offered by the International Association of Animal Behavior Consultants. "I was also among the first trainers in the country to achieve the designation of certified pet dog trainer through the Certification Council for Professional Dog Trainers," she says. "Certification is certainly becoming more and more important in the industry."

Racehorse trainers must be licensed by the state in which they work. Otherwise, there are no special requirements for this occupation.

Internships and Volunteerships

Internships are an excellent way to learn more about the demands of a career in animal training while you are still in school. Internships last between one and two semesters. Students aren't usually paid for their work, but they receive credit hours for their participation.

Volunteering offers an opportunity to begin training animals and learn firsthand about the tasks and routines involved in managing animals. Part-time or volunteer work in animal shelters, pet-training programs, rescue centers, pet shops, or veterinary offices gives potential trainers a chance to discover whether they have the aptitude for working with animals. Teoti volunteered for many years before she landed her first paying job in dog training. "My first job as a volunteer was as an assistant for dog training classes," she says. "I helped people with the class exercises and assisted the instructor. My first paying job was when I started a business with a fellow dog trainer."

You can also acquire experience by working in a summer job as an animal caretaker at a zoo, aquarium, museum that features live animal shows, amusement park, or stable (if you have an interest in horse racing).

WHO WILL HIRE ME?

Typical employers for animal trainers include dog-training and companion-pet programs, zoos, aquariums and oceanariums, amusement parks, rescue centers, pet shops, and circuses. Many (57 percent) are self-employed, and a few very successful animal trainers work in the entertainment field, training animal "actors" or working with wild and/or dangerous animals. A number of these positions require a great deal of traveling and even relocating.

The threat of terrorism has created demand for bomb-sniffing dogs and their trainers. An increasing number of animal trainers and handlers will be employed by government agencies such as the Federal Aviation Administration and U.S. Customs & Border Protection, Fortune 500 companies, amusement parks, and sports arenas.

People who wish to become animal trainers generally start out as animal keepers, stable workers, or caretakers and are promoted to the position of trainer only after acquiring experience within the ranks of an organization. You can enter the field by applying directly for a job as an animal keeper, letting your employer or supervisor know of your ambition so you will eventually be considered for promotion. The same applies for volunteer positions. Learning as a volunteer is an excellent way to get hands-on experience, but you should be vocal in your interest in a paid position once you have gotten to know the staff and they have gotten to know you.

When considering a position, it is important to observe the training methods used by the organization. No reputable organization, regardless of what it trains animals for, should use physical injury to train or discipline an animal. The techniques you learn at your first job determine the position you will qualify for after that. You want to be sure that you are learning from an organization that has a sound philosophy

A Rewarding Experience

• • • • • • • • • • • • • •

Kellyann Payne, a dog trainer and past-president of the Association of Pet Dog Trainers, describes one of the most memorable experiences in her career:

About 12 years ago I was asked to evaluate a young feral dog that had been pulled out of a sewer. Indeed the dog seemed "wild." He was very afraid of people, choosing to run away rather than approach as most dogs would. I agreed to foster the dog to see if he could be put up for adoption after spending some time around people in a controlled environment.

Our first night together was memorable. When we first came home, it took him more than three hours to leave his crate. Those three hours were the best investment of time I ever spent. I remember the moment he popped his head out, sniffed the air, and darted across the room to snatch a piece of meat from my hand. Then he quickly ran back to his crate.

Each day he improved and each day I grew closer to him. It did not take long for me to become very attached to the little guy. While I foster many dogs, I am typically quite good about keeping an emotional distance. This little guy was different for me, though. Ultimately I adopted him and named him Nemo.

Fast forward 12 years and he is lying at my feet as I type this. He is still very timid when he meets someone new, but he has come a long, long way. He has been featured in commercials and training videos for Animal Planet. He has learned a number of fun tricks and skills that are far more advanced than most dogs will ever learn. (And he still loves to learn new tricks!) He has taught me more about patience and potential than any dog I have ever trained. My best analogy is that if the average dog is like a book, Nemo is a library.

Facts About Pacific White-Sided Dolphins

Pacific white-sided dolphins are some of the most popular animals at ocean-ariums and aquariums. Here are some interesting facts about this species and dolphins in general:

- Dolphins are not fish, they are mammals.

- They swim in herds, which can number in the thousands.

- Pacific white-sided dolphins can be distinguished from other dolphin species by their black backs, gray sides, white bellies, and a stripe that runs down each side of their body.

- Pacific white-sided dolphins are known for being gregarious and athletic. They can swim as fast as 25 miles per hour and jump 15 to 20 feet in the air.

- All dolphins use echolocation to find their way in the water and hunt for food. They send out a series of high-frequency clicks that bounce back off objects that are around them in the water. Their forehead and lower jaw receive the return-ing sound waves, which allows them to determine an object's size, shape, and proximity.

- Dolphins do not have vocal chords. They make sounds using muscles inside their blowholes.

Source: Monterey Bay Aquarium, Shedd Aquarium

and training method for working with animals.

The most sought-after positions depend on the animals you want to train. Dog-training programs are probably the most plentiful and offer the widest range of training philosophies and techniques. Check out books on dog training meth-ods to learn what the differences are. Sea mammals are exhibited at oceanariums and aquariums, and it is very difficult to land a job in this specialty.

WHERE CAN I GO FROM HERE?

Opportunities for advancement are lim-ited because most establishments have very small staffs of animal trainers. The typical career path is from animal keeper to animal trainer. A trainer who directs or supervises others may be designated head animal trainer or senior animal trainer.

Some animal trainers start their own training businesses and, if successful, hire other trainers to work for them. Oth-ers become agents for animal acts. But promotion may mean moving from one organization to another and may require relocating to another city, depending on what animal you specialize in.

WHAT ARE THE SALARY RANGES?

Animal trainers earn a wide range of sal-aries based on their specialty and place of employment. Salaries for all animal trainers ranged from less than $16,700 to $51,400 a year or more in 2008, according to the U.S. Department of Labor. The median salary for animal trainers was $27,270 in 2008. Those who earn higher salaries are in upper management and spend more time running the business than working with animals.

In the field of racehorse training, however, trainers are paid an average fee of $35 to $50 a day for each horse, plus 10 percent of any money their horses win in races. Depending on the horse and the races it runs, this can exceed the average high-end earnings for a trainer. Show horse trainers may earn as much as $30,000 to $35,000 a year. Trainers in business for themselves set their own fees for teaching both horses and owners.

Animal trainers who work full time receive benefits such as vacation days, sick leave, health and life insurance, and a savings and pension program. Self-employed trainers must provide their own benefits.

WHAT IS THE JOB OUTLOOK?

Employment for animal trainers is expected to be mixed in the coming years, with opportunities predicted to be very good for dog trainers and slower than average for horse and marine mammal trainers.

An increasing number of animal owners are seeking training services for their pets. The field of dog training (the largest employer of animal trainers) is expected to grow much faster than the average for all careers through 2016, according to the U.S. Department of Labor. "Future employment appears to be strong," says Mychelle Blake. "It is estimated that there are about 6 million dogs born in the United States each year and that only a very small percentage of these dogs ever attend a training class or see a trainer one on one. As the benefits of training continue to be emphasized in the media, the percentage of dog owners seeking trainers will only continue to expand."

Threats of terrorism have created a strong demand for search-and-rescue and bomb-sniffing dogs. Search-and-rescue programs, although expanding, are not permanent work positions for the handler. These teams are used intermittently, as the need arises. But an increasing number of trainers will be needed to train teams. There will be strong demand for bomb-sniffing dogs and their trainers and handlers to ensure the safety of airports, government buildings, corporations, amusement parks, sports facilities, and public utilities.

Employment for marine mammal trainers and horse trainers is expected to grow more slowly than the average for all careers through 2016, according to the U.S. Department of Labor. Both fields are small and employ only a few trainers. Positions such as marine mammal trainer are highly sought after, and there is little turnover in this field.

Aquarists

SUMMARY

Definition
Aquarists maintain aquatic exhibits. Among other duties, they check water quality, clean tanks, feed the animals, and collect and transport new specimens.

Alternative Job Titles
Animal keepers
Marine life keepers

Salary Range
$15,140 to $27,000 to $40,000

Educational Requirements
Bachelor's degree

Certification or Licensing
Required

Employment Outlook
More slowly than the average

High School Subjects
Biology
Earth science

Personal Interests
Animals
Science
Wildlife

Aquarists such as Freya Smith really need to be on their toes when participating in activities such as the Monterey Bay Aquarium's White Shark Research Project. This "collaborative multi-year study of white sharks off the California coast has two primary goals: tagging and field studies and exhibiting a white shark." (Visit http://www.montereybayaquarium. org/cr/whiteshark.asp for more information on the project.)

Freya served as a field team leader on the project and had to be on call in the event that a juvenile shark was located for potential inclusion in the study.

"Last summer," she recalls, "the Monterey Bay Aquarium set out to bring back its fourth young-of-the-year (less then one year old) white shark to temporarily display in our million-gallon exhibit, the Outer Bay.

"When a fisherman in Southern California caught a white shark accidentally, I had to hop in a car with a coworker and drive down seven hours at a moment's notice, sacrificing all plans I had for that day and possibly the weekend to come. Once we arrived, we were transported by a Boston Whaler boat one hour to the site where our ocean sea pen was set up. This is where the juvenile white shark was placed by our rapid response team. The pen was one mile from shore, and the boat that tended the pen, the *Bar-*

bara H., was our home for the next four to seven days."

During this time, Freya lived in a cabin with the boat's crew and her coworker and never went back to shore. "My job," she says, "was to go to the pen every morning, attempt to get visuals on the white shark from the surface to do observations, collect and record weather and ocean conditions, and check the bait I had left out overnight to see if it had been eaten by the shark. Then I would call the aquarium, give them my morning updates, and as a team we would decide if we would dive that day in the pen to get more visual observations on the shark's health and appearance. We would also repair nets if needed, and take video of the shark swimming in the pen."

During this time, Freya and her colleague would ferry back and forth to the pen from the boat. "We would check baits, put out fresh baits as needed (sustainable, restaurant-quality salmon and mackerel), do more surface observations of the white shark, if possible, and collect more weather and ocean data," she says. "At night, I would enter all the observations and field data from my log book into the computer and fish off the *Barbara H.* for fresh mackerel for the next day. I would repeat this day after day until we got the shark to feed and/or a team of my coworkers would come from Monterey to relieve us. Eventually, the white shark did feed several times in the ocean pen. After the aquarium's veterinarian performed a thorough physical on the shark, we made a decision to get a team together to transport the shark back to the Mon-terey Bay Aquarium and put it on display in our Outer Bay Exhibit."

Lingo to Learn

aquarium A place where living aquatic plants and animals are studied and exhibited. Also, a tank, bowl, or other water-filled structure in which living aquatic plants and animals are exhibited.

breeding The sexual pairing of two members of the same species for the purpose of producing offspring.

conservation The practice of preserving natural resources.

specimen A small sample of a living organism or nonliving object.

tidal pool A pool of seawater left on rocks near the ocean when the water (or tide) recedes. A variety of animals live in these temporary pools, including crabs, starfish, barnacles, small fish, and sea urchins.

wetsuit A garment that protects the wearer from the harsh conditions of the ocean or other bodies of water.

WHAT DOES AN AQUARIST DO?

Aquarists (pronounced, like "aquarium," with the accent on the second syllable) are employed by aquariums, oceanariums, and marine research institutes. Aquarists are not animal trainers and do not work on marine shows. They do, however, support the staff that does this work. Their job is generally technical and requires a strong science background. With increased experience and education, aquarists may, in

To Be a Successful Aquarist, You Should...

- be able to work well with others
- be willing to travel for your work
- be in good physical shape
- not be afraid to get dirty on the job
- have good hearing and vision
- have excellent communication skills
- be self-motivated
- be willing to occasionally work outdoors in all types of weather
- be able to follow directions
- have a strong love of animals

time, become involved in research efforts at their institution or advance to a higher professional position, such as curator.

Aquarists' job duties are similar to those of zookeepers. Aquarists feed fish, maintain exhibits, and conduct research. They work on breeding, conservation, and educational programs.

Aquarists clean and take care of tanks daily. They make sure pumps are working, clean glass, check water temperatures, and sift sand. Aquarists have to scrub some exhibits by hand. They also change the water and vacuum tanks routinely. They water plants in pond or marsh exhibits.

Food preparation and feeding are important tasks for aquarists. Some ani-mals eat live food. Others eat cut-up food mixtures. Some animals require special diets and may have to be individually fed.

Aquarists carefully observe all the animals in their care. They must understand their normal habits (including feeding, sleeping, mating, and moving) in order to be able to know when something is wrong. Aquarists write daily reports and maintain detailed records of animal behavior.

Many aquarists are in charge of collecting and stocking plants and animals for exhibits. They may have to make several trips a year to gather live specimens.

Aquarists may work indoors or outdoors, depending on the facility for which they are employed and the exhibit to which they're assigned. Aquarists spend a lot of time in the water. Their day will be filled with a variety of tasks, some repetitive, like feeding, others unusual, such as working with rescued marine mammals. In the beginning, aquarists work under the supervision of a senior aquarist or supervisor and may work as part of a team.

WHAT IS IT LIKE TO BE AN AQUARIST?

Julie Christie is a marine life keeper at the Oregon Zoo (http://www.oregonzoo.org) in Portland, Oregon. She has worked in the field for 12 years, including more than seven years at the Oregon Zoo. "I have always been interested in coastal life," she says, "and when I started volunteering at the Oregon Coast Aquarium I realized how much care went into keeping these animals physically and mentally stimulated. I also saw the dedication and passion of many of the staff members, and it inspired me to get involved, learn, and apply everything I could to provide better animal care.

"As keepers," she continues, "it is our job to maintain the best quality animal care. We prepare and administer diets and medications daily (even on holidays and weekends); clean exhibits and ensure safety; observe animal behavior throughout the day; and keep thorough records about every aspect of each individual animal (for example, medical changes, breeding behavior, lethargy, increased appetite, observed limping, new enrichment, etc.). We continually try to further our education and update our animal care. Keepers must be highly effective communicators to many different types of people."

Keepers are very involved in the daily enrichment of the animals. "We are continually researching, acquiring, and providing different and novel items to these animals," says Julie. "This gives the animals change to their exhibit, choices of items to interact with, some control over their environment, and mental and physical challenges. Animal keepers are also highly involved in training animals. These behaviors could be anything from fun behaviors to encourage more learning (retrievals), to veterinary care behaviors to increase the animals' medical care in a low-stress environment, to moving the animals from one area to another for cleaning purposes. Keepers are animals' caretakers, activity coordinators (for both

animals and visitors), public educators, animal advocates, record keepers, conservationists, behaviorists, and much, much more."

One of Julie's most rewarding career moments came when she and other staff were tasked with providing 24-hour-a-day care for more than a month to a sick female sea otter named Thelma. "Thelma had stopped eating one morning and was very 'off' behaviorally," Julie recalls. "She was taken to the vet hospital, and the vets discovered that one of her lungs had collapsed. We all worked very hard to care for her, and Thelma was able to have surgery to remove the collapsed lung. This procedure had never been done on a sea otter, and after the surgery there were many things we would have to take slowly to ensure her health. One of the things was Thelma's diving and how it would affect her one remaining lung. Through time and dedication by many we are lucky to say Thelma is still with us and living her otter life just as she was before this all happened."

Freya Smith is a senior aquarist at Monterey Bay Aquarium in Monterey, California. "I became a certified scuba diver at age 12," she recalls, "and that's what helped start my passion and inspired me to become a marine biologist. When I was pursuing my marine biology degree at the University of California at Santa Cruz, I knew that entering this field would not make me rich, but that I could help make a difference in the world's oceans and with the many creatures that inhabit them. I have worked as an aquarist at the aquarium for eight and a half years. An aquarist is responsible for performing general aquarium husbandry duties. These responsibilities include setting up, maintaining, and caring for aquarium exhibits; preparing and dispensing food; treating organisms for diseases; and assisting with the collecting effort."

Freya's main and secondary job duties change on a yearly basis. "This year," she says, "my main job is to take care of the Bat Ray Touch Pool Exhibit and the Waves & Tides Exhibit. Caring for the bat rays entails putting on hip wader boots and climbing into the Bat Ray Exhibit to clean it daily, doing daily hand feeding of the animals and getting the public involved, doing daily observations on each individual bat ray's health, and helping with collecting bat rays, if needed. Taking care of the Waves & Tides Exhibit entails cleaning and maintaining the six exhibits that make up this area. This includes scrubbing windows, siphoning, daily feedings of the fish and invertebrates, and adding new plants and animals, as needed. For the collections of this exhibit, I go tide-pooling and scuba-diving out in Monterey Bay to gather plants and invertebrates to enhance those exhibits (the aquarium has a collecting permit through the California Department of Fish and Game).

"My secondary duties are as follows: feeding and training sea otters; feeding sharks in the Outer Bay Exhibit, which include scalloped hammerheads and Galapagos sharks; and scuba diving in the Monterey Bay Habitats Exhibit to do an underwater shark feeding for the seven-gill sharks, bat rays, and leopard sharks."

Advice for Aspiring Aquarists

Freya Smith, a senior aquarist at Monterey Bay Aquarium, offers the following advice to young people who are interested in the field:

- I strongly encourage anyone who is interested in this career to volunteer in the field. Volunteering is one of the most important ways to get on-the-job training and experience. And volunteering will allow you to sample a career and see if it's one you like.

- Become scuba certified at the first chance you get and continue to dive as much as possible.

- Read the book *The Marine Aquarium Handbook: Beginner to Breeder*, by Martin A. Moe Jr., cover to cover. (It's out of print, but you can easily find a copy online.)

- Go to college and earn a degree in biology.

- Don't get discouraged on the road to this career; you can achieve anything you put your mind to. There are stories of many aquarists who went to college, had all the required skills, and had to volunteer for years until a position opened up, and then they got their dream job (a full-time, paid position).

Freya says that there are many pluses and no drawbacks to working as an aquarist. "By working in this field, I get to do something I love," she says. "I'm excited to go to work every day, and look forward to working with many cool animals at the aquarium. I also get to work outside sometimes, going boating to collect kelp, going scuba diving out in the field, and tide pooling. Another great thing about working in this field is that I get to help inspire the public about conservation of the world's oceans."

DO I HAVE WHAT IT TAKES TO BE AN AQUARIST?

Julie Christie believes that the most important qualities for marine life keepers include a "good attitude, being a hard worker, self-motivation, creativity, good communication skills (both written and oral), being a team player, the commitment to continually develop one's skills, the ability to accept constructive criticism, and being physically able to perform necessary skills."

Freya Smith cites the following professional qualities as most important for successful aquarists: "a bachelor of science degree in biology or related field; knowledge of marine flora and fauna; an ability to do exhibit maintenance and collection records; an understanding of the basic taxonomy of marine fish, invertebrates, and plants; the ability to assess basic invertebrate and fish health; an understanding of basic, aquarium-related water quality and water chemistry; knowledge of the mathematics necessary for metric conversions and water-volume calculations; an understanding of biological, mechanical, and chemical filtrations; an ability to perform numerous types of field collections; and scuba diving certification."

Facts About the Monterey Bay Aquarium

- The aquarium opened on October 20, 1984.

- Nearly 2 million people visit the aquarium each year.

- Approximately 550 different species of plants and animals are on display.

- It was the first aquarium in the world to exhibit a living kelp forest.

- The aquarium has more than 400 employees and nearly 1,000 volunteers.

- *Parents Magazine* named the Monterey Bay Aquarium the best aquarium for kids in 2007.

Source: Monterey Bay Aquarium

In terms of personal qualities, Freya says that the following are most important: "an ability to function professionally with a positive attitude in a team environment; the ability to communicate effectively in person and in writing; an ability to share both positive and negative feedback and to resolve interpersonal professional concerns; and self motivation."

Aquarists need to be in good physical shape, with good hearing and visual acuity. Some employers also require a certain strength level—say, the ability to regularly exert 100 pounds of force—since equipment, feed, and the animals themselves can be heavy and often unwieldy. Throughout the year, aquarists may be required to travel at different times to collect specimens, participate in research expeditions, and attend educational seminars.

HOW DO I BECOME AN AQUARIST?

Education

High School

Take as many science classes as you can in high school. Biology, chemistry, and zoology are especially important. Mathematics, computer science, and English classes will also be useful.

Postsecondary Training

You will need at least a bachelor's degree in one of the biological sciences—preferably with course work in such areas as parasitology, ichthyology, or other aquatic sciences—to work at top employers such as aquariums. The care of captive animals has become a complex discipline, and it's no longer viable to apply without a four-year degree. "There are many different avenues you can pursue in college" says Julie Christie, "but definitely get a college degree. Fish and wildlife, biology, zoology, and psychology are some typical degrees. Many employers require job applicants to have a degree or many years of paid experience."

Certification or Licensing

Aquarists must be able to dive, in both contained water (to feed fish and maintain tanks) and in open water (on trips to collect new specimens). This means that you'll need to have scuba certification, with a rescue diver classification. Potential employers will expect you to be able to pass a diving physical examination before you are hired. You may also need to have a special collector's permit from the state in which you work that allows you to gather samples for your aquarium.

Internships and Volunteerships

You will most likely participate in an internship at an aquarium, zoo, or other

---

Pros and Cons

● ● ● ● ● ● ● ● ●

Julie Christie, a marine life keeper at the Oregon Zoo, details what she likes most and least about her job:

Pros in this field are definitely the animals. We are very fortunate to interact with a wide variety of animals daily. We have created bonds with them and get to observe many different aspects of their lives. I personally feel this also motivates me to look at my own life and try to make sure I am aware of my impact on the earth and attempt to minimize it. Another pro is when you have a great team you work with that continually brings new ideas to animal care.

In terms of cons, resources are often hard to come by due to money, staffing, or time limitations. Sometimes it is hard when you are trying to provide the best care possible. Of course, a big con is animal loss; the bonds we have with these animals make it very difficult during times of health decline.

marine science facility as part of your college education. Internships allow you to learn more about the field and work closely with aquarists and other professionals. Most internships are unpaid, but many colleges award course credit for their successful completion.

In addition to formal education, many aquariums seek applicants who have demonstrated a strong interest in the field during their high school and college years. Most often, they look for a history of volunteering. That means you need to look for every avenue you can find to work around fish or other animals. "Try to volunteer at a zoo, aquarium, rehabilitation center, animal areas within your school, or get a job at a pet store," Julie recommends. "It always helps to have animal experience, and sometimes this field isn't for everyone. These are good ways to help you decide if you really want to pursue this field."

You can also ask your career guidance counselor for information on marine science careers and opportunities for summer internships or college scholarships offered by larger institutes.

Facts About the Oregon Zoo

- The zoo opened in 1887.
- It is the oldest zoo west of the Mississippi River.
- More than 1.4 million people visited the Oregon Zoo in 2006.
- Approximately 200 species of birds, mammals, reptiles, amphibians, and invertebrates are on display. There are also 1,000 species of exotic plants on display in its botanical garden.
- The zoo's Trillium Creek Family Farm opened in 2004. It is the first U.S. zoo exhibit that is run entirely by teen volunteers.
- Its Steller Cove Exhibit "replicates Oregon's unique coastal landforms, including coastal waves, a dramatic blowhole, tide pools, and rocky shorelines." It has 387,000 gallons of water.

Source: Oregon Zoo

WHO WILL HIRE ME?

Aquarists most often work in public aquariums, zoos, or in research jobs with marine science institutes.

Full-time jobs for aquarists can be scarce, especially for those just starting in the field. Part-time or volunteer positions with zoos, aquariums, science institutes, nature centers, or even pet stores could provide valuable preliminary experience that may eventually lead to a full-time position.

WHERE CAN I GO FROM HERE?

The typical career path for an aquarist progresses from intern/volunteer through part-time work to full-fledged aquarist, senior aquarist, supervisor, and finally, curator. Each step along the path requires additional experience and, often, additional education. Curators are generally expected to have a Ph.D. in a relevant marine science discipline, for example. The career path of an aquarist depends on how much hands-on work they like to do with animals. Aquarists who enjoy working closely with animals may prefer not to seek advancement into positions, such as curator, that take them away from daily, hands-on work with animals. Instead, they may advance by seeking employment at larger or more prestigious facilities.

WHAT ARE THE SALARY RANGES?

Aquariums are often nonprofit institutions, somewhat limiting the earnings ability in this job. In general, aquarists earn between $23,000 and $40,000 a year. Salaries for nonfarm animal caretakers (a career category that includes aquarists) ranged from less than $15,140 to $31,590 or more in 2008, according to the U.S. Department of Labor.

Aquarists receive fairly extensive benefits, including health insurance, 401(k) accounts, tuition reimbursement, continuing education opportunities, and reciprocal benefits with many other cultural institutions.

WHAT IS THE JOB OUTLOOK?

The number of positions for aquarists is not expected to change much in the next decade. While terrestrial zoos have begun to add aquarium complexes to their sites in growing numbers, an actual boom in the construction of new aquariums is unlikely at this time. Many aquarists advance to other positions, however, so openings do become available. Aquarists with advanced degrees and training who are willing to relocate will have the best employment opportunities.

Park Workers

SUMMARY

Definition
Park workers are employed by national, state, and local parks in jobs dedicated to preserving our nation's natural and cultural resources and sharing them with the public.

Alternative Job Titles
(Note: The following are a small sampling of career opportunities; there are dozens of unique job opportunities available.)
Backcountry rangers
Biologists
Interpreters
Park superintendents
Scientists

Salary Range
$24,611 to $34,953 to $89,000+

Educational Requirements
High school diploma; bachelor's degree recommended

Certification or Licensing
None available

Employment Outlook
More slowly than the average

High School Subjects
English (writing/literature)
Physical education
Science
Speech

Personal Interests
Animals
Botany
Business management
Camping/hiking
The environment
Science
Teaching
Wildlife

Dr. Donna Shaver, chief of the Division of Sea Turtle Science and Recovery at Padre Island National Seashore, says that one of the most interesting and rewarding things that has happened to her while working in the field was the return of Kemp's ridley sea turtles, which had been experimentally imprinted to Padre Island National Seashore, and the significant increase in nesting there. "When I began working with the Kemp's Ridley Sea Turtle Recovery Project at Padre Island National Seashore in 1980 as a volunteer," she recalls, "the Kemp's ridley population was plummeting. Some feared that it would go extinct. I decided that I wanted to dedicate my career to helping save this and other sea turtle species. After years of effort by many people in the United States and Mexico, the Kemp's ridley population is increasing. Scientists believe that with continued conservation efforts on the nesting beaches and in the marine environment, it will be possible to recover the population and remove the Kemp's ridley sea turtle from the endangered species list in several years." (Visit http://www.nps.gov/archive/pais/pphtml /9highlights471.html to learn more about the National Park Service's Division of Sea Turtle Science and Recovery and its programs.)

WHAT DOES A PARK WORKER DO?

Park workers help protect our nation's natural and cultural resources. They edu-cate visitors about the parks and their nat-ural resources. Park workers are employed at local and state parks, as well as for the National Park Service (NPS). Our country's National Park System covers more than 84 million acres. With only one exception (Delaware), every state in our country is home to at least one national park. Most of these parks welcome hundreds of thousands of visitors each year. All NPS areas are given one of the following designations: National Park, National Historical Park (NHP), National Battlefield, National Battlefield Park, National Battlefield Site, National Military Site, National Memorial, National Historic Site (NHS), National Monument, National Preserve, National Seashore, National Parkway, National Lakeshore, National Reserve, National River, National Wild and Scenic River, National Recreation Area, or just Park.

Park workers who deal with the environment (or manage employees that work with environmental issues) include scientists (such as bear management specialists, biological technicians, biologists, ecologists, fisheries biologists, marine biologists, oceanographers, physical science technicians, seabird biologists, and zoologists), law enforcement rangers, interpreters, resource managers, and park superintendents—to name just a few.

Scientists are behind-the-scenes heroes within local, state, and national parks. Scientists help us better understand the ecosystems and wildlife within our parks so that we can manage and use them more wisely. They protect endangered species, create conservation plans, and study animals and environmental conditions in parks.

To Be a Successful Park Worker, You Should...

- have comprehensive knowledge of animals and the environment
- love nature and enjoy working with the public
- be friendly, confident, and able to communicate clearly with coworkers and the general public
- be willing to work in a variety of natural environments, as well as adverse weather such as extreme heat or cold, rain, snow, and high winds
- be flexible about work schedules and work locations
- be willing to continue to learn throughout your career
- be able to react quickly and effectively in crisis situations

A Proud Heritage

● ● ● ● ● ● ● ● ● ●

In 1872 Congress enacted an historical measure, establishing Yellowstone National Park as "a public park or pleasuring ground for the benefit and enjoyment of people." This landmark act marked the first time that our country—or any other country in the world—officially recognized the importance of preserving our most awe-inspiring natural resources in their natural state.

On August 25, 1916, President Woodrow Wilson signed an act creating the National Park Service, a new federal bureau in the Department of the Interior. The mandate of this fledgling bureau was to protect the 40 national parks and monuments then in existence and any that would subsequently be created. According to this act, the purpose of these parks was "to conserve the scenery and the natural and historic objects and the wildlife therein and to provide for the enjoyment of the same in such manner and by such means as will leave them unimpaired for the enjoyment of future generations."

An Executive Order in 1933 transferred an additional 63 monuments and military sites from the authority of the Forest Service and the War Department to that of the National Park Service. This order laid the cornerstone for the National Park Service we know today, which includes historical sites as well as scenic areas.

Throughout the years, the National Park Service has remained committed to the ideal of conserving our country's natural and cultural resources and has developed a mission statement that reflects this ideal. The mission statement of the National Park Service is as follows: *The National Park Service is dedicated to conserving unimpaired the natural and cultural resources and values of the National Park System for the enjoyment, education, and inspiration of this and future generations. The Service is also responsible for managing a great variety of national and international programs designed to help extend the benefits of natural and cultural resources conservation and outdoor recreation throughout this country and the world.*

Today, the National Park Service includes 391 distinct areas in 49 states, the District of Columbia, American Samoa, Guam, Puerto Rico, and the Virgin Islands. Wilson's "Organic Act" of 1916 has since inspired more than 100 other nations to create similar parks and preserves.

Park rangers have the most contact with visitors. Though all rangers are trained to respond to emergency situations, there are actually two distinct kinds of rangers: those who enforce the rules and protect the park resources and those who interpret the resources to the public.

Enforcement rangers patrol the vast expanses of our nation's parks, helping visitors have safe, enjoyable experiences in the wilderness. They are responsible for visitor protection, resource protection, law enforcement, and overseeing special park uses, such as commercial filming. They also collect park fees, provide emergency medical services, fight fires, and conduct wilderness rescues. In order to perform their responsibilities, they must spend a great deal of time in the field. Fieldwork may involve hiking the park's trails, patrolling the park's waters in boats, or interacting with visitors (some of whom get too close to wild animals or dangerous natural features such as geysers).

Interpretive rangers are responsible for helping visitors understand the natural and cultural resources within our national parks. They try to educate the public about the history and value of the resources. They also try to help visitors learn how to have enriching, enjoyable experiences in the parks without harming animals and the environment. Interpretive rangers give presentations, lead guided hikes, and answer questions. Some conduct orientation sessions for visitors as they first enter the park. Some also give presentations before community groups and schools in order to help neighboring communities appreciate their parks.

The many employees and functions within each park all are overseen by one individual. This person, called the *park superintendent* or *park manager*, is charged with making sure that our parks maintain the delicate balance between welcoming visitors and preserving natural resources. He or she may, in larger parks, work with an assistant superintendent. In addition to supervising the various operations within a park, the superintendent handles land acquisitions, works with resource managers and park planners to direct development, and deals with local or national issues that may affect the future of the park.

WHAT IS IT LIKE TO BE A PARK WORKER?

Dr. Donna Shaver is the chief of the National Park Service's Division of Sea

---

Lingo to Learn

national historic park A national historic park is an area that preserves the location of an event or activity that is important to our country's heritage.

national historic site A national historic site is similar to a national historic park, but is usually smaller.

national memorial These areas commemorate events or individuals of national significance.

national monument National monuments cover smaller areas than the national parks and do not have as great a diversity of attractions.

national park National parks cover large areas and contain a variety of resources. Most are chosen for the natural scenic and scientific values.

national parkway A national parkway is a scenic roadway designed for leisurely driving.

national preserve A national preserve is an area set aside for the protection of specific natural resources.

national recreation area An area or facility that has been set aside for recreational use.

national seashore A marine area that is set aside for the protection of specific natural resources.

Turtle Science and Recovery at Padre Island National Seashore. She has worked with sea turtles for the last 29 years, and has led the Kemp's Ridley Sea Turtle Recovery Project at Padre Island National Seashore since 1986. Dr. Shaver supervises a variety of sea turtle research and conservation projects in Texas. "I decided to enter this career because I was interested in the conservation of threatened and endangered species," she explains. "I wanted to contribute to recovery efforts for these imperiled species.

"The pros of working in this field," she continues, "are that you are helping make a difference in the survival of individual animals, species, habitats, and ecosystems. You get the opportunity to meet and work with a wide range of interesting people, including scientists, government officials, environmental groups, media representatives, community members, and others. You develop partnerships and cooperative working relationships with others to accomplish your goals, and in so doing have the chance to interact with many dedicated people. You are challenged to develop creative solutions to problems and to manage multiple priorities. You sometimes get the opportunity to work outdoors, which can be a pro when the weather is nice or a con when it is inclement. Another con is that sometimes the work can require very long hours and tiring physical labor. It also can sometimes be difficult to find a job in this career and sometimes these jobs do not pay much money."

DO I HAVE WHAT IT TAKES TO BE A PARK WORKER?

Park workers must successfully combine two very different characteristics. They must have a keen appreciation for nature and they must enjoy working with the public.

Because many park employees deal extensively with the public, they must be friendly, confident, and able to communicate clearly. Since they usually are responsible for a wide variety of tasks, they must also be exceptionally versatile. The fact that they work closely with nature, which can be unpredictable, means that these people must be creative problem solvers.

In addition to these general requirements, each of the positions within parks also involves a set of characteristics and abilities that are unique to that position. Scientists, for instance, must have excellent research skills and have encyclopedic knowledge of the species or ecosystem that they are responsible for studying and protecting. Superintendents must be excellent administrators and must have the vision to make long-term plans for a park. Enforcement rangers must be able to react quickly and effectively in crisis situations, and they must be able to convey authority to individuals who are violating park rules. Interpreters must have extensive knowledge about the resources in their parks and must be excellent educators. They must also have excellent communication skills.

Dr. Shaver says that scientists must have a variety of personal and professional qualities to be successful in the field. "They need to have a good educational background; have the drive to continue to learn and to excel at the activities that they undertake; and be enthusiastic, trustworthy, hard working, dedicated, and punctual. They also need to be able to work well alone and with others. They should be able to communicate and work well with others of varying educational levels, ethnic backgrounds, and age groups and able to communicate well verbally and in writing. They need to have good attention to detail and accuracy. They must have the ability to not give up when activities get repetitious or discouraging."

HOW DO I BECOME A PARK WORKER?

Almost no one enters the National Park Service or state or local parks in the position they would ultimately like to hold. Students who hope to one day serve as a scientist, ranger, or an interpreter must begin by getting a foot in the door. Most people begin as seasonal employees, working for three to four months a year in parks that receive more visitors during either the summer or winter seasons. This seasonal experience enables people to gain an understanding of the park system's mission and determine whether they would enjoy a career within the park system.

Those who choose to continue usually try to get experience in a variety of entry-level positions or in several different parks. This process helps individuals become familiar with the park system. It also allows park managers to gauge their strengths and abilities. When a person has gained experience through seasonal positions, he or she may be considered for a permanent position when one becomes available. Once an individual has gained permanent employment within the park system, he or she will receive on-the-job training. Rangers also undergo fire, search and rescue, and law-enforcement training.

Until that first opportunity becomes available, however, there are many ways for individuals to prepare themselves for a career in state or local parks or the National Park Service.

Education
High School
Students who hope to work in local, state, or national parks should study science and history during high school. They should also take classes that help them to develop their communication skills. Because interaction with the public is such a significant part of many park careers, students may also want to take psychology, education, and sociology courses. Those who plan to become rangers should also concentrate on physical education courses; physical fitness is a definite asset for people who must hike miles of backcountry trails, fight fires, and climb rocks to perform rescues.

Dr. Shaver advises high school students to "work hard at their studies and stay in school. They need to finish high school and get a college degree. Advanced degrees (MS and Ph.D.) can be helpful if they wish to lead a program or conduct research or more technical activities. Math and science courses are critical, but English, foreign language, business, management, speech, computer science, art, and many other courses are useful in preparation to enter this field. I also advise that, if they are interested in this career, they need to work hard in the volunteer or job positions that they get and do not give up. They must stay enthusiastic, positive, and committed to their goals. It may take a few years to get a permanent job in this career."

Hands-on experience can be a distinct advantage for a person who is trying to enter a competitive field. Students who are interested in working for the National Park Service should seek this experience by volunteering for a national park through the Volunteers-in-Parks (VIP) program (http://www.nps.gov/getting-involved/volunteer). Park volunteers can help park employees in any number of ways, including answering phone calls, welcoming visitors, maintaining trails, building fences, painting buildings, or picking up litter. Volunteer opportunities also are available at state and local parks.

Students who do not live near a park should contact the Student Conservation Association (SCA), which provides volunteers to assist federal and state natural resource management agencies. The SCA brings together students from throughout the United States to serve as crew members within the national parks. These students live and work within the parks for four to 12 weeks at a time. Dr. Shaver began her career at Padre Island National Seashore as an SCA volunteer in 1980. Other volunteer programs are available through the Youth Conservation Corps, Job Corps, Boy Scouts, Girl Scouts, and Public Land Corps.

The VIP, SCA, and other volunteer experiences can help a student prepare for a career in the parks and determine whether he or she would enjoy such a career.

Postsecondary Training

Prospective park employees would be well advised to obtain a bachelor's degree.

Most rangers currently in the National Park Service are college graduates and many believe that this will one day become a requirement. Any individual who hopes to serve as a scientist within the parks must have a college degree, with a major in the relevant discipline. Dr. Shaver received a bachelor of science degree in wildlife biology from Cornell University, a master of science degree in biology from Texas A&I University, and a Ph.D. in zoology from Texas A&M University.

Though there is no specific curriculum for people hoping to enter the National Park Service or work in state and local parks, students should continue to study science, with an emphasis on environmental science and wildlife management. History, public speaking, and business administration courses would all be useful for anyone entering this field.

Because there is so much competition for park jobs, especially those with the National Park Service and particularly ranger jobs, many people put themselves through additional training programs to distinguish themselves from other candidates. Some enroll in medical technician training programs or police academies. Others attend independent ranger academies to learn the fundamentals of law enforcement, emergency procedures, and fire fighting. These training programs can offer an excellent foundation for a prospective ranger.

Certification or Licensing

There is no general certification requirement for park employees. Individuals

Efforts to Save an Endangered Turtle

Dr. Donna Shaver, chief of the Division of Sea Turtle Science and Recovery at Padre Island National Seashore, details the recovery program for the endangered Kemp's ridley sea turtle:

The Kemp's ridley (Lepidochelys kempii) is the most endangered of all the species of sea turtle. Its principle nesting area is a 16-mile stretch of beach at Playa de Rancho Nuevo, Tamaulipas, Mexico, where approximately 40,000 Kemp's ridleys nested in a single day in 1947. The Kemp's ridley population dwindled to a low of only 702 nests in 1985. Numbers have been increasing in Mexico since that time, but are still far less than formerly recorded.

To save the Kemp's ridley, the U.S. federal government, the state of Texas, and the Republic of Mexico joined forces in an attempt to re-establish a nesting population at Padre Island National Seashore and provide a safeguard against extinction. The program was designed around the theory that mature sea turtles return to the beach where they hatched to lay their own eggs. From 1978 to 1988, a total of 22,507 eggs were collected at Rancho Nuevo and placed in Styrofoam boxes containing Padre Island sand. The eggs were then transported to a laboratory at Padre Island National Seashore for incubation and experimental imprinting.

After hatching, the young turtles were released on the beach and allowed to crawl into the surf, hopefully leaving them with a lasting impression of the beach. The hatchlings were recaptured and transported to the National Marine Fisheries Service Laboratory in Galveston, Texas. They were raised for about one year in Galveston, growing large enough to avoid most predators and also to be tagged for future recognition. Finally, they were released into the Gulf of Mexico.

After years of effort, a nesting population is being re-established at Padre Island National Seashore. The first two recorded returnees from the 1978–1988 project were documented nesting at Padre Island National Seashore in 1996. Nesting is increasing rapidly, with more Kemp's ridley nests found at Padre Island National Seashore than any other location in the United States. Although a few of these turtles are from the 1978–1988 project, most are turtles that are naturally repopulating the area.

From April through mid-July, National Park Service volunteers and staff search the beaches of North Padre Island from 6:30 A.M. to 6:30 P.M. each day to detect and protect nesting sea turtles, eggs, and hatchlings. These patrols occur during the day since Kemp's ridleys nest mostly during the day, in contrast to the other sea turtle species, which nest mostly at night. Eggs from most nests found on North Padre Island and northward on the Texas coast are transported to Padre Island National Seashore for protected care. Resulting hatchlings are released on the beach at the National Seashore and allowed to enter the surf and go free.

This work also involves an extensive educational component since beach visitors locate up to half the Kemp's ridley nests found on the Texas coast each year. We work to educate the public on how they can aid with our conservation efforts and how they can avoid inadvertently harming the turtles and their eggs.

who become rangers may be given emergency medical training. Those who work in parks with underwater resources, such as the Channel Islands, may become certified divers.

Internships and Volunteerships

The best way to learn about a career as a park worker is to obtain an internship or volunteer opportunity in a local, state, or national park.

The National Park Service lists available internships in the Support Your Park section of its individual Web sites. The NPS offers more than 25 volunteer programs for people between the ages of five and 24. The programs, such as the Youth Conservation Corps and Public Land Corps, will help educate you about the environment while you work with conservation workers to improve national parks. Visit http://www.nps.gov/getting-involved/volunteer to learn about the wide range of programs that are available and to view photos of past projects.

If you are unable to land an internship or a volunteership with the NPS or a state or local park, you can try to seek out a position with private environmental organizations, other government agencies (such as the Bureau of Land Management), and government organizations at the state and local level.

WHO WILL HIRE ME?

If you are interested in applying for a National Park Service job, contact your local Federal Job Information Center or the federal Office of Personnel Management (http://www.usajobs.gov) in Washington, D.C., for application information.

Although the National Park Service is the only employer for people who would like to pursue this career at the national level (similar jobs are available at state and local parks), there are many radically different national parks. People who pursue this career may work in mountainous areas like Grand Teton National Park in Wyoming; desert locales like Saguaro National Park in Arizona; marine areas such as the Channel Islands National Park in California; and urban parks such as Independence National Historical Park in Pennsylvania. (It is important to remember that not all parks are nature-oriented; many focus on a historical event or figure.)

The skills necessary for many positions within the local, state, and national parks are highly transferable. Interpretive rangers, for instance, may pursue careers as botanists, educators, or naturalists. Law enforcement rangers may consider careers as police officers, firefighters, or emergency medical personnel. The scientists who study our parks' resources may move into private research, or, like historians and archaeologists, they may consider becoming educators.

WHERE CAN I GO FROM HERE?

As is true of most professions, advancement within the National Park Service and at state and local parks usually means assuming managerial and administrative responsibilities. Rangers, for instance, may become subdistrict rangers, district rangers, and then chief rangers. Chief rangers may one day become park superintendents. Superintendents, in turn, may assume regional responsibilities or become directors of an entire state park system. While this is the traditional path to advancement, it is not one that anyone treads very quickly. The opportunities for upward mobility within parks are limited because the turnover rates at upper levels tend to be quite low. While this may hinder an ambitious employee's advancement, it is indicative of a high level of job satisfaction.

WHAT ARE THE SALARY RANGES?

According to the National Association of State Park Directors, rangers employed by state parks had average starting salaries of $24,611 in 2004 (the most recent data available from the NASPD). Local and state park workers usually receive benefits such as paid vacations, sick leave, paid holidays, health and life insurance, and pension plans.

The salaries for National Park employees are based on individuals' level of responsibility and experience. Employees are assigned salary grade levels. As they gain more experience, they are promoted to higher grade levels, or to higher salary steps within their grade levels.

The National Park Service uses two categories of levels. The first, called the General Schedule (GS), applies to professional, administrative, clerical, and tech-

Did You Know?

Wrangell-St. Elias National Park and Preserve (http://www.nps.gov/wrst) in Alaska is the largest national park—it is 13.2 million square acres in size. This stunning wilderness has the largest number of peaks and glaciers above 16,000 feet on the continent. Additionally, an amazing number and variety of animals live in the park, including Dall sheep, mountain goats, caribou, moose, brown/grizzly bears, black bears, bison, lynx, wolverines, river otters, martens, wolves, marmots, beavers, porcupines, snowshoe hares, bats, geese, trumpeter swans, ducks, golden and bald eagles, peregrine falcons, gyrfalcons, pine grosbeaks, black-capped chickadees, woodpeckers, willow ptarmigan, spruce grouse, ravens, goshawks, great horned owls, salmon, rainbow trout, lake trout, Dolly Varden, and burbot.

nical employees and is fairly standard throughout the country. Firefighters and law enforcement are included in the General Schedule. The other, called the Wage Grade (WG), applies to employees who perform trades, crafts, or manual labor and is based on local pay scales.

Most rangers begin at or below the GS-5 level, which, in 2009, translated to earning between $27,026 and $31,401. The average ranger in 2009 was on the second step of the GS-7 level, which translates to a salary of $34,953. The most experienced rangers can earn $43,521, which is the highest salary step in the GS-7 level. To move beyond this level, most rangers must become supervisors, subdistrict rangers, district rangers, or division chiefs. At these higher levels, people can earn more than $89,000 per year. These positions are difficult to obtain, however, because the turnover rate for positions above the GS-7 level is exceptionally low.

National Park Service employees receive benefits such as paid vacations, sick leave, paid holidays, health and life insurance, and pension plans. The NPS often provides housing to employees who work in remote areas.

WHAT IS THE JOB OUTLOOK?

Employment opportunities at state and local parks should be only fair in coming years. Some states or communities have closed parks due to budget cuts, and turnover in top positions is typically low.

Although it covers a lot of ground, the National Park Service is really a very small government agency. Because the agency is small, job opportunities are limited and, although they are not highly lucrative, they are considered very desirable among individuals who love outdoor work and nature. Consequently, competition for National Park Service jobs is very intense. This is not a situation that is likely to improve since turnover rates are low and new parks are seldom added.

Students interested in working in local, state, and national parks should not be discouraged, however. Determined people will always be able to land a park job if they really want to; they just have to be willing to take a seasonal or entry-level position and to relocate to a park that has an opening.

Pet Care Workers

SUMMARY

Definition
Pet care workers care for pets in a variety of ways, including managing their welfare in pet stores, grooming them, walking them, and taking care of them when their owners are unable to.

Alternative Job Titles
Varies by career

Salary Range
$15,080 to $21,000 to $30,000+ (pet shop workers)
$14,520 to $18,890 to $31,600+ (pet groomers)
$5,000 to $20,000 to $100,000+ (pet sitters)

Educational Requirements
High school diploma

Certification or Licensing
Voluntary

Employment Outlook
About as fast as the average (pet store workers)
Faster than the average (pet groomers, pet sitters)

High School Subjects
Business
Mathematics

Personal Interests
Animals
Business

Cindy Vet, owner and operator of PET BUDDY Pet Sitting, LLC, cares for many special needs and geriatric pets that have chronic diseases or other serious problems. Their owners are often faced with the difficult decision of allowing their pets to continue suffering or to euthanize them. "It is an agonizing decision to have to make," Cindy says. "When a client calls me in with their family and vet to help be a part of that decision-making process, it is very emotional, but it is also very important to me because I know that I am truly a part of that pet's family, too. The greatest thank you a client can give me is to ask me to be there with them when they let their pet go. That lets me know that they realize how much I have loved and cared for their pet—as if it were my own."

WHAT DOES A PET CARE WORKER DO?

There are three types of pet care workers covered in this article: *pet store workers*, *pet groomers*, and *pet sitters*. While job duties and work settings vary for each career, all pet care workers share a common concern for the well-being of animals.

Pet store workers are employed in pet stores that range from mom-and-pop storefront businesses to major chains such as PETCO, Petland, and PetSmart. Larger pet stores may employ a sizeable staff, including cashiers, managers, stock workers, bookkeepers, pet groomers, animal caretakers, and animal trainers. Smaller stores may employ a few individuals trained to perform a variety of responsibilities—from ringing up customer purchases to cleaning fish tanks. Regardless of the size of the store or the duties of its staff, all pet shop workers must be knowledgeable about animals and products and friendly and helpful to customers. All members of the pet shop staff contribute to the running of the shop through their various responsibilities, such as assisting customers, stocking shelves, ordering products, cleaning cages and aquariums, and maintaining records. Some pet shops offer specialized services such as training, grooming, and boarding. Most shops sell smaller animals such as birds, fish, and hamsters. Some shops do sell larger animals like cats and dogs, but most buyers will turn to breeders or shelters for these pets. Pet shop workers are in the retail business, so people skills may be more important for this type of work than for some other careers in animal care.

Pet groomers comb, cut, trim, and shape the fur of all types of dogs and cats. They may also groom birds and other animals. Although all dogs and cats benefit from regular grooming, shaggy, longhaired dogs provide pet groomers with the bulk of their business. Some types of dogs—such as poodles, schnauzers, cocker spaniels, and many types of ter-

riers—need regular grooming for their standard appearance. Show dogs, or dogs that are shown in competition, are groomed frequently. Before beginning grooming, the *dog groomer* talks with the owner to find out the style of cut that the dog is to have. The dog groomer also relies on experience to determine how a particular breed of dog is supposed to look.

The dog groomer places the animal on a grooming table. To keep the dog steady during the clipping, a nylon collar or noose, which hangs from an adjustable pole attached to the grooming table, is slipped around its neck. The dog groomer talks to the dog or uses other techniques to keep the animal calm and gain its trust. If the dog doesn't calm down but snaps and bites instead, the groomer may have to muzzle it. If a dog is completely unmanageable, the dog groomer may ask the owner to have the dog tranquilized by a veterinarian before grooming can begin.

After calming the dog, the groomer brushes it and tries to untangle its hair. If the dog's hair is very shaggy or overgrown, such as an English sheepdog's, the groomer may have to cut away part of its coat with scissors before beginning any real grooming. Brushing the coat is good for both longhaired and shorthaired dogs, as brushing removes shedding hair and dead skin. It also neatens the coat so the groomer can tell from the shape and proportions of the dog how to cut its hair in the most attractive way. Hair that is severely matted is actually painful to the animal because the mats pull at the animal's skin. Having these mats removed is necessary to the animal's health and comfort.

Once the dog is brushed, the groomer cuts and shapes the dog's coat with electric clippers. Next, the dog's ears are cleaned and its nails are trimmed. The groomer must take care not to cut the nails too short because they may bleed and cause the dog pain. If the nails do bleed, a special powder is applied to stop the bleeding. The comfort of the animal is an important concern for the groomer.

The dog is then given a bath, sometimes by a worker known as a *dog bather*. The dog is lowered into a stainless steel tub, sprayed with warm water, scrubbed with a special shampoo, and rinsed. This may be repeated several times if the dog is very dirty. The dog groomer has special chemicals that can be used to deodorize a dog that has encountered a skunk or has gone for a swim in foul water. If a dog has fleas or ticks, the dog groomer treats them at this stage by soaking the wet coat with a solution to kill the insects. This toxic solution must be kept out of the dog's eyes, ears, and nose, which may be cleaned more carefully with a sponge or washcloth. A hot oil treatment may also be applied to condition the dog's coat.

The groomer dries the dog after bathing, either with a towel, hand-held electric blower, or in a drier cage with electric blow driers. Poodles and some other types of dogs have their coats fluff-dried, then scissored for the final pattern or style. Poodles, which at one time were the mainstay of the dog grooming business, generally take the longest to groom because of their intricate clipping pattern. Most dogs can be groomed in about 90 minutes, although grooming may take several hours for shaggier breeds whose coats are badly matted and overgrown.

More and more cats, especially long-haired breeds, are now being taken to pet groomers. The procedure for cats is the same as for dogs, although cats are not dipped when bathed. As the dog or cat is groomed, the groomer checks to be sure there are no signs of disease in the animal's eyes, ears, skin, or coat. If there are any abnormalities, such as bald patches or skin lesions, the groomer tells the owner and may recommend that a veterinarian check the animal. The groomer may also give the owner tips on animal hygiene.

Pet owners and those in pet care generally have respect for pet groomers who do a good job and treat animals well. Many people, especially those who raise show dogs, grow to rely on particular pet groomers to do a perfect job each time. Pet groomers can earn satisfaction from taking a shaggy, unkempt animal and transforming it into a beautiful creature. On the other hand, some owners may unfairly blame the groomer if the animal becomes ill while in the groomer's care or for some malady or condition that is not the groomer's fault.

Pet sitters offer peace of mind to owners who can't bear to leave their dogs or cats at kennels or boarders while they are away from home. With a pet sitter, pets can stay in familiar surroundings, as well as avoid the risks of illnesses passed on by other animals. The pets are also assured routine exercise and no disruptions in their diets. Because dogs and cats are the world's most common companion animals, pet sitters usually work mostly with these two species, but pet sitters are also called on to care for birds, reptiles, gerbils, fish, and other animals.

With their own set of keys, pet sitters let themselves into the homes of their clients and care for their companion animals while the pet owners are away at work or on vacation. (Some pet sitters care for animals owned by elderly people or those with disabilities who cannot leave their houses or care for the pets as well as they would like.) Pet sitters feed the animals, make sure they have water, and give them their medications. They clean up any messes the animals have made and clean litter boxes. They give the animals attention, playing with them, letting them outside, and taking them for walks. Usually a pet sitter can provide pet owners with a variety of personal pet care services—they may take a pet to the vet, offer grooming, sell pet-related products, and give advice. Some pet sitters take dogs out into the country, to mountain parks, or to lakes, for exercise in wide-open spaces.

Pet sitters typically plan one to three visits (of 30 to 60 minutes in length) per day, or they may make arrangements to spend the night. In addition to caring for the animals, pet sitters also look after the houses of their clients. They bring in the newspapers and the mail; they water the plants; they make sure the house is securely locked. Pet sitters generally charge by the hour or per visit. They may also have special pricing for overtime, emergency situations, extra duties, and travel.

> ## To Be a Successful Pet Care Worker, You Should...
>
> - enjoy working with animals
> - have good business skills
> - not be afraid to get your hands dirty
> - have good customer service skills
> - be able to take direction and work independently
> - be willing to perform sometimes repetitious tasks
> - be able to lift heavy animals, supplies, or equipment
> - be willing to work on holidays and weekends (especially pet sitters)
> - be willing to work outdoors in all types of weather (pet sitters)

Many pet sitters work alone, without employees, no matter how demanding the work. Though this means getting to keep all the money, it also means keeping all the responsibilities. A successful pet-sitting service requires a fair amount of business management.

WHAT IS IT LIKE TO BE A PET CARE WORKER?

Jerry Wentz is the co-owner of Homesitters of Raleigh & Cary, a pet-sitting business that has served the Wake County,

North Carolina, area since 1985. "Our mission," he says, "is 'Happy Pets, Happy Pet Parents.'" Jerry says that work in this field was a natural fit. "My wife graduated from North Carolina State with a degree in animal science and I graduated From East Carolina University with a degree in business administration. We both love animals."

Jerry's business, which is bonded and insured, currently has 19 employees serving thousands of homes, owners, and animals each year. "The services we offer," he explains, "include visits (approximately 30 minutes) for dogs and cats while the owners are traveling, or in some cases they may be home but unable to care for their pets on their own; midday dog walking for owners who cannot come home to allow a potty break for their dog; overnight stays in the owner's home for those who really want to spoil their pets; and visits for homeowners without pets who are traveling for extended periods and wish to have their premises checked periodically. All visits where pets are present include feeding, providing fresh water, scooping the cat's litter box, exercising, and play time. Also included are bringing in the mail, newspaper, and packages; watering house plants; and leaving a note after each visit to document the situation and activities for the client's understanding of the service we provide."

"This business, like most, is all about a lot of details," Jerry continues, "so following up to make sure those details are properly managed is important. Visit days and times for thousands of visits, service details such as exercise and feeding routines, medications, alarm codes, emergency contacts, and last-minute changes are just some of the things that must be right each and every time."

Jerry spends a significant part of his day looking for exactly the right people to work for his business. "I have approximately 100 initial contacts for every person hired," he says, "but this results in an average employee tenure of more than five years."

Rachel Diller is a pet groomer in Littleton, Colorado. "I have managed boarding kennels and worked in retail through wholesale within the pet industry," she says. "Becoming a pet groomer seemed to be the next logical step. Being involved with American Kennel Club Conformation events also led me to have a desire to groom. I've watched several breeder friends work on their show progeny, and it was an art form I couldn't wait to learn. Over the years, I had bathed dogs and done basic grooming, but now it is a passion.

"I own, manage, and groom at my business," she continues. "The Poodle Shop, purchased with that name, was a good investment for me to be able to run my own business. At first, I wanted to change the name because it seemed so vague. But, with so many people calling for appointments that sought me as a specialist, I couldn't do it. On average, I groom 20 standard poodles a month; miniatures and toys are countless. I also specialize in Kerry blue terriers and cats. Cats are very dangerous to groom. This is the biggest reason why most groomers will not groom cats. I have always had good luck grooming felines. They either tolerate it or they don't. Plain and simple.

"When I purchased my business there was a client list of 300," she adds. "When I actually went through those cards, *maybe* 75 were actually alive. I have grown from that 75 on the initial list to well over 1,000 clients in a period of three years. My clients come to me as a professional in the industry who understands the needs of their pets. If you are good at something you do, there is no limit to the potential."

Cindy Vet is the owner/operator of PET BUDDY Pet Sitting, LLC, in Georgia. She has worked in the field for more than five years. "I pet sit mostly dogs and cats," she says, "but I do have some lizards, guinea pigs, hamsters, gerbils, fish, birds, and ferrets that I sit for as well. No snakes though! That is about the only pet I won't sit because they scare me to death! I entered the field because I wanted to put my graduate degree in management to use in my own company, and I have always wanted to work with animals. (My last name kind of lends itself to that anyway!) I had read that one of the five fastest-growing industries was pet professional services.

"The pros of my job are that I am my own boss," Cindy says. "I can make my own decisions and set my own hours to a certain degree, and I get to play with, love on, and take care of the furry kids all day. The one con is that, in this industry, you work almost all the holidays and it is hard sometimes because you can't spend the time with your own family that you would like to spend."

The Ups and Downs of Owning a Pet-Sitting Business
● ● ● ● ●

The editors of *What Can I Do Now? Animal Careers* asked Jerry Wentz, owner of Homesitters of Raleigh & Cary in North Carolina, to detail the pros and cons of owning a pet-sitting business:

The pros and cons of owning a pet-sitting business are the same as owning almost any business. More so than in a "regular job" you are in charge of your own success or failure; you also have the responsibility of helping others succeed; and your efforts are enhanced or diminished to the degree that you wisely choose good people to carry out the details of providing your service. This type of business operates 365 days a year, but most business owners have a mentality of hard work, and the fact that business is done every day doesn't mean the owner never takes a day off. I work most days, but many weekend days just a couple of hours. Some very large pet-sitting business owners have a management staff in place and only manage their managers. They are not involved in day-to-day operations.

DO I HAVE WHAT IT TAKES TO BE A PET CARE WORKER?

Successful pet care workers share several common traits. The main quality for a person who wants to work with pets is a love of animals. Animals can sense when someone does not like them or is afraid of them. A person needs certain skills in order to work with aggressive, nervous, or fidgety animals. They must be patient with the animals, able to gain their respect, and enjoy giving the animals a lot of love and attention. In addition to a deep interest in caring for animals, pet care workers must also have strong communication and customer service skills—whether they are working in a pet store, pet grooming shop, or interacting with customers on the phone or in their homes.

"The most important quality of a pet groomer is patience," says Rachel Diller. "You have to be tremendously patient when working with moving targets. The second most important quality is a natural intuitive connection with pets. Like I said, it's an art form and part of being artsy is understanding where the dog is coming from. If you have a puppy who is scared— you're not doing that 'puppy cut' all owners seek. If you have an older dog who is having a hard time standing, you work with that pet and have a gentle touch doing it. A pet's care should come before the vanity of grooming. Groomers also need to understand dog and cat behavior and have breed knowledge. This is a must. Groomers need to be aware of correct coat type, correct breed standards to groom, and, most importantly, how those apply to the owners and their lifestyles. Lastly, you must be mentally and physically strong—lifting, holding onto moving parts, and being quick. This is a hard job to do and it's not for the average pet lover. Find someone to learn from who is current in the industry and take it all in. Decide for yourself if this is something you'd be willing to do."

"Many people start a pet-sitting business thinking this will be a way for them to work just with pets," says Jerry Wentz. "Nothing could be further from the truth. Any service business requires strong interpersonal and excellent communication skills. Pet sitting is not just about playing with pets all day. You have to be able to deal effectively with people. You need to be an ambassador for your business, be able to convince potential clients that you offer their best alternative to caring for their pets (and sometimes you have to delicately tell them you don't want their business), motivate the people working for you, and solve problems as they arise. And it is true that most problems are really opportunities in disguise. The key to turning a problem into an opportunity is to use it as a chance to demonstrate your commitment to satisfying the client. When clients know you really care about them and their pets, they are loyal."

As a pet sitter (and sometimes a pet groomer), you'll be in business for yourself. You won't have a boss to give you assignments, and you won't have a secretary or bookkeeper to do the paperwork. You also won't have employees to take over on weekends, holidays, and days when you're not feeling well. Though some pet sitters and groomers are successful enough to afford assistance, most must handle all the aspects of their businesses by themselves. So, you should be self-motivated and as dedicated to the management of your business as you are to the animals. "If you are going to start your own pet-sitting business," advises

The Benefits of Accreditation

The editors of *What Can I Do Now? Animal Careers* discussed accreditation with Ellen Price, editor of *Pet Sitter's WORLD* and academic manager at Pet Sitters International (PSI).

Q. Can you provide us with a general overview of PSI's Accreditation Program?

A. PSI's Accreditation Program is an in-depth educational coursework that has been tailored exclusively for pet sitters. The coursework manual was developed with input from the most knowledge-able and experienced professionals in the pet care industry. The accreditation process includes a home-study coursework and a proctored final exam. The curriculum includes topics on:

- Pet care for a wide range of companion animals, including dogs, cats, cage pets, birds, barnyard pets, reptiles and amphibians, rabbits, livestock, horses, and ferrets.

- Health and nutrition, including animal diseases, first aid/health, sanitation, and parasites.

- Additional services a pet sitter can add to the core business of in-home pet care, including basic grooming, mid-day dog walking, and pet loss and grief counseling.

- Business and office procedures, including employee hiring and management, customer relations, advertising and marketing, disaster planning, ethics, and legal issues.

After obtaining the PSI accredited pet sitter designation, a PSI member will be cer-

tified for three years. For recertification, 30 approved credit units (ACUs) must be accumulated during the three-year certification period. ACUs can be obtained through PSI-designated continuing education credits, pet first aid courses, pet-related publishing, involvement in pet industry events and activities, educational conferences and seminars, and community service.

Q. How important is certification to career development and advancement?

A. How many parents would leave a child at a daycare center without checking the qualifications of the owner and caregivers? Or leave an infant in the care of a stranger with no proof of that person's qualifications in child care? Well, today's companion animals are considered part of the family by their owners. And those pet owners are becoming more particular about the caregivers they hire to look after their furred, feathered, and finned family members.

The pet-sitting industry is not controlled by government regulations and licensing procedures. So how is a pet parent to know about the qualifications of a potential pet sitter? It's a question pet sitters are being asked with increasing frequency. Here is the answer a PSI member can give: "As a PSI member, I have access to educational programs and professional support that help me take the best care possible of your companion animals. These benefits have been developed

(continues on next page)

(continued from previous page)

specifically to help ensure my success as a professional pet sitter—and that means your satisfaction as a loving pet owner."

Here's a partial list of the vital member benefits PSI makes available to its members: PSI membership certificate, liability insurance and bonding, pet first aid certification, PSI's accredita-tion program, and background checks for staff sitters.

While all these benefits are important, the accreditation program is one of the most powerful tools in the professional pet sitter's toolbox. It is a definitive measure of a pet sitter's knowledge and professionalism—and one that sets PSI accredited pet sitters apart from those who have not attained certification.

Cindy Vet, "take some business classes at a local college. It is so valuable to be able to have marketing, time management, and communication skills in this industry. You should have people skills and customer service skills as well."

As a pet sitter, pet owners entrust you with the care of their pets and their homes, so you must be reliable and trustworthy. You should also be prepared for emergency situations. For example, you need to know what to do if a pet becomes ill. Pet sitters should also expect a good amount of dirty work. You'll be cleaning litter boxes and animal messes within the house and picking up after dogs as you walk them on the street. You may be giving animals medications. You'll also be cleaning aquariums and bird cages.

HOW DO I BECOME A PET CARE WORKER?

Education

High School

To be a successful pet store worker, you should take accounting, marketing, and other business-related courses in high school. Math classes will help you learn how to manage money and calculate the proper feed and medication amounts for the animals. Science classes are also important for anyone working with animals. A knowledge of chemistry will come in handy when preparing medications and chemicals for the aquariums. Biology will introduce you to the biological systems of various kinds of animals. Geography and ecology courses can also add to your understanding of animals by introducing you to their natural habitats and origins.

You do not need a high school diploma to work as a pet groomer, but a diploma or GED certificate can be a great asset to people who would like to advance within their present company or move to other careers in animal care that require more training, such as veterinary technicians. Useful courses include English, business, math, general science, anatomy and physiology, health, zoology, psychology, bookkeeping, office management, typing, art, and first aid.

High school courses such as accounting, marketing, and business will be especially useful to pet sitters who own their own businesses. Computer science classes will help you learn about the software you'll use to manage accounts and create schedules. Joining a school business club will introduce you to business practices and local entrepreneurs. Science courses such as biology and chemistry, as well as health courses, will give you some good background for developing animal care skills. As a pet sitter, you'll be responsible for overseeing the health of the animals, their exercise, and their diets; at an owner's request, you may also be preparing medications and administering eye and ear drops.

Postsecondary Training

You do not need to attend college or receive special training to work in entry-level positions at a pet store. As with most retail businesses, pet shops often employ high school students for part-time and summer positions. Store owners usually hire people with a love of animals, and some knowledge of their care, for entry-level positions such as clerk, cashier, and salesperson. Aspiring pet shop managers should consider earning an associate's or bachelor's degree. It is also easier to advance into management positions if you have a college degree. Though any college degree will be valuable for higher-level pet shop positions, you'll want to take courses in marketing, accounting, merchandising, and other business-related areas. Some pet shops also like to hire people with veterinary tech training. Students pursuing a pre-veterinary sciences degree often work part time in a pet shop to gain experience with animals and their owners.

A person interested in pet grooming can be trained for the field in one of three ways: enrolling in a pet grooming school; working in a pet shop or kennel and learning on the job; or reading one of the many books on pet grooming and practicing on his or her own pet.

To enroll in most pet grooming schools, a person must be at least 17 years old and fond of animals. Previous experience in pet grooming can sometimes be applied for course credits. Students study a wide range of topics including the basics of bathing, brushing, and clipping; the care of ears and nails; coat and skin conditions; animal anatomy terminology; and sanitation. They also study customer relations, which is very important for those who plan to operate their own shops. During training, students practice their techniques on actual animals, which people bring in for grooming at a discount rate. You can access a list of pet grooming schools by visiting http://www.petgroomer.com. Many other grooming schools advertise in dog and pet magazines. It is important for students to choose an accredited, state-licensed school in order to increase both their employment opportunities and professional knowledge.

Students can also learn pet grooming while working at a grooming shop, kennel, animal hospital, or veterinarian's office. They usually begin with tasks such as shampooing dogs and cats and trimming their nails, and then gradually work their way up to brushing and basic haircuts. With experience, they may learn more difficult cuts and use these skills to earn more pay or start their own business.

The essentials of pet grooming can also be learned from any of several good books available on grooming. These books contain all the information a person needs to know to start his or her own pet grooming business, including the basic cuts, bathing and handling techniques, and the type of equipment needed. Still, many of the finer points of grooming, such as the more complicated cuts and various safety precautions, are best learned while working under an experienced groomer. There still is no substitute for on-the-job training and experience.

Many pet sitters start their own businesses after having gained experience in other areas of animal care. Vet techs and pet shop workers may promote their animal care skills to develop a clientele for more profitable pet-sitting careers. Graduates from a business college may recognize pet sitting as a great way to start a business with little overhead. But neither a vet tech qualification nor a business degree is required to become a successful pet sitter. And the only special training you need to pursue is actual experience. A local pet shop or chapter of the ASPCA may offer seminars in various aspects of animal care; the National Association of Professional Pet Sitters (NAPPS) offers a mentorship program, as well as a newsletter, while Pet Sitters International (PSI), in addition to educational publications, also sponsors educational conferences, correspondence programs, and teleconferences.

Certification or Licensing

There is no specialized certification available for pet store workers. The National Retail Federation offers the following voluntary designations to sales workers who successfully pass an assessment and meet other requirements: national professional certification in sales, national professional certification in customer service, and basics of retail credential. Contact the federation for more information.

The National Dog Groomers Association of America (NDGAA) offers certification to groomers who pass written and practical examinations. To start a grooming salon or other business, a license is needed from the city or town in which a person plans to practice. The International Society of Canine Cosmetologists also offers certification.

PSI offers the accredited pet sitter designation to applicants who pass an open book examination that covers topics in four major categories: pet care, health and nutrition, business and office procedures, and additional services. Additionally, the NAPPS offers the certified pet sitter designation to applicants who complete a home-study course and pass an online examination. Certification tells prospective clients that you have met industry standards, and it may increase your chances of being hired.

Though there is no particular pet-sitting license required of pet sitters, insurance protection is important. Liability insurance protects the pet sitter from lawsuits; both the NAPPS and PSI offer group liability packages to their members. Pet sitters should also be bonded. Bonding assures the pet owners that if anything is missing from their homes after a pet-sitting appointment, they can receive compensation if their pet sitter is found to be at fault.

The Pet Care Services Association also offers several certifications to workers who care for pets.

Internships and Volunteerships

Colleges and universities, along with professional organizations, are sources of information on work-study projects and student internships. Any type of volunteer work with animals is beneficial for future pet care workers. Often it is the only way for entry-level workers to receive important hands-on experience. Most cities have local divisions of the Humane Society, which are frequently in need of volunteers.

The Most Popular Services Provided by Pet Sitters

According to Pet Sitters International, the top eight services requested by pet owners in 2008 were:

1. Basic pet care
2. Dog walking
3. Care of special needs pets
4. Pet transportation
5. Overnight pet sitting
6. House-sitting while no pet is present
7. Errand services
8. Pooper-scooper services

WHO WILL HIRE ME?

Pet store workers work in pet stores that range from "mom and pop" establishments to large chains such as PETCO, Petland, and PetSmart. One way to land a job in a pet store is to check the classified ads in your paper for pet shop jobs, but a better approach is to fill out applications at all the pet stores in your neighborhood, and then check back on a regular basis so that the manager or store owner gets to know you. That way, when there is a job opening, the manager will have you in mind. For management positions, you should have some background in entry-level retail positions and some college education. While pursuing that education, you can take part-time work in pet stores or other retail businesses. Though any retail experience is valuable, experience in a small pet store will involve you directly with many of the main concerns of a business; in a larger pet "megastore" your experience may be limited to a few duties.

Pet groomers are employed by grooming salons, kennels, pet shops, veterinary practices, animal hospitals, and grooming schools. The pet care industry is thriving, and opportunities for groomers are expected to increase steadily in the coming years. Although most employers can offer attractive benefits packages, many pet groomers choose to go into business for themselves rather than turn over 40 to 50 percent of their fees to their employers. Graduates of accredited pet grooming schools benefit from the schools' job placement services, which can help students find work in the kind of setting they prefer. Classified ads in daily newspapers and listings in dog and pet magazines are other sources of job information. Job leads may be available from private or state employment agencies or from referrals of salon or kennel owners. People looking for work should phone or send letters to prospective employers, inform them of their qualifications, and, if invited, visit their establishments.

Nearly all pet sitters are self-employed, although a few may work for other successful pet sitters who have built up a large enough clientele to require help. It takes most pet sitters a significant amount of time to build up a business substantial enough to make a living without other sources of income. However, the outlook for this field is excellent and start-up costs are minimal, making it a good choice for animal lovers who want to work for themselves. For those who have good business sense and a great deal of ambition, the potential for success is good. Jerry Wentz and his wife both worked for the previous owner of his business before deciding to purchase it. "This is a step I think any potential business owner should take," he says. "If you are thinking of owning a clothing store, for example, you should work in one to see what the business is actually like. Preconceived ideas are not always accurate reflections of what the day to day activities involve."

You're not likely to find job listings under "pet sitter" in the newspaper. Most pet sitters schedule all their work themselves. However, you may find ads in the classifieds, in weekly community papers, or online, from pet owners looking to hire pet sitters. Some people, such as Cindy Vet, who become pet sitters have backgrounds in animal care—they may have worked for vets, breeders, or pet shops. "I actually talked to my vet about starting my pet-sitting business," she recalls, "and they told me to get bonded and insured and do this professionally and they would help with referrals. They do not board because they believe the pet does better in its own home environment. In fact, one vet who takes care of all my cats handles a lot of special needs and geriatric pets. These pets often need medications, insulin shots, and subcutaneous fluids for thyroid and renal disease, as well as diabetes. He showed me how to administer these types of medications and actually started referring a lot of his clients to me over my first Christmas holidays. Of course, the joke after the first of the year was that I had the geriatric pets down now, so could they please start referring puppies and kittens. I am truly blessed because my vets helped me get started in this business. And I even went to work for them to help supplement my pet-sitting income when I first started my own company. I am now pet sitting full time, but I still work one Saturday a month to stay up-to-date on everything new in the vet field."

A person who has a background in animal care usually enters the business with a client list already in hand, having made contacts with many pet owners. But, if you're just starting out in the field, you need to develop a list of references. This may mean volunteering your time to friends and neighbors, or working very cheaply. If you're willing to actually stay in the house while the pet owners are on vacation, you should be able to find plenty of pet-sitting opportunities in the summertime. Post your name, phone number, and availability on the bulletin boards of grocery stores, colleges, and coffee shops around town. Once you've developed a list of references, and have made connections with pet owners, you can start expanding, and increasing your profits.

WHERE CAN I GO FROM HERE?

As they gain more experience, pet store workers will be assigned more responsibilities. After starting as a stock worker or cashier, you may eventually be asked to open and close the store, place orders, design advertisements, order new products, and negotiate with distributors. Your work in the many different areas of the store may lead to advancement from an entry-level position to a management position, even if you don't have a college education. As a manager, you may be allowed to expand the store in new directions. With the understanding of a store and its clientele, you can introduce such additions as an animal training or grooming program, sponsorship of adopt-a-pet and animal-assisted therapy programs, and new product lines.

Pet groomers who work for other people may advance to a more responsible position such as office manager or dog trainer. If dog groomers start their own shops, they may become successful enough to expand or to open branch offices or area franchises. Skilled groomers may want to work for a dog grooming school as an instructor, possibly advancing to a job as a school director, placement officer, or other type of administrator. With more education, a groomer may get a job as a veterinary technician or assistant at a shelter or animal hospital. Those who like to train dogs may open obedience schools, train guide dogs, work with field and hunting dogs, or even train stunt and movie dogs. People can also open their own kennels, breeding and pedigree services, gaming dog businesses, or pet supply distribution firms. Each of these requires specialized knowledge and experience, so additional study, education, and work is often needed.

The adage "You get back what you put into it" applies well to advancement opportunities for pet sitters. It will take hard work to build your business; the more time you dedicate to your business, the bigger the business will become. It is important to remember that the success of any small business can be very unpredictable. For some, a business can build very quickly, for others it may take years. Some pet sitters start out part time, perhaps even volunteering, and then may find themselves with enough business to quit their full-time jobs and devote themselves entirely to pet sitting. Once your business takes off, you may be able to afford an assistant, or an entire staff. Some pet sitters even have franchises across the country. You may even choose to develop your business into a much larger operation, such as a dog day care facility.

Did You Know?

Americans spent $43.2 billion on their pets in 2008, according to the American Pet Products Association. Here is how this money was spent by pet sector:

- Food: $16.8 billion

- Veterinary care: $11.1 billion

- Supplies/over-the-counter medications: $10.0 billion

- Pet services (grooming/boarding): $3.2 billion

- Live animal purchases: $2.1 billion

WHAT ARE THE SALARY RANGES?

Experience, level of education, job title, employer, and work performed determine the salary ranges for pet care workers.

Entry-level pet shop workers earn minimum wage, and even those with experience probably won't make much more than that. Pet store managers make less than $30,000 annually on average, but many larger pet stores are beginning to reward managers for their varied responsibilities and extra hours. The size of the store also makes a difference; stores with larger volumes pay their managers considerably more than stores with volumes of less than $1 million. The size of the store also determines the number of benefits for a full-time employee. In smaller stores, pet shop workers may not receive any health benefits or vacation pay,

while a bigger store may have group health plans for managers.

Groomers charge either by the job or the hour. If they are on the staff of a salon or work for another groomer, they get to keep 50 to 60 percent of the fees they charge. For this reason, many groomers branch off to start their own businesses. The U.S. Department of Labor reports that median hourly earnings of nonfarm animal caretakers (the category in which pet groomers are classified) were $9.31 (or $19,360 annually) in 2008. Salaries ranged from less than $7.28 (or $15,140 annually) to more than $15.19 per hour (or $31,590 annually). Those who own and operate their own grooming services can earn significantly more, depending on how hard they work, the clientele they service, and the economy of the area in which they work.

Pet sitters set their own prices, charging by the visit, the hour, or the week. They may also charge consultation fees and additional fees on holidays. They may have special pricing plans in place, such as for emergency situations or for administering medications. Depending on the kinds of animals (sometimes pet sitters charge less to care for cats than dogs), pet sitters generally charge between $8 and $20 for a 30-minute visit. The average per-visit rate for dog walking was $18.08 in 2008, according to Pet Sitters International (PSI). Pet sitters charged $19.86 for a 33-minute visit caring for pets with special needs. PSI conducted a survey of annual salaries and discovered that the median revenue is $20,000. Some very successful pet sitters have annual salaries of more than $100,000, while others only make $5,000 a year. Though a pet sitter can make a good profit in any area of the country, a bigger city will offer more clients. Pet sitters in their first five years of business are unlikely to make more than $10,000 a year; pet sitters who have had businesses for eight years or more may earn more than $40,000 a year.

Pet groomers and sitters who work for a company usually receive benefits such as vacation days, sick leave, health and life insurance, and a savings and pension program. Self-employed workers must provide their own benefits.

WHAT IS THE JOB OUTLOOK?

Almost every area of the country has pet stores, pet groomers, and pet sitters. Turnover, especially among part-time workers in these businesses, is high. Dedicated and qualified pet care workers, particularly those with lots of hands-on experience, will be in high demand.

The employment of retail sales personnel in all industries should grow about as fast as the average for all careers through 2016, according to the U.S. Department of Labor. Many smaller, traditional, "mom and pop" pet shops are closing because they cannot compete with large chains that can afford to offer special pricing, inexpensive grooming facilities, and free training programs. This trend is likely to continue, but small stores will survive if they are able to promote a more personalized and knowledgeable assistance not available from the larger stores. The pet retail industry, in some form, will grow along with the retail industry in general.

The demand for skilled dog groomers has grown faster than average for all occupations, and is expected to continue to grow at this rate through 2016, according to the U.S. Department of Labor. The number of dogs and cats being kept as pets continues to increase each year. Owners are spending more money on pet care and often don't have enough free time or the inclination to groom their pets themselves. Grooming is not just a luxury for pets, however, because regular attention makes it more likely that any injury or illness will be noticed and treated. Also, as nontraditional pets become more mainstream, innovative groomers will need to take advantage of new techniques and facilities for bringing animals other than dogs and cats into the pet salon.

The career of pet sitters is expected to enjoy good growth in the next decade. Most pet sitters charge fees comparable to kennels and boarders, but some charge less. And many pet owners prefer to leave their pets in the house, rather than take the pets to unfamiliar locations. This has made pet sitting a desirable and cost-effective alternative to other pet care situations. "Even in the downturn in the economy, there is still a good deal of growth in this industry," says Cindy Vet. "Some sitters are offering other types of services other than just sitting, such as midday dog walks, pet transportation to vets and doggie day cares, and grooming and training. I have been lucky in that my business has not taken a hit with the economy. I have a lot of business travelers in addition to my vacation clients, so that helps balance it out."

Veterinarians

SUMMARY

Definition

Veterinarians diagnose and control animal diseases, treat sick and injured animals medically and surgically, prevent transmission of animal diseases, and advise owners on proper care of pets and livestock.

Alternative Job Titles

Companion-animal veterinarians

Doctors of veterinary medicine

Large-animal veterinarians

Small-animal veterinarians

Salary Range

$46,610 to $79,050 to $143,660+

Educational Requirements

Medical degree

Certification or Licensing

Required

Employment Outlook

Much faster than the average

High School Subjects

Biology

Chemistry

Mathematics

Personal Interests

Animals

Science

Wildlife

Between her junior and senior year in veterinary school, Dr. Bernadine Cruz participated in an externship at the Los Angeles Zoo. "I was privileged to go on daily rounds with the staff veterinarian," she recalls. "I assisted in the treatment of everything from snapping turtles, birds, and African hoof stock, to the most fascinating patient, a lowland gorilla named Caesar. He got his name because he was delivered Caesarian section by a team of veterinarians and M.D.s. He had an injury that required repeated sedation administered via a blowgun dart. I would spend my lunch hour sitting next to his hospital cage. His eyes were mesmerizing. I don't know if it was more me watching him or Caesar watching me. Caesar instilled in me the belief that I am not superior to any of the life forms I encounter, only different. It is my responsibility to treat all of them fairly and with empathy."

WHAT DOES A VETERINARIAN DO?

Veterinarians care for a wide range of animals—from farm animals and those in zoos and aquariums, to pets such as dogs, cats, and birds.

Approximately 80 percent of veterinarians work in private clinical practice. Although some veterinarians treat all kinds of animals, about half limit their practice to companion animals such as dogs, cats, and birds. Of the veterinarians in private practice, about 11 percent work mainly with horses, cattle, pigs, sheep, goats, and poultry. Veterinarians may also treat llamas, catfish, or ostriches. Others are employed by wildlife management groups, zoos, aquariums, ranches, feedlots, fish farms, and animal shelters.

The remaining 20 percent of veterinarians work in public and corporate sectors. Many veterinarians are employed by city, county, state, provincial, or federal government agencies that investigate, test for, and control diseases in companion animals, livestock, and poultry that affect both animal and human health.

Veterinarians in private clinical practice become specialists in surgery, anesthesiology, dentistry, internal medicine, ophthalmology, or radiology. Many veterinarians also pursue advanced degrees in the basic sciences, such as anatomy, microbiology, and physiology. Veterinarians who seek specialty board certification in one of 20 specialty fields must complete a two- to five-year residency program and must pass an additional examination. Some veterinarians combine their degree in veterinary medicine with a degree in business (MBA) or law (JD).

Veterinarians work at pharmaceutical and biomedical research firms to develop, test, and supervise the production of

To Be a Successful Veterinarian, You Should...

- have good powers of observation
- have an aptitude and interest in the biological sciences
- be willing to continue to learn throughout your career
- enjoy working with people, as well as animals
- have a curious nature
- have compassion
- have good leadership skills

drugs, chemicals, and biological products such as antibiotics and vaccines that are designed for human and animal use. Some veterinarians are employed in management, technical sales and services, and marketing in agribusiness, pet food companies, and pharmaceutical companies. Still other veterinarians are engaged in research and teaching at veterinary and human medical schools, working with racetracks or animal-related enterprises, or working within the military, public health corps, and space agencies.

Veterinarians are employed in various branches of federal, state, provincial, county, or city government. The U.S. Department of Agriculture has opportunities for veterinarians in the Food Safety and Inspection Service and the Animal and Plant Health Inspection Service, notably in the areas of food hygiene and safety, animal welfare, animal disease control, and research. Veterinarians are also employed by the Environmental Protection Agency to deal with public health and environmental risks to the human population.

WHAT IS IT LIKE TO BE A VETERINARIAN?

Dr. Bernadine Cruz has been a companion-animal veterinarian for more than 20 years. She practices in Orange County, California. "It is a busy practice with six veterinarians and a staff of 15," she says. "I have a marvelous clientele and see a combination of cats and dogs.

"When I entered college," she continues, "I initially thought that I wanted to become a physician, but I decided that taking care of men and women—large and small—didn't hold the same appeal as being able to work on all the species of animals in the world. I could be a pediatrician, gerontologist, surgeon, or dermatologist. I could also be guaranteed sloppy wet kisses from puppies with their sour milk breath—heaven. As a veterinarian, I knew that I would be able to address the health issues of creatures with fins, fur, feathers, and scales, while at the same time being able to safeguard the health and well-being of people and the environment. Now *that* was exciting. I have never regretted my career choice."

Dr. Cruz spends the majority of her day educating her clients about how to provide the best care possible for their pets.

"Preventative medical care is my forte," she says. "I also see dogs and cats that have become ill for myriad reasons. It is my responsibility to acquire a thorough medical history from the owner, determine which diagnostic tests are required, and then interpret the results of those tests. Depending on the diagnosis, I will institute treatment either in the hospital or at home. I always strive to establish a team approach to pet health with the owner."

When she is not working directly with pets, Dr. Cruz is involved in several other pet-owner educational outreach programs. "These," she says, "may include serving as a spokesperson for major pharmaceutical companies, acting as a host for the in-clinic educational series 'PetCareTV,' or hosting my own Internet-based radio show, called 'The Pet Doctor,' which is heard on PetLifeRadio.com. I am also involved with my national veterinary medical association, the American Veterinary Medical Association (AVMA). This has been very rewarding. A person can make a major impact on the profession, and the public in general, by getting involved."

Dr. Jim Rasmussen is the senior veterinarian at the Minnesota Zoo (http://www.mnzoo.com). The zoo has more than 2,400 animals and 388 species from around the world. Dr. Rasmussen graduated from veterinary school in 1990. He worked in private practice for a year and then entered a two-year residency program in primate medicine before accepting a job at the Minnesota Zoo. "I always enjoyed animals and wanted to become a veterinarian since an early age," he says. "I specifically liked working with nondomestic animals and had been involved with wildlife rehabilitation for quite some time prior to entering veterinary school. My main job duty is to oversee the medical care of the collection of zoo animals. I still provide clinical/hands-on care to the collection animals, but the associate veterinarians are more extensively involved with the hands-on medical care. In my current position I also am the supervisor for the veterinary department and am more involved with management issues at the zoo."

Dr. Rasmussen says that the best parts of his job are "being able to work with very interesting and unique animals, being able to be involved with conservation projects, working with other animal professionals who are very committed to the field, and the fact that there are always new challenges to deal with so work is never dull."

Dr. Greg Hammer has been a veterinarian for 35 years. He is a partner at Brenford Animal Hospital, a small-animal and equine practice in Dover, Delaware, that employs nine doctors. At Brenford, he practices clinical medicine and surgery. "I chose this career at a very young age, probably when I was around seven," he says. "Much of my life has mirrored my uncle's, who was a veterinarian in Nebraska. I grew up watching him and knowing that my love of science, people, and animals would be a perfect career match as a veterinarian.

"What I do now is much different than when I first graduated from veteri-

nary school at Kansas State University," he continues. "The first year, I practiced mixed animal medicine—all creatures great and small. The next two years, I was a veterinarian/captain in the Air Force Veterinary Corps. After discharge, I joined Brenford and have been a partner there ever since."

A typical day for Dr. Hammer begins at 7 A.M. with rounds and treatments in the hospital. "I usually see appointments for two hours," he says, "and then start surgery. In the afternoon, I see appointments again and usually go home around 6 P.M. My main duties are clinical medicine and surgery on dogs and cats. I share secondary administrative duties with four other partners. One of the greatest things about working as a veterinarian is having the opportunity to help people by taking care of their friends—their pets. Every day, I get the chance to teach people about medicine and prevent problems in their pets. It's also a great pleasure to be able to make a decent living enjoying every minute of what I do. As for the cons, I can honestly say that I really haven't found any yet."

Dr. Hammer says that one of his most rewarding experiences in organized veterinary medicine occurred when he became president of the 78,000-member American Veterinary Medical Association. "In that role," he says, "I represented veterinary medicine all over the world. I had the opportunity to speak to members of the U.S. Congress, to thousands of veterinarians all over the U.S., and to the public through the media. It can't get more rewarding than that. On a day-to-day basis, just going in to my hospital and helping my clients and their pets is all the reward I need!"

Dr. Kimberly May is the director of professional and public affairs in the Communications Division of the American Veterinary Medical Association. She graduated from veterinary school in 1994. "I had always wanted to be a veterinarian for as long as I can remember," she says. "A love of animals, coupled with an inquisitive and scientific mind, made it a perfect choice for me."

Dr. May practiced as an equine veterinarian and surgeon until fall 2005, at which time she began working for the American Veterinary Medical Association. "This job offered me the perfect combination of veterinary medicine, communications, outreach, and creativity," she says. "I still work in the veterinary field, but I'm not working on animals every day. I'm still using my veterinary education; actually, I'm probably using it *more* now—or at least a wider range of it.

"When I was in practice as a surgeon," she continues, "my day began at 7 A.M. (assuming we weren't still working on emergency cases from the night before) with rounds, where we'd go through all of the hospitalized cases, get updated on their status, and determine the day's course of action. We'd then spend our day between appointments conducting exams and doing what was needed for the hospitalized cases, whether that be surgery, blood work, endoscopy, or X rays. If an emergency came in, that patient took precedence because they required urgent care. The days could be long if emergen-

cies came in because our day didn't end until all of the animals had been cared for and plans had been determined for overnight care. We had a round-the-clock staff of technicians to provide animal care and treatment. Over the night, we might be called in to examine a hospitalized horse with a problem or for an emergency that would come to the hospital. Horses don't just get sick or injured during the day, and we got a fair share of late-night and early morning emergencies. My main job duty was to provide veterinary care for the hospitalized horses. This included medical and surgical treatment."

In her current employment with the American Veterinary Medical Association, Dr. May's daily activities vary widely and can change from hour to hour. "Some of the things I do," she says, "include providing media interviews on hot topics and issues of interest to veterinary medicine and the AVMA; crisis communications (including the identification of potential crises and the establishment of communication plans); environmental scanning to evaluate issues of interest to the public, media, and the profession; reviewing materials produced by the AVMA for educating the public; interacting with veterinarians needing assistance from the AVMA; generating educational materials for the profession and the public; managing several electronic communications channels; and developing new programs to improve our interactions with members, the profession, and the public."

Dr. Rexanne Struve is the owner and a practitioner at Veterinary Associates of Manning in Manning, Iowa. She has been a veterinarian for approximately 33 years. "Veterinary Associates is a general practice clinic," she explains, "providing care to all kinds of animals. I am also the owner of Struve Laboratories, which is a separate business, but run out the same facility as the clinic. I have been head of the laboratories since 1981. The purpose of Struve Labs is to provide cesarean derived, colostrum deprived piglets. These piglets are born into a sterile bubble, and then transported into a lab to be used for research. The benefit of being born via cesarean is that they are very clean—they are not exposed to the viruses or bacteria of the mother's birth canal. These piglets also do not receive colostrum, or first milk, from the mother. Clean piglets are used by different pharmaceutical companies that need to trial test various vaccines for effectiveness as mandated by the U.S. Department of Agriculture and the Food and Drug Administration.

"I am at the clinic every day, but spend the majority of my time with the work associated with Struve Labs. I have a veterinarian employed at the clinic who handles many of the daily calls and provides treatments. I handle all night and weekend calls, and most of the emergency work. At the clinic we see all kinds of animals. We treat all the large animals such as horses, cattle, pigs, sheep, llamas, and ostriches. We also treat the whole gamut of small animals such as dogs, cats, birds, and exotic animals."

Dr. Struve says that the best part about her job is delivering live healthy baby animals. "Sometimes the mother may be in trouble—whether she is a cow

Pros and Cons
● ● ● ● ● ● ● ●

The editors of *What Can I Do Now? Animal Careers* asked Dr. Bernadine Cruz what she likes best and least about her job:

The pros definitely outweigh any negatives. I have the pleasure of developing long-lasting relationships with people who are devoted to their pets. I often become an honorary member of their families. I interact with marvelous animals, and every day is always challenging and mentally stimulating. There are constant advances in veterinary medicine, so there is always something new to learn. With my involvement in educational outreach projects, I have been able to travel extensively, and my multimedia endeavors have allowed me to update the public on pet health issues. As a veterinarian, I have even been able to serve as a medical aid provider for the Iditarod and Yukon Quest 1,000-mile sled dog races. Both races were an experience of a lifetime.

The hours can be long, and it is not always possible to save every pet. It can be frustrating to know that there is more that can be done to aid a pet, but that it's not always financially feasible to do so.

or a dog or lamb—and I do what I can to help her deliver a live healthy baby. That's really the most rewarding part of my job. The cons of my job would be the emergency calls and night calls. Sometimes these emergencies happen during the holidays and someone has to be there to take care of them. In my practice, weather can be another unpleasant factor. I may have to work outside in a storm or in severe cold."

DO I HAVE WHAT IT TAKES TO BE A VETERINARIAN?

To be successful as a veterinarian, you should have an inquiring mind and keen powers of observation. Veterinarians should be able to interact well with a variety of people—from veterinary technicians, to support staff, to a pet's owner. An ability to communicate with people is as important for a veterinarian as diagnostic skills. "On my first day of veterinary school," recalls Dr. Cruz, "the dean addressed us and said that if we entered veterinary medicine because we liked medicine but didn't like interacting with people, we should 'get up and leave now, because this is a people-service profession.' Good communication skills are of paramount importance to having a successful practice (the same is true for life in general). It is also important to always have an open and inquiring mind." Dr. Rasmussen agrees. "You have to like working with a wide variety of people," he says. "As a zoo vet you deal with other zoo staff, the public, sometimes news people, and other medical professionals. You also need to be a good communicator in this field, both in written and oral communication. You need to like to learn on a continuous basis as there are always new things to learn and unique problems to solve."

"You need a strong scientific mind and good math and communications skills," advises Dr. May. "Veterinarians have to be able to interact effectively with animal owners. It is also important to be com-passionate and have strong leadership skills."

Veterinarians use cutting-edge medical equipment, such as electron microscopes, laser surgery, radiation therapy, and ultrasound, to diagnose animal diseases and to treat sick or injured animals. Although manual dexterity and physical stamina are often required, especially for farm vets, important roles in veterinary medicine can be adapted for those with disabilities.

Veterinarians may have to euthanize (that is, humanely kill) an animal that is very sick or severely injured and cannot get well. When an animal such as a beloved pet dies, the veterinarian must be compassionate when dealing with the owner's grief and loss.

HOW DO I BECOME A VETERINARIAN?
Education

Dr. Rasmussen advises students interested in veterinary science to "obtain a good science-based education, but also get good information technology and communication training. I also tell those interested in the profession that they should pursue other interests—whether it be literature, music, art, history, etc.—while they are in undergraduate college as those courses are not available as part of the curriculum once you enter veterinary school."

High School

High school students who are interested in a career in veterinary science should take a college preparatory curriculum. A strong emphasis on science classes such as biology, chemistry, and anatomy is highly recommended. "At the high school level," says Dr. Struve, "I think it is important for students to have a well-rounded background. Students who only spend their time studying may get straight A's, but they are not well-rounded students. They don't have to join a sport or be president of a club, but they should join something or get involved in an activity that interests them. I would recommend that students who are interested in this type of career get involved in a biology club, 4-H club, or the National FFA Organization."

Postsecondary Training

The doctor of veterinary medicine (DVM) degree requires a minimum of four years of study at an accredited college of veterinary medicine. Although many veterinary colleges do not require a bachelor's degree for admission, most require applicants to have completed 45 to 90 hours of undergraduate study. It is possible to obtain preveterinary training at a junior college, but since admission to colleges of veterinary medicine is an extremely competitive process, most students receive degrees from four-year colleges before applying. In addition to academic instruction, veterinary education includes clinical experience in diagnosing disease and treating animals, performing surgery, and performing laboratory work in anatomy, biochemistry, and other scientific and medical subjects.

There are 28 colleges of veterinary medicine in the United States that are accredited by the Council on Education of the American Veterinary Medical Association. Each college of veterinary medicine has its own preveterinary requirements, which typically include basic language arts, social sciences, humanities, mathematics, chemistry, and biological and physical sciences. Veterinarians in private clinical practice become specialists in surgery, anesthesiology, dentistry, internal medicine, ophthalmology, or radiology. Many veterinarians also pursue advanced degrees in the basic sciences, such as anatomy, microbiology, and physiology.

Applicants to schools of veterinary medicine usually must have grades of "B" or better, especially in the sciences. Applicants must take the Veterinary College Admission Test. Only about one-third of applicants to schools of veterinary medicine are admitted, due to small class sizes and limited facilities. Most colleges give preference to candidates with animal- or veterinary-related experience. Colleges usually give preference to in-state applicants because most colleges of veterinary medicine are state-supported. There are regional agreements in which states without veterinary schools send students to designated regional schools.

"You really need to be dedicated to get through veterinary school," says Dr. Struve. "It's not any one subject that is difficult, but rather the amount of work and information that is given throughout the course of the four years. You'll need a good background and interest in science and math, as well as communications. I would also recommend taking a second language as I am increasingly coming into contact with people whose first language is not English. Spanish is a good choice for a second language."

Certification or Licensing

Veterinarians who seek specialty board certification in one of 20 specialty fields must complete a two- to five-year residency program and pass an additional examination. Some veterinarians combine their degree in veterinary medicine with a degree in business (MBA) or law (JD).

All states and the District of Columbia require that veterinarians be licensed to practice private clinical medicine. To obtain a license, applicants must have a DVM degree from an accredited or approved college of veterinary medicine.

Interesting Experiences

The editors of *What Can I Do Now? Animal Careers* asked Dr. Kimberly May to detail some of her most interesting experiences as a veterinarian:

- The most rewarding experiences come from saving the life of a beloved companion. I was in charge of caring for a horse that was severely ill. He had severe diarrhea, and was very dehydrated and very sick. He was in the hospital for more than two weeks in our intensive care unit, and I spent much of those two weeks with him. He was getting high volumes of intravenous fluids to keep him from getting dehydrated. Although he was eating, he couldn't eat enough to provide the nutrition he needed, so we had to give him food and protein through his veins, too. It was a roller-coaster ride with him, where he'd look really good one hour and look like he was going to die the next hour. We spent a lot of time and effort helping him, and I lost a lot of sleep worrying about him and constantly designing and redesigning the plan for treating him to try and save his life. In the end we were able to save him and watch him go back home to the owner who loved him so much.

- I worked on a pregnant mare that had a uterine torsion (a twisted uterus). If we couldn't fix it, her foal would die and she might, too. We took her to surgery and untwisted her uterus. Three months later, she gave birth to a beautiful, healthy foal. They named the foal after me.

- Although my current employment doesn't offer me the opportunity to tell stories of the animals I'd directly saved or helped, my reward comes from feedback we receive. We produce materials that educate people and help them help their pets. It's very rewarding to hear from someone that the information we provided to them helped their pet. For example, during the massive pet food recall that began in March of 2007, the AVMA became the source of information for millions of people seeking reliable and accurate information. We worked directly with the U.S. Food and Drug Administration, pet food companies, and reporters around the country to get up-to-date, accurate information to veterinarians, their clients, and the general public.

They must also pass one or more national examinations and an examination in the state in which they plan to practice.

Some states issue licenses without further examination to veterinarians already licensed by another state. Approximately half of the states require veterinarians to attend continuing education courses in order to maintain their licenses. Veterinarians may be employed by a government agency (such as the U.S. Department of Agriculture) or at some academic institutions without having a state license.

Internships and Volunteerships

"When I was in veterinary school, internships were encouraged, but not required," Dr. Struve recalls. "Today, however, students are required to do an internship or externship to acquire clinical experience. This experience may be obtained in a clinical or practice setting with an experienced veterinarian. Internships and externships last about two to four months, often done in the summer before the final year of veterinary school. Your internship should be in a field of practice interest."

Dr. Rasmussen advises students to "obtain job experience by volunteering or working at veterinary clinics, zoos, farms, and animal rehabilitation centers. Many veterinary schools look at this experience when they rank applicants." Participation in extracurricular activities such as 4-H are good ways to learn about the care of animals. Such experience is important because, as already noted, many schools of veterinary medicine have established experience with animals as a criterion for admission to their programs.

WHO WILL HIRE ME?

Veterinarians are employed by zoos, aquariums, schools and universities, wildlife management groups, ranches, feedlots, fish farms, pet food or pharmaceutical companies, and the government (mainly in the U.S. Departments of Agriculture, Health and Human Services, and Homeland Security, and the armed forces). The vast majority, however, work at veterinary clinical practices or hospitals. Many successful veterinarians in private practice are self-employed and may even employ other veterinarians.

New graduate veterinarians may enter private clinical practice, usually as employees in an established practice, or become employees of the U.S. government as meat and poultry inspectors, disease control workers, and commissioned officers in the U.S. Public Health Service or the military. New graduates may also enter internships and residencies at veterinary colleges and large private and public veterinary practices or become employed by industrial firms.

Job leads can be obtained by contacting veterinary employers directly. Many veterinary college career services offices also provide veterinary students with employment leads. Job listings are available in newspaper classified ads, industry trade journals, and at the Web sites of professional associations such as the American Veterinary Medical Association.

Dr. Kimberly May advises new graduates to "look for a position with an employer who will mentor you and encourage you to develop new knowledge and skills. Take the time to find a job that fits your needs."

An Interesting Experience

The editors of *What Can I Do Now? Animal Careers* asked Dr. Jim Rasmussen, senior veterinarian at the Minnesota Zoo, to detail one of his most interesting experiences as a zoo veterinarian:

An example of a unique animal story, and one in which I gained some fame, was how I removed a stuffed animal toy from a Komodo dragon. We had an adult male Komodo monitor lizard that had been eating and was in eating mode when a guest accidentally dropped some stuffed toys into the exhibit. The Komodo ran over and gobbled one of the toys down before he realized it wasn't food. We thought he might regurgitate the toy, but I was concerned that it could possibly plug him up as well. So we monitored him and x-rayed him to see how things were progressing, but several days later we decided we would need to intervene and remove the toy.

We assembled a team to anesthetize the Komodo and try to remove the toy by passing an endoscope into his stomach.

While we could see the toy, it had lodged in the distal portion of his stomach, and it would not come loose with the endoscopic instruments after 30 minutes of trying.

At that point we were feeling some frustration so I volunteered my arm as a retrieval instrument. I wasn't quite sure I could reach it as the Komodo was 8.5 feet long, but I was quite sure my arm would fit down his esophagus as these animals often swallow large chunks of meat or whole prey. I donned a long, plastic, arm-length glove, wrapped it with duct tape to protect my arm from his razor-sharp teeth, and passed my arm through a padded PVC tube, which had been placed in his mouth to further protect my arm. I was just able to reach the toy and manipulate it to the point of retrieving it. When my arm came out intact with the highly slimy, but whole, toy, a cheer from all the observers went up in the room. The Komodo recovered fine from the anesthesia and the rest of the ordeal and is still doing well, although he now lives at another zoo.

WHERE CAN I GO FROM HERE?

Veterinarians who work for government agencies or the military may advance in grade and salary after acquiring time and experience on the job. Veterinarians in private clinical practice can advance by expanding their practices, which will generate higher income. They may also own and operate several practices.

Those who teach or do research may obtain a doctorate and move from the rank of instructor to that of full professor, or they may advance to an administrative position.

WHAT ARE THE SALARY RANGES?

Median annual earnings of veterinarians were $79,050 in 2008, according to the U.S. Department of Labor. Salaries ranged from less than $46,610 to more than $143,660. The mean annual salary for veterinarians working for the federal government was $81,610 in 2008.

According to a survey by the American Veterinary Medical Association, the average starting salary for veterinary medical college graduates who worked exclusively with small animals was $64,744 in 2008. Those who worked exclusively with large animals earned an average of $64,424. Equine veterinarians earned an average of $41,636 to start.

Benefits include paid vacation, health insurance, disability insurance, life insurance, and retirement or pension plans.

WHAT IS THE JOB OUTLOOK?

Much-faster-than-average employment growth for veterinarians is expected through 2016, according to the U.S. Department of Labor. "The future is very bright for veterinarians and veterinary technicians," says Dr. Hammer. "A recent survey listed them at number 4 and number 2, respectively, as recession-proof jobs. With the national shortage of veterinarians that our nation is experiencing, the job market is wide open for those who want to work."

"The job outlook is very good," says Dr. May. "Veterinarians are always needed, and some areas, such as research, government service, and academia, are experiencing shortages that are projected to worsen over the next few years. There is a marked demand for veterinarians interested in rural practice and food supply veterinary medicine."

The number of pets (especially cats) is expected to increase because of rising incomes and an increase in the number of people aged 34 to 59, among whom pet ownership has historically been the highest. Approximately 63 percent of U.S. households owned a pet in 2008, according to the American Pet Products Association. Many single adults and senior citizens have come to appreciate animal ownership. Pet owners may also be willing to pay for more elective and intensive care than in the past. In addition, emphasis on scientific methods of breeding and raising livestock, poultry, and fish, and continued support for public health and disease control programs, will contribute to the demand for veterinarians.

The outlook is good for veterinarians with specialty training. Demand for specialists in toxicology, laboratory animal medicine, and pathology is expected to increase. Most jobs for specialists will be in metropolitan areas. Prospects for veterinarians who concentrate on environmental and public health issues, aquaculture, and food animal practice appear to be excellent because of perceived increased need in these areas. Positions in small animal specialties will be competitive. Opportunities in farm animal specialties will be better. Most of these positions are located in remote, rural areas, and many veterinarians prefer to work in urban areas.

Despite the availability of additional jobs, competition among veterinarians is likely to be stiff. The number of students in graduate-degree and board-certification programs has risen dramatically.

Veterinary Technicians

SUMMARY

Definition
Veterinary technicians perform a variety of duties to assist veterinarians in the care of animals.

Alternative Job Titles
Animal technicians
Wildlife technicians
Zoo technicians

Salary Range
$19,770 to $28,900 to $41,490+

Educational Requirements
Associate's degree

Certification or Licensing
Required by certain states

Employment Outlook
Much faster than the average

High School Subjects
Biology
Chemistry
Mathematics

Personal Interests
Animals
Science
Wildlife

Veterinary technician Joel Pond says that he finds it especially rewarding when he can adapt a veterinary procedure to the zoo animal by using its behavior or physiology to his advantage. "One day," he recalls, "I was asked to take X rays of a chameleon (a small African lizard). When taking X rays one needs to take a side view and a top-to-bottom view so the doctor can see internal structures from different directions." Joel's task was complicated by the fact that he was not allowed to anesthetize the animal in order to get him to hold still long enough to take the picture. Also, the lizard did not like to walk or stand on flat surfaces, like the x-ray table. "But he had no problem staying on a twig in his transport container," Joel says. "While handling this creature, I noticed that when I moved my hand close by him, he would stop and freeze for a while. I decided I could use that behavior to my advantage. I knew X rays could pass through some plastics, so I constructed an artificial twig using a plastic rod attached to two crosspieces made from plastic medicine bottles. This created a bridge on which the chameleon could walk upright on top of the x-ray plate that held the film. Once I had a means to place the animal on the film I was able to get him to stand still merely by moving my hand overhead. Then I could take the X ray."

WHAT DOES A VETERINARY TECHNICIAN DO?

Veterinary technicians work with veterinarians to assist with the health care of animals. They may work in animal hospitals, private veterinary clinics, zoos, aquariums, kennels, horse farms, wildlife sanctuaries, shelters, and research laboratories. Although most veterinary technicians work with domestic animals, some work settings may involve treating exotic animals or endangered species. Veterinary technicians may work with small animals such as dogs and cats at a small-animal hospital, or they may work with large animals such as horses, cows, pigs, and sheep at a clinic for farm animals. Often veterinary technicians who work with large farm animals are required to travel to the farm, as these animals are typically treated on site. Some veterinary technicians work in an environment that involves caring for both small and large animals.

During examinations, veterinary technicians often help to restrain the animal and perform routine visit procedures. They may administer injections, clean wounds, apply and change dressings, and clean teeth. Veterinary technicians often talk with the animal's owner and write down information for the animal's file. In many clinics and private practices, it is the veterinary technician who explains treatment and animal care to the owner.

Veterinary technicians assist veterinarians in performing surgery. They prepare the animal for surgery and may administer local, regional, or general anesthesia and monitor the animal's vital signs. The veterinarian often asks the technician to provide specific supplies and instruments when needed. In addition, it is often the duty of technicians to monitor sick animals and animals recovering from surgery. In some cases, when an animal is very ill or injured without chance of survival, or in an overcrowded shelter, a veterinary technician may be required to euthanize the animal.

One of the main duties of veterinary technicians is to perform laboratory procedures. Laboratory work may compose up to 50 percent of a veterinary technician's job. This work involves taking samples from an animal's body to look for such problems as parasites, diseases, and infections. Laboratory work may also include assisting the veterinarian with necropsies to determine the cause of an animal's death, as well as taking and developing X rays.

In some facilities, veterinary technicians are responsible for overseeing supplies and equipment. These duties may include recording, replenishing, and maintaining equipment, supply, and pharmaceutical inventories. Veterinary technicians can also schedule appointments, organize patient files, and keep books for billing and payment records.

Some veterinary technicians work in zoos or with wildlife. Because there are only a few zoos in each state and each zoo only employs a few technicians, zoo jobs are highly competitive and the field is difficult to break into. Like veterinary technicians at a clinic or hospital, a *zoo* or *wildlife technician* may be responsible

To Be a Successful Veterinary Technician, You Should...

- enjoy working with animals
- have a strong stomach
- stay calm and think clearly in emergency situations
- be a good listener
- follow instructions well
- be careful, precise, and detail-oriented
- have good communication skills
- be patient
- be compassionate
- have a strong interest in and aptitude for science and medicine

for a great deal of laboratory work. However, these technicians typically will not have the duties of explaining treatments to owners, gathering information for the animal's file, or scheduling appointments. Instead, zoo and wildlife technicians may be asked to discuss cases with curators and other zoo professionals. Zoo and wildlife technicians often observe and work with animals in their "habitats," and this involves working outdoors.

Veterinary technicians work in other unexpected or less common settings. These include obedience schools, circuses, the military, and in information systems technology, where information on animals is compiled and provided by a veterinary technician via a computer network.

WHAT IS IT LIKE TO BE A VETERINARY TECHNICIAN?

Joel Pond works as a certified veterinary technician at a world-renowned zoo in the Chicago area. He is also the executive director of the Association of Zoo Veterinary Technicians. "I have had a lifelong interest in animals that was fostered by my father," he says. "I more or less fell into the position I hold today. I had a sick turtle that needed a veterinarian. The only veterinarian in the city who treated exotic animals was the part-time zoo veterinarian. One day, I asked him where he learned to treat turtles. He replied, 'I am the veterinarian at a zoo. Would you like to accompany me on my rounds some afternoon?' I took him up on his gracious offer four decades ago. What I did not learn in college, I was taught by that veterinarian and other veterinary technicians."

A typical day for Joel lasts from 8 A.M. to 5 P.M. with an hour for lunch. "Of course," he says, "we deal with emergencies and are often called upon to work late or begin the day earlier." In the morning, Joel and his colleagues meet with the three veterinarians and others to go over the day's cases. "With three veterinary technicians we divide up our work load so none of us gets bored," he explains. "One of us takes the clinic cases. These usually entail an anesthetic procedure in order to perform a routine physical exam. The clinic technician induces, maintains, and monitors anesthesia; may take blood and urine samples; and takes and develops radiographs (X rays). The second technician may be involved in an identical procedure on a cage mate at the same time, or he or she may be working on special projects involved in maintaining the zoo animal hospital. The third technician works primarily in the zoo's clinical laboratory running the laboratory tests on the blood, urine, feces, and tissue samples collected from the anesthetized animals or submitted to the lab by the animal keepers. All of the technicians in our practice can do the job of the other." In the afternoons, Joel and the other technicians clean up from the day's procedures, write patient records, and set up for the next day's work.

Joel says that zoo veterinary technicians "typically work in a veterinary hospital that consists of office spaces, a laboratory, animal treatment room, sterile surgery suite, a radiology room with dark room for developing the X rays, a pharmacy, a place to clean and sanitize the surgical equipment and to wash our clothing, a diet kitchen for the animals, along with animal holding facilities capable of housing animals as small as a baby mouse or as big as an elephant. Most zoo animal hospitals have separate quarantine facilities to house newly arrived animals. Many of us go out into the zoo to perform our jobs, performing the anesthesia (sometimes known as immobilizations) where the animals live. This is especially true of large hoof stock, such as giraffes and hippos. We also work with aquatic animals from polar bears to penguins, as well as all sorts of fish. Some of the animals we work with are venomous (vipers and tarantulas). Some are very large or very strong (elephants and rhinoceroses). Some are creepy (Madagascar hissing cockroaches), and some are extraordinarily cute (koalas). Some are highly endangered or even extinct in the wild (such as the Micronesian kingfisher)."

DeeAnn Wilfong is the head veterinary technician at Littleton Equine Medical Center (http://www.littletonequine.com) in Littleton, Colorado. The facility, which was founded in 1950, exclusively treats horses. DeeAnn is also the president of the American Association of Equine Veterinary Technicians and Assistants. "I began college with the intention of becoming a veterinarian," she says, "but took another career path. I continued on to receive my bachelor of science degree in biology and had intentions of working with wildlife or within the zoo system. The medical side of the industry was something I was still interested in so I took another look at veterinary medicine and found a school where I could receive a degree in veterinary technology. The nursing side of veterinary medicine is exactly the compromise I was looking for between being a veterinarian and being a biologist. I still planned on working in the wildlife industry, but it is extremely competitive with very few positions so I went into equine medicine and found my love."

DeeAnn's work as a veterinary technician is atypical since she is also a technician manager, publication editor, association

Lingo to Learn

companion animals Household pets, typically cats and dogs—as opposed to large animals such as farm animals, or exotics such as zoo animals.

euthanize To kill an animal in a relatively painless way as an act of mercy. Typically done for terminally sick or injured animals.

feline distemper (panleukopenia) An acute, usually fatal, viral disease, especially of cats, characterized by extensive destruction of white blood cells.

inpatient A patient who is lodged at the hospital or clinic due to surgery or illness.

necropsy An examination done on a dead animal to determine cause of death.

outpatient A patient who is treated and released directly after examination.

parasitosis Infestation or disease caused by parasites. In animals this may include flea infestation, heartworm, lyme disease, tick fever, and many others.

pathology The study of diseases and the changes produced by them.

president, and heavily involved in the industry. "I do travel quite a bit for my industry obligations," she says, "but as an equine technician, there is no travel unless you work for more than one practice. A very generic typical day is spent receiving patients including emergencies, setting up for procedures including surgery, attending to the hospitalized cases, and providing customer service for our clients. I work in a large equine surgical referral facility so we have a high surgical and emergency caseload. In my practice, veterinary technicians run all anesthetic cases, take radiographs, run the MRI unit, staff the intensive care unit, and are responsible for all hospitalized and critical care patients. They function as circulating nurses in surgery and work with the veterinarians, assisting them with exams (for lameness, ophthalmology, neurology, pre-purchase, reproductive, neonatal, endoscopy, and the diagnostics that are involved). The day begins early and ends late as horses don't injure themselves within our office hours. The hospital is staffed 24/7, 365 days per year."

Margot Monti is a veterinary technician at the Oregon Zoo (http://www.oregonzoo.org) in Portland, Oregon. She has worked as a technician for 19 years—and the past 16 years at the Oregon Zoo. "This career is really something I've known I wanted to do since I was about four years old," she says. "I was always the kid down at the creek catching crayfish, collecting Japanese beetles from the neighbors' roses, tending to the minor wounds of the neighborhood dogs—anything that had to do with animals."

Margot has a very large range of job duties. These include assisting the veterinarians in surgery; taking radiographs; giving medication; filling prescriptions; doing dental cleanings on animals with teeth; monitoring anesthesia; drawing and performing laboratory testing on blood, feces, and tissues; aiding in necropsy examinations on dead animals; and participating in any necessary veterinary care. "When not directly working with animals," she says, "I clean cages and floors, keep good records, order supplies, present educational programs, and participate in planning for our new veterinary hospital. Basically, I do anything that has to do with the veterinary hospital except make diagnoses, prescribe medication, or perform surgery. These are the veterinarians' responsibilities, though they do a lot more than that, too."

DO I HAVE WHAT IT TAKES TO BE A VETERINARY TECHNICIAN?

"Working with some of the world's most endangered species or animals with highly specialized physical needs is challenging for all involved, including zoo veterinary technicians," says Joel Pond. "Therefore, we need to be intelligent, adaptable, and resilient. A good 'animal sense' is also valuable; but not everyone has the ability to read animals. Zoo vet techs must be willing to continue to learn their craft as veterinary medicine continues to evolve and more knowledge is gained about the animals in zoos throughout their career."

"Self-motivation and an ability to prioritize an endless 'to-do' list are crucial," says Margot Monti. "So is creativity, because we continually face problems and challenges that no one has ever seen before. You have to know what, when, and how to get things done before anyone even tells you. One also has to be extremely flexible. Emergencies happen, priorities change, and you have to be ready to drop whatever you're doing

or change course without missing a beat. Empathy is key, as is being able to detect even the most subtle changes in behavior and know whether it's significant. Beyond that, of course, it helps immensely not to be queasy, not to become too emotionally involved in all the ups and downs of animal care, and to have a really good educational background in basic biology, anatomy, and physiology. A taste for adventure also never hurts."

Veterinary technicians must be able to work with blood, hypodermic needles, and open wounds and incisions. In addition, the technician must be prepared for emergencies, many of which may be unpleasant and even gory. For this reason, anyone interested in becoming a veterinary technician should have a strong stomach and not wince at the sight of blood or panic in medical emergencies. Anyone who loves animals but cannot handle unpleasant medical situations will have a difficult time as a veterinary technician.

Even if an animal is badly injured, a veterinary technician must be able to think on his or her feet and remain calm enough to perform the job well. Therefore, an aptitude for science and medicine, in addition to an interest in working with animals, is necessary for this job.

Veterinary technicians must also be able to accept the fact that no matter what they do during a medical emergency, the animal they are taking care of many not survive. DeeAnn Wilfong says that the least rewarding aspect of her job is "the emotional pain and exhaustion that comes with working in the medical

Career Memories

The editors of *What Can I Do Now? Animal Careers* asked DeeAnn Wilfong, head veterinary technician at Littleton Equine Medical Center, to detail one of the most rewarding experiences she has had during her career:

I've been doing this for about 10 years, so I have a lot of stories and a lot of them are a bit gory, but one of my favorites is about a mare that was pregnant with twins. Horses are not built to have more than one foal at a time, and it can cost the mare and both foals their lives. Nature often eliminates one of the twins, or we can do a procedure very early on to be sure that only one foal develops.

Unfortunately for the mare, neither was true in her case. She was admitted to the hospital to have the foals and several teams were put on standby, prepared for a worst-case scenario, and the clients were dealing with the possibility that they might lose the mare and both foals.

The night the call came in, I was about 15 minutes away from the hospital. The surgical, anesthesia, reproductive, and internal medicine teams were called in, and I was one of the first to arrive.

Preparing myself for the worst, I took a deep breath and walked into the barn. As I got to the mare's stall, I peaked in to see not one, but two, perfectly healthy and alive foals in the straw. The mare had foaled them out without any assistance and was doing fine. The foals were small, but equally healthy (often one is normal and the other has health issues or doesn't survive) and the mare was no worse for the wear. Within a few hours they were running around the stall, bucking and kicking and terrorizing their mother. We had gone from expecting the worst outcome to being blessed with the best-case scenario, and I often think of those foals when times get tough and I wonder why I do what I do.

industry. You deal with life and death, and this can be hard on a person."

Veterinary technicians are an important part of a medical team. For example, the typical profile of a private veterinary practice consists of three veterinarians, two technicians, and three other assistants. Because of this, veterinary technicians should be good listeners and communicators, able to follow precise instructions from the veterinarian, and able to discuss cases with owners and other veterinary professionals.

HOW DO I BECOME A VETERINARY TECHNICIAN?
Education

High School

Because postsecondary education is required for the job, it is important that students interested in becoming veterinary technicians complete high school. While still in high school, you will want to begin building a strong foundation in the sciences, especially anatomy, chemistry, and biology. Not only will these courses provide you with the background needed for postsecondary training, they will also help you discover whether you have an aptitude for the field of medicine. For example, if you faint while dissecting a frog or feel woozy while watching a video on the cardiovascular system, you might want to reconsider your interest in the field of veterinary technology. In addition, health classes are important, as they introduce you to a variety of medical concepts.

Fixing Tusko

Margot Monti, a veterinary technician at the Oregon Zoo, recalls one of her most memorable experiences as a veterinary technician:

One of our elephants, named Tusko, had an infected tusk, and we decided that it needed to be removed for his health. He had been walking around for years with these jagged edges of broken tusk sticking out of a hole on the side of his face, and they were cutting into his lip. On top of that, the hole was always dripping with really stinky nasty goo and just had to be all kinds of unpleasant for him.

Because one can't just take an elephant to the dentist and give him a little shot of Novocain to pull out a tooth, we spent months making plans for how and where to anesthetize him and how to keep him asleep. We had a huge elephant-sized waterbed made for him to lie on while he was asleep so he didn't crush his internal organs, and assembled and made some crazy elephant-sized tusk extraction tools (we did most of our shopping for these at the hardware store rather than in a medical supply catalog).

In the meantime, the elephant keepers worked to train Tusko to allow the vet crew (i.e., me) to place an IV catheter into his ear to deliver medication, then lie down in the right place on the floor. We assembled different teams of people to help us—one crew to do anesthesia, one to operate all the necessary heavy equipment, one to actually do the dental work, and someone to coordinate the flock of reporters that were assigned to cover the story for TV and newspapers. All in all, I think there were about 40 people involved, and I was one of the ones who actually oversaw the "big picture" of the procedure and knew where all the equipment and supplies we needed were located.

It's a pretty risky thing to anesthetize an elephant; a lot can go wrong. We ended up having to do the procedure twice. The first time we anesthetized Tusko, we weren't able to get all the pieces of tusk out because there was so much of it way up inside his head that we realized we needed a whole new set of bigger and better tools.

But, because we had planned well and had a great team of people working on Tusko, we were able to (not once but twice) anesthetize him; get up into the tusk cavity with (yes, really) huge drill bits and little chainsaws and chisels and sledgehammers; clean out all the slabs and chunks of infected tusk, bone, and tissue; and make Tusko more comfortable. And the best part was that he woke up and stood up and began to eat right away and didn't die. Twice.

You should also study mathematics in high school. In college and on the job, technicians use mathematics in a variety of ways, especially when working with pharmaceuticals to make sure an animal is receiving the correct dosage of medicine, and in determining radiation calculations and exposure time of X rays. Computer-science skills are also important, as technicians at many clinics and hospitals use computers to analyze data when helping veterinarians make diagnoses on laboratory specimens.

Good communication skills are important because veterinary technicians must communicate with animal owners and other members of the veterinary team and record information on patient charts. While in high school, you should take college-preparatory courses in English or language arts. "My most important advice to anyone in high school pursuing any career," says Margot Monti, "is first to pay attention in English class. Learn to write. Get your basic grammar, punctuation, and spelling down and you'll be miles ahead of the vast majority of people. Proficiency in English will get you jobs, advance your career, and make you a better communicator."

Postsecondary Training

Currently, more than 130 academic institutions offer two- or four-year postsecondary programs for veterinary technicians. These programs are accredited by the American Veterinary Medical Association (AVMA) and lead to an associate in applied science or other appropriate degree, with four-year degrees available at some programs.

Courses in veterinary technician programs are usually taught by veterinarians or veterinary technicians. The instructors in the program are aware of what employers expect technicians to know, and they teach toward these goals.

The core curriculum of these programs includes fundamentals of chemistry, biological science, communication skills, humanities or liberal arts, and applied mathematics. Within these basics, there are more than 20 required areas of study, including ethics in veterinary medicine, animal nutrition and feeding, medical terminology, and surgical nursing and assisting, just to name a few. The programs involve reading, lecture, memorization, and test taking, as well as laboratory sessions and hands-on work with live animals.

Zoo animal veterinary technicians take the standard veterinary technician curricula. "There are no schools that teach zoo veterinary technology as such," says Joel Pond. "One adapts veterinary technology learned for domestic animals, such as dogs, cats, horses, cattle, and chickens to related zoo animals. We are learning something new every day about our animals. We have to adapt methods, medications, and theories derived from domestic species and apply them to zoo animals. While learning these methods may be difficult and challenging, it is that very challenge and learning process that is most rewarding to those of us who are fortunate enough to work in a zoo or aquarium."

Some employees in veterinary hospitals and other animal care facilities have not completed a two-year AVMA program, but instead gained their experience on the job. These workers usually have the title of veterinary assistant, animal health assistant, animal attendant, or animal caretaker, among others. However, they are not considered to be veterinary technicians and their duties and salaries typically don't match those of a technician from an accredited program.

Certification or Licensing

Although the AVMA determines the majority of the national codes for veterinary technicians, state codes and laws vary. Most states offer registration or certification, and the majority of these states require graduation from an AVMA-accredited program as a prerequisite for taking the National Veterinary Technician Examination or a similar state or local examination. Most colleges and universities assist graduates with registration and certification arrangements. To keep abreast of new technology and applications in the field, practicing veterinary technicians may be required to complete a determined number of annual continuing education courses.

The American Association for Laboratory Animal Science offers certification to veterinary technicians who are interested in working in research settings. The American Association of Equine Veterinary Technicians and the Academy of Veterinary Emergency and Critical Care Technicians also offer certification.

Internships and Volunteerships

The most common way to obtain experience with animals while in high school is to have pets. This is probably the easiest

Advancement Possibilities

Physician assistants provide health care services to patients under the direction and responsibility of the physician. They examine patients, perform comprehensive physical examinations, and compile patient medical data, including health history and results of physical examination.

Veterinarians diagnose animal illnesses, treat diseased and injured animals medically and surgically, inoculate animals against diseases, and give advice on the care and breeding of animals.

Zookeepers provide day-to-day care for animals in zoological parks. They prepare diets, clean animal housing or enclosures, and monitor the behavior of the animals. They might also assist in research projects with the animals.

way to learn to care for and understand animals. But if you can't or don't have any pets, there are still plenty of opportunities to work with animals before deciding whether or not to enter an AVMA-accredited program.

College veterinary technology programs often require students to complete an internship. Most internships are unpaid, but many colleges offer course credit for their successful completion.

Another way to get experience in animal care is through a part-time job or volunteering. Students who have access to a farm might try getting work there, either in the summer or after school. This experience will not only provide you with an opportunity to work with animals, but also a head start once you enter college.

Participating in 4-H is also a good way to gain experience working with animals. Students in 4-H raise, train, and care for a variety of animals, including farm animals and seeing-eye dogs or other "helping dogs." To find local 4-H chapters, students should ask their guidance counselors, look up 4-H in the phone book, or visit its national Web site (http://4-h.org). In addition, private veterinary clinics, animal shelters, pet shops, and kennels often accept high school interns or even hire employees to help groom animals, clean cages, and walk boarders.

WHO WILL HIRE ME?

Approximately 91 percent of veterinary technicians are employed in veterinary services. Others work in animal shelters, stables, boarding kennels, zoos, aquariums, grooming salons, state and private educational institutions, and local, state, and federal agencies.

Besides finding job openings by word-of-mouth or sending resumes out to a variety of employers, you should also search newspaper classified ads for technician jobs at clinics. These ads may list openings under such categories as "Small Animals," "Animals," "Veterinary Technicians," "Animal Shelters," and others.

Advice for Young People

Margot Monti, a veterinary technician at the Oregon Zoo, offers the following advice to people who are interested in entering the field:

- Take as many biology and zoology classes as you can.

- Volunteer at a veterinary clinic or wildlife rehabilitation center. Work somewhere busy that teaches you how to be part of an effective team.

- Make contact with people who can help you get your foot in the door and impress them with your competence and ability to learn.

- Listen to those more experienced than you; really listen to what they have to say, because they'll teach you more than any textbook ever could.

- Love things that other people think are "gross." I, for example, think parasites are the coolest things in the world. Really. Get out there and get your hands dirty and love it!

There are also many national, state, and regional veterinary medical associations that maintain lists of job openings—often at their Web sites. Applicants can also call state boards of veterinary medicine to find out if they maintain a list of job openings or if they know of an organization that does.

Often, college career services offices will assist recent graduates in securing positions as veterinary technicians. Technicians-in-training who have done internships in clinics or hospitals may get hired by these clinics, if space permits, once they have graduated from their program and passed the exam. For this reason, it is wise for student technicians to find summer employment or a school-year internship at a location where they would be interested in working once they graduate.

Technicians who are interested in working in zoos or research facilities should look in specialized field publications, such as *The NAVTA Journal* (contact the National Association of Veterinary Technicians in America) and *Journal of Zoo & Wildlife Medicine* (contact the American Association of Zoo Veterinarians). People interested in zoo jobs may also want to contact the Association of Zoo Veterinary Technicians. Technician jobs in zoos, however, are highly competitive and relatively scarce.

WHERE CAN I GO FROM HERE?

A veterinary technician may have such a love of the work that he or she chooses to remain in the position as a permanent career. In this case, advancement usually comes in the form of increases in salary and responsibilities. However, the job of veterinary technician also allows for a wide variety of other job advancement possibilities.

Going back to school to receive a bachelor of science degree, a technician can become a veterinary technologist. Or, a technician could even attend four years of veterinary school after receiving a bachelor of science degree to become a doctor of veterinary medicine.

Veterinary technicians may also make a variety of lateral (i.e., on the same level) career moves. Technicians may have to receive some supplemental training to make a lateral career move, but these usually do not entail extensive schooling. Lateral moves for a veterinary technician may include careers in veterinary pharmaceutical sales, obedience or assistance animal training, or kennel or pet supply store ownership or management. Veterinary technicians are also hired as instructors by colleges and universities that have veterinary technician programs, as consultants with pet food manufacturers, and as agents or adjusters for large-animal insurance companies.

Some technicians may even choose to stay in the field of medicine but leave veterinary science. This move presents the opportunity of training for careers such as hospital laboratory technician, medical researcher, nurse, paramedic, or physician

FYI

Until the 1960s, veterinarians trained their own employees on the job. These employees were often called veterinary assistants. In the early 1960s, to meet the increasing technical demands of the veterinary field, colleges and universities developed formal academic programs to train veterinary technicians.

Related Jobs

- animal breeders
- animal caretakers
- animal trainers
- dog groomers
- horseshoers (farriers)
- kennel operators
- laboratory assistants
- livestock farm workers
- obedience trainers
- ranchers
- stable attendants
- wildlife biologists
- zoologists

assistant. Through their jobs, veterinary technicians become well-acquainted with both animal care and medical science and will find a variety of careers related to one or both of these fields.

WHAT ARE THE SALARY RANGES?

Median annual earnings for veterinary technicians and technologists were $28,900 in 2008, according to the U.S. Department of Labor. Salaries ranged from less than $19,770 annually to $41,490 or more annually.

In addition to salary, veterinary technicians may receive health benefits, free animal care and boarding, paid vacation, and sick leave, among other benefits. However, these benefits will vary depending on the employer.

WHAT IS THE JOB OUTLOOK?

Veterinary medicine is a field that is not usually affected by the economy. In times of recession, people may postpone a large purchase or cut back on personal expenditures, but most people will continue to provide their animals with health care. For this reason, certified veterinary technicians can expect to find job stability. The number of American households with one or more pets is on the rise, creating a need for more veterinary technicians in the companion animal field. An increased concern for animal welfare also means that more technicians will be hired by animal shelters and animal welfare societies. Veterinary technicians who work with farm animals will also be in strong demand.

The employment outlook for zoo veterinary technicians is not as good. "Obtaining a job in a zoo can be challenging as many zoo veterinary technicians remain at their positions for long periods," says Joel Pond. "There are usually several job openings somewhere in the U.S. at any given time. People planning to work in the zoo field should expect to relocate once finished with veterinary technology school. Getting experience in zoo work is beneficial—whether it is volunteering for a zoo or working in a wildlife facility."

Zoo and Aquarium Curators and Directors

SUMMARY

Definition
Curators and directors work as managers in zoos and aquariums. They supervise employees, animals, and business operations.

Alternative Job Titles
Chief animal officers
Chief executive officers
Chief operating officers
Managers
Presidents
Supervisors
Vice-presidents

Salary Range
$20,000 to $55,000 to $150,000+

Educational Requirements
Bachelor's degree; master's degree required for top positions

Certification or Licensing
None available

Employment Outlook
More slowly than the average

High School Subjects
Biology
Business
Speech

Personal Interests
Animals
Science
Wildlife

"Everything we do here is special," says Anthony Godfrey, president and chief operating officer of the Georgia Aquarium. "We conduct research that helps all mankind, we educate our guests so they can have a better understanding of the environment and, most importantly, we touch the lives of our guests in a positive way." As the leader of the aquarium, Anthony had the opportunity to touch the life of a sick nine-year-old boy and his family. "Before we opened the aquarium, I took the boy and his family on a tour of the aquarium," Anthony recalls. "He had stage-four cancer and

did not have long to live, so he wanted to see the world's largest aquarium. We were not allowed to take guests through the aquarium yet because we were still months away from opening, but this was a very special situation. The boy and his family spent three hours enjoying the aquarium. We did not have a gift shop yet, so I gave the boy a hat and T-shirt with our name and logo on it. He was so happy to receive these gifts that he put them on before he left. The family also received special tickets for opening day; however, the young boy did not make it to opening day. He died shortly after his visit wearing his Georgia Aquarium T-shirt because he would not take it off. On opening day, the family thanked me for the special day they spent with their son at the aquarium months earlier."

WHAT DOES A ZOO AND AQUARIUM CURATOR OR DIRECTOR DO?

Zoo and aquarium curators are the chief employees responsible for the daily care of the creatures. They oversee the various sections of the animal collections, such as mammals, birds, and fish. *Zoo and aquarium directors*, or *chief executive officers*, are administrators who coordinate the business affairs of these centers. Directors execute the institution's policies, usually under the direction of a governing authority. They are responsible for the institution's operations and plans for future development and for such tasks as fund-raising and public relations. They also serve as representatives of, and advocates for, their institutions and their entire industry.

General curators of zoos and aquariums oversee the management of an institution's entire animal collection and animal management staff. They help the director coordinate activities, such as education, exhibit design, collection planning, research, new construction, and public services. They meet with the director and other members of the staff to create long-term strategic plans. General curators may have public relations and development responsibilities, such as meeting with the media and identifying and cultivating donors. In most institutions, general curators develop policy; other curators implement policy.

Animal curators are responsible for the day-to-day management of a specific portion of a zoo's or aquarium's animal collection (as defined taxonomically, such as mammals or birds, or eco-geographically, such as the forest edge or the desert trail); the people charged with caring for that collection, including assistant curators, zookeepers, administrative staff such as secretaries, as well as researchers, students, and volunteers; and the associated facilities and equipment.

For example, the curator in charge of the mammal department of a large zoo would be responsible for the care of such animals as lions, tigers, monkeys, and elephants. He or she might oversee nearly 1,000 animals representing 200 different species, manage scores of employees, and have a multimillion-dollar budget.

Assistant curators report to curators and assist in animal management tasks and decisions. They may have extensive supervisory responsibilities.

Curators have diverse responsibilities; their activities vary widely from day to day. They oversee animal husbandry procedures, including the daily care of the animals, establish proper nutritional programs, and manage animal health care in partnership with the veterinary staff. They develop exhibits, educational programs, and visitor services and participate in research and conservation activities. They maintain inventories of animals and other records, and they recommend and implement acquisitions and dispositions of animals. Curators serve as liaisons with other departments.

Curators prepare budgets and reports. They interview and hire new workers. When scientific conferences are held, curators attend them as representatives of the institutions for which they work. They are often called upon to write articles for scientific journals and perhaps provide information for newspaper reports and magazine stories. They may coordinate or participate in on-site research or conservation efforts. To keep abreast with developments in their field, curators spend a lot of time reading.

Curators meet with the general curator, the director, and other staff to develop the objectives and philosophy of the institution and decide on the best way to care for and exhibit the animals. They must be knowledgeable about the animals' housing requirements, daily care, medical procedures, dietary needs, and social and reproduction habits. Curators represent their zoos or aquariums in collaborative efforts with other institutions, such as the more than 110 Association of Zoos and Aquariums (AZA) Species Survival Plans that target individual species for intense conservation efforts by zoos and aquariums. In this capacity, curators may exchange information, negotiate breeding loans, or assemble the necessary permits and paperwork to effect the transfers. Other methods of animal acquisition coordinated by curators involve purchases from animal dealers or private collectors and collection of nonendangered species from the wild. Curators may arrange for the quarantine of newly acquired animals. They may arrange to send the remains of dead animals to museums or universities for study.

Curators often work on special projects. They may serve on multidisciplinary committees responsible for planning and constructing new exhibits. Curators interface with colleagues from other states and around the world in collaborative conservation efforts.

Working under the supervision of a governing board, *directors* are charged with pulling together all the institution's operations, development of long-range planning, implementation of new programs, and maintenance of the animal collection and facilities. Much of the director's time is spent meeting with the volunteer governing board and with departmental staff who handle the institution's daily operations.

Directors plan overall budgets, which includes consideration of fund-raising programs, government grants, and private financial support from corporations, foundations, and individuals. They work with the board of directors to design major policies and procedures, and they meet with the curators to discuss animal acquisitions, public education, research projects, and developmental activities. In larger zoos and aquariums, directors may give speeches, appear at fund-raising events, and represent their organizations on television or radio.

A major part of the director's job is seeing that his or her institution has enough money to operate. Where zoos and aquariums were once funded largely by local and state governments, the amount of tax money available for this purpose is dwindling. Generally, zoos and aquariums need to generate enough revenue to pay for about two-thirds of their operating expenses from sources such as donations, membership, retail sales, and visitor services.

As zoos and aquariums endeavor to improve facilities for animals and visitors alike and to present the conservation message to the public in a more effective manner, renovation of existing structures and construction of new exhibits is an ongoing process. Directors spend much of their time working with architects, engineers, contractors, and artisans on these projects.

Directors also inform the public about what is going on at the zoo or aquarium. This involves participating in interviews with the media, answering questions from individuals, and even resolving complaints. In addition to being interviewed by journalists and other writers, directors do writing of their own for inhouse newsletters and annual reports or for general circulation magazines and newspapers.

Although not directly involved in animal management within his or her own institution, the director may play a significant role in conservation at a regional, national, or international level. Directors work on committees for various conservation organizations, such as AZA Species Survival Plans. They may be involved at a higher level of the AZA, working on such things as accreditation of other institutions, developing professional ethics, or long-range planning. Directors work with other conservation groups as well and may serve in leadership positions for them too.

As zoos and aquariums expand their conservation role from only the management of captive animals to supporting the preservation of the habitats those animals came from, directors are working with universities and field biologists to support research.

Other directorial personnel include *assistant directors* and *deputy directors*. Like curators, these workers are responsible for a specific duty or department, such as operations, education, or animal management. They also manage certain employees, supervise animal care workers, and take care of various administrative duties to help the director.

The work atmosphere for curators and directors of animal facilities will always center on the zoo or aquarium in which they work. Curators spend most of their time indoors at their desks reading email, talking on the phone, writing reports, meeting deadlines for budgets, planning exhibits, and so forth. Particularly at large institutions, the majority of their time is spent on administrative duties rather than hands-on interaction with animals. Like other zoo and aquarium employees, curators often work long hours tending to the varied duties to which they are assigned.

When the unexpected happens, curators must respond to their share of animal emergencies. In difficult situations, they may find themselves working late into the night with keepers and veterinarians to help care for sick animals or those that are giving birth.

Curators are sometimes required to travel to conferences and community events. They might also travel to other zoos throughout the country or lead trips for zoo members to wilderness areas in the United States and abroad.

Directors tend to spend a great deal of time in their offices conducting business affairs. They attend a lot of meetings. Directors are sometimes required to travel to conferences and community events. They might also travel to other institutions throughout the country or abroad to attend meetings of professional

Rewarding Experiences

Diane Fusco, marine mammal supervisor at the Minnesota Zoo, details some of her most rewarding experiences in the field:

- Every morning I have the privilege of caring for these fantastic animals. I have the time to spend with them to get to know their behavior as a group and individually, learn some of their specific characteristics, spend time teaching them, and at other times spend time learning from them. Interacting with them in the water is an experience that is always rewarding.

- Spending 24 hours watching a dolphin go into labor, deliver a healthy calf, and several weeks later having the mom bring the calf over to meet the trainers is a memory not to be forgotten.

- Being able to present the animals as ambassadors of the ocean environment to zoo guests and sharing my experiences with them is rewarding and challenging at the same time. I want to be able to create an awareness of the ocean environment and its inhabitants; sometimes that is not always easy to do.

- Part of my job involves supervising the mammal training team. It is rewarding to see a novice trainer make a training breakthrough with their animal and reach their training goal.

organizations and conservation groups or to discuss animal transfers and other matters. Often, directors lead groups on trips around the United States or to developing countries.

WHAT IS IT LIKE TO BE A ZOO AND AQUARIUM CURATOR OR DIRECTOR?

Anthony Godfrey is the president and chief operating officer for the Georgia Aquarium (http://www.georgiaaquarium.org) in Atlanta, Georgia. It is the largest aquarium in the world. "I have worked in finance and business for 26 years and four-and-a-half of those years have been working for an aquarium," he says. "I have always enjoyed the challenges that come from running a business. The aquarium is a dream job because I have a strong interest in science and business. It is very rewarding to watch employees grow and see company goals being met. It is also rewarding running an educational facility where guests enjoy their experience."

Anthony says that being president of the aquarium is similar to being a basketball coach. "My main duty," he explains, "is making sure that I have the right players on the team, and that each player correctly executes the plan that we have laid out. It is very simple—we can only be as good as our team. My goal is making sure that everyone knows the aquarium's mission and what each player can do to help us achieve this mission. I want employees to enjoy and take pride in what they do, as well as be excited about the future. To sum it up, my main duties are to assemble the right team, create the vision for the team, decide what the team wants to accomplish, make sure everyone plays their position well, and cheer the entire process along."

Anthony believes that there are many pros to being an aquarium director. "We are unique in that we can do research to learn more about animals and their habitats," he says, "which helps ensure that future generations can continue to enjoy them as we do. This research benefits the animal kingdom as well as humans. The research we conduct in animal pathology is very similar to human pathology. In addition to research, we get the privilege of educating and entertaining our guests at the same time. The word *edutainment* is what we do best. People come here to learn and can also create lifetime memories with the people who they care about the most. Since we are also in the entertainment business, we are constantly trying to think of new programs, animals, and other changes that we can bring to our guests. In this industry, you can never stop the process of change or stand still. The cons in this field are animal deaths—just like in the wild. It is important to remember the circle of life and that all living things eventually die."

Billy Hurley is the senior vice president and chief animal officer for the Georgia Aquarium. He has worked in the field for 21 years. "I decided on this career because my mother instilled in me the desire to work with animals and the environment," he says. "This interest led me into this industry. My main job is animal acquisition and animal care. Locating and moving animals comes with a set of challenges. I take extreme pride in knowing we are able to create an environment in which we can provide greater care and better health opportunities for animals than they receive in the wild with all of today's ecological problems. My secondary duty is to create an innovative and immersive experience for our guests during their time at the Georgia Aquarium."

Billy says that there are a lot of pros to working in this field. "One would be the gratification of knowing you are inspiring others to protect the environment and the animals that live in it," he says. "I also enjoy the unique relationships I develop with these extraordinary animals. One con of working in this field is the financial challenges for biological research. This research does not come with lots of money; however, the research is very rewarding in the end. Another mild con would be that this job is 24/7. I'm always on call to help animals."

One of Billy's most rewarding experiences occurred when he worked on a research project off the island of Bermuda. "We were catching bottlenose dolphins for health assessments," he recalls. "We placed tags on all of the dolphins to track their movements and behaviors. From these animals, we discovered that dolphins can dive a lot deeper then we ever imagined. It was exciting to learn something new in a world where we think we know it all."

Diane Fusco works at the Minnesota Zoo (http://www.mnzoo.com) in Apple Valley, Minnesota. She has worked in the zoo and aquarium field for many years, starting at a zoo in New York State as a zookeeper in 1972. "As a biology major in college and having an interest in animal behavior," she says, "zoo work seemed like a perfect fit. In 1977 I moved to Min-

nesota specifically to begin work at the Minnesota Zoo as a zookeeper. My zookeeper experience overall involved caring for multiple species of mammals, birds, saltwater fish, and marine mammals. It was at the Minnesota Zoo where I settled into my current job working with the marine mammals. I started out as one of the training team members working with beluga whales, harbor seals, and dolphins. Today, I am supervisor of the zoo's marine mammals, which includes bottlenose dolphins and northern sea otters.

"This is not a nine to five job," she continues. "Sometimes your life is consumed with the job. Your skin will never be the same again—whether it's from baking in the hot sun or plunging your hands into frozen clam meat. There's probably a lot more time spent cleaning animal service and living areas than you can imagine. Despite these rather unattractive descriptions, the opportunity to work with these animals far outweighs the negative aspects of the job.

"I primarily supervise the marine mammal program to ensure optimal animal care. This includes designing, implementing, and evaluating their nutritional program; training and enrichment; veterinary and preventative medical care; maintaining animal records; and monitoring water and ambient environment in coordination with the animal management team. I also supervise seven trainers who are tasked with the care and training of the animals." Another important aspect of Diane's job is managing the interpretive programs that are created to give zoo guests an educational and entertaining experience. "As a team," she explains, "we develop and evaluate our dolphin presentations, dolphin encounter program, and the sea otter daily demonstrations. As a supervisor I also spend a great deal of time with paperwork. This might include submitting a budget for the department, staff scheduling, managing inventory, submitting documents for animal transactions, and representing the zoo in specific professional organizations."

Jonathan Scoones is the director of exhibits and volunteers at Mystic Aquarium & Institute for Exploration (http://www.mysticaquarium.org) in Mystic, Connecticut. He has worked in the field for 10 years. "I entered the field to showcase the fascinating animal world to children of all ages; to demonstrate their important role in the world; and to help protect animals for future generations," he says. "My main job duties are designing and coordinating the production of new exhibits that fascinate and involve guests, and meeting the mission of the organization. I am also developing a strong, self-supporting volunteer program that will enable volunteers to provide significant, vital roles in the organization." Jonathan says that taking part in the transport of seven whales and four dolphins from Shedd Aquarium in Chicago, Illinois, to Mystic, Connecticut, has been one of his most memorable experiences in the field. "The animals 'vacationed' here while Shedd's Oceanarium—their home—underwent renovations," he says. "We were awake for 36 hours, in the rain, driving down the road at 4 A.M. with a state police escort

and several trucks in order to get all the animals here safely—which we did!"

Dean Treangen is the farm supervisor at the Minnesota Zoo. He has worked at the zoo since the farm exhibit opened in 2000 and has been involved in the animal industry his entire life. "I have always had an interest in animals and love working with them," he says. "I grew up on a farm, went to the University of Minnesota, and worked in the dairy industry until coming to the zoo. My main job is supervising the farm exhibit. This includes taking care of and maintaining the exhibit, supervising and hiring staff, dealing with all the visitors that come through the farm, working with the volunteers, and, most importantly, attending to the health and well-being of the animals here at the farm." Some of Dean's secondary duties include assisting other zoo departments when necessary, serving on zoo committees, and promoting the zoo by attending events and meetings. "One of the most interesting and rewarding experiences I have had has been the births of the foals here at the farm," says Dean. "Additionally, seeing children, sometimes for the first time, interacting with the animals is very rewarding."

Allan Maguire is the supervisor of aquariums and life support at the Minnesota Zoo. He started in the zoo field in 1981 as a zookeeper, and in subsequent years, he was promoted to the positions of zoologist assistant, zoologist, and, finally, zoo supervisor in 2004. "I grew up in Iowa on a small farm with livestock and pets, as well as aquariums," he says. "This lifestyle growing up gave me an appreciation for the outdoors and keeping domestic and wild animals alive and healthy in captivity. The allure of working with exotics and domestics in a public setting was a natural extension of my life. Working with animals gives me a rewarding feeling. Knowing the actions I take have a direct impact on the welfare and survivability of the animal collection and give the zoo an opportunity to educate the public about important biological information is also rewarding to me. My workdays have some regularity, but most parts of each day are different. This keeps the job from getting stale." Allan says that one drawback to working at a zoo is the long and unpredictable hours. "Zoos are 24/7 operations," he says, "and can take you away from other things in life because you work weekends and or holidays. The hours can be long in some situations. Additionally, the pay scale is low compared to other types of jobs with similar education and skills."

Donnie Harrington is curator of fish and invertebrates at Mystic Aquarium & Institute for Exploration. "When I was young," he recalls, "I was always interested in the oceans and the system on which they worked. At the age of 15 I decided to open my own business with my twin brother taking care of aquariums. After continuing to grow our company and going to school for physical education, we built the company, Something Fishy Inc. from two to 20 staff, and we're now working throughout the country. Our company has expanded

---

Facts About the Minnesota Zoo

- The zoo was founded in 1978.
- Approximately 1 million people visit the zoo each year.
- It has more than 2,400 animals and 388 species from five continents.
- Approximately 225 employees and more than 1,100 volunteers work at the zoo.
- The zoo is a member of the Association of Zoos and Aquariums.

Source: Minnesota Zoo

---

from maintenance to design, consulting, retailing, animal management, and public aquarium work. Mystic Aquarium and Something Fishy Inc. have teamed up to make our Fish and Invertebrates Department world class. My personal goal is to achieve success in all that I do and my passion for my company, and Mystic Aquarium will not let me fail. My main job duties are overseeing the day-to-day operation of fish and invertebrates, which includes employee management, animal care, record keeping, tracking inventory, scheduling, managing intern and volunteer programs, monitoring fish health, overseeing new exhibits, maintaining cleanliness for all exhibits, diving, building relationships, and other tasks."

DO I HAVE WHAT IT TAKES TO BE A ZOO AND AQUARIUM CURATOR OR DIRECTOR?

To be a successful curator, you should have a fondness and compassion for animals. But as managers of people, curators must also have strong interpersonal skills, including conflict management and negotiating. They must have excellent leadership skills, the ability to get the best out of their workers, and the ability to create and maintain a team atmosphere and build consensus. They also need excellent oral and written communication skills and should be effective and articulate public speakers. "Although your job may involve working with animals, it is also very important to be able to get along with others and be respectful," advises Diane Fusco. "Most training programs are extremely team oriented, therefore having effective written and oral communication skills will be key. Being able to think clearly and quickly and the ability to follow directions are also needed in this job. I also think having a sense of humor and not taking oneself so seriously all the time goes a long way, as does patience. Most training teams also evaluate one another on their skills and job performance, so you must be able to receive constructive review and coaching and then use that information effectively. You must be able to work holidays, weekends, nights, or stay past your shift to assist as needed. Having a positive attitude is paramount as that is a characteristic that will be with you through whatever path you choose.

Finally, having a strong commitment to the animals and the profession will assist you throughout your career."

"People in the zoo field need to have diverse work skills," says Allan Maguire. "A variety of biological and mechanical skill sets are very important for aquarium keepers of all levels. They need to be personable and able to work with their fellow employees, as well as the general zoo visitor. They must be able to interpret information about their jobs and the animals in their care, to all ages and groups of visitors and staff."

Curators should have an in-depth knowledge of every species and exhibit in their collections and how they interact. Modern zoo and aquarium buildings contain technologically advanced, complex equipment, such as environmental controls, and they often house mixed-species exhibits. Not only must curators know about zoology and animal husbandry, they must understand the infrastructure as well.

It takes a lot of effort and diligence to become a zoo or aquarium curator. Students need to have perseverance in order to meet educational challenges, get their foot in the door at a zoo or aquarium, and work their way up the career ladder. "If this is a career you are interested in pursuing and really passionate about then never take no for an answer," advises Billy Hurley. "There are always a lot of people who want to swim with 'Flipper,' but not a lot of people who will do the work necessary for this to happen."

Zoo and aquarium directors have excellent leadership and communication skills. They are skilled at inspiring oth-

be able to build bridges between these various groups and put together a consensus. They need to be flexible and open-minded without losing sight of their role as advocate for their institution. Directors must have outstanding time management skills, and they must be willing and able to delegate.

Directors must be articulate and sociable. They must be able to communicate effectively with people from all walks of life. Much of their time is spent cultivating prospective donors, so they must be comfortable dealing with those with wealth and power.

HOW DO I BECOME A ZOO AND AQUARIUM CURATOR OR DIRECTOR?

Education

High School

High school students who want to prepare for careers in middle and upper management in zoos and aquariums should take classes in the sciences, especially biology, microbiology, chemistry, and physics, as well as in mathematics, computer science, language, and speech.

"In high school," Diane Fusco advises, "take advantage of classes that will expose you to animal behavior, biology, and ecology. Marine-mammal training is based on operant conditioning, so look at taking some psychology classes. If you are leaning toward working in a zoo or aquarium, having good public speaking skills will be a benefit. Develop strong swimming skills and, if able, take that a step further and become scuba certified."

> ### Facts About the Mystic Aquarium & Institute for Exploration
>
> - The aquarium was founded in 1973.
> - Approximately 750,000 people visit the aquarium each year.
> - It has more than 70 exhibits, 425 species, and 12,175 specimens.
> - The aquarium is a member of the Association of Zoos and Aquariums and the International Association for Aquatic Animal Medicine.
>
> Source: Mystic Aquarium & Institute for Exploration

---

ers and promoting their institution. Their most important traits include leadership ability, personal charisma, people skills, and public speaking ability.

"This industry requires someone who can embrace change and likes working with animals and people," says Anthony Godfrey. "It is certainly helpful for someone to have an interest in science and the ability to maintain a high energy level. People skills and teamwork skills are also very important. Students need to learn early in their education how to work on a project with a team, including electing a team leader."

Directors need to be politically savvy. They interact with many different groups, each with their own agendas. They must

It is also a good idea to participate in extracurricular activities that will help you develop your leadership and communication skills. These include student body associations, service clubs, debate teams, and school newspapers.

"Students who are interested in working in this field should take the opportunity to visit and speak with employees of an aquarium," advises Anthony Godfrey. "Aquarium professionals are thrilled to talk about what they do. Taking science classes, working on team projects, and volunteering at an aquarium are all great things a student can do to help decide if this is the right field for them."

Postsecondary Training

Curators need at least a bachelor's degree in one of the biological sciences, such as zoology, ecology, biology, mammalogy, and ornithology, to work in the field. Course work should include biology, invertebrate zoology, vertebrate physiology, comparative anatomy, organic chemistry, physics, microbiology, and virology. Electives are equally important, particularly writing, public speaking, computer science, and education. Even studying a second language can be helpful.

Curators employed at larger institutions must have an advanced degree; many curators are required to have a doctoral degree. But advanced academic training alone is insufficient; it takes years of on-the-job experience to master the practical aspects of exotic animal husbandry. Also required are management skills, supervisory experience, writing ability, research experience, and sometimes the flexibility to travel.

Several major zoos offer formal keeper training courses as well as on-the-job training programs to students who are studying areas related to animal science and care. Such programs could lead to positions as assistant curators.

A director's education and experience must be rather broad, with a solid foundation in animal management skills. Therefore, a good balance between science and business is the key to finding a position in this field. Directors need courses in zoology or biology as well as business courses, such as economics, accounting, and general business, and social sciences, such as sociology.

Today most directors have a master's degree; many at larger institutions have doctoral degrees. Directors continue their education throughout their careers by taking classes as well as reading and learning on their own.

Certification or Licensing

No certification or licensing is available for this profession.

Internships and Volunteerships

A few institutions offer curatorial internships designed to provide practical experience. Contact the AZA for further information about which schools and animal facilities are involved in internship programs. "Gain some practical experience before deciding on a career choice by volunteering and interning at different facilities," advises Diane. "Often these positions are unpaid; however, they are one of the first ways to be able to build your experience. Joining professional organizations at a student level will also keep you up to date on the business. I would highly suggest membership in the International Marine Animal Trainers' Association or American Association of Zoo Keepers."

Volunteering at zoos or aquariums, animal shelters, wildlife rehabilitation facilities, stables, or veterinary hospitals demonstrates a serious commitment to animals and provides firsthand experience in caring for them.

WHO WILL HIRE ME?

Neither the position of zoo and aquarium curator nor the position of director is an entry-level job. Although there are exceptions, most curators start their careers as zookeepers or aquarists and move up through the animal management ranks.

Although the competition for zoo and aquarium jobs is intense, there are several ways to pursue such positions. Getting an education in animal science is a good way to make contacts that may be valuable in a job search. Professors and school administrators can often provide advice and counseling on finding jobs as a curator. The best sources for finding out about career opportunities at zoos and aquariums are trade journals (AZA's *Connect Magazine* or the American Association of Zoo Keepers Inc.'s *Animal Keepers' Forum*), the Web sites of specific institutions, and special-focus periodicals. Most zoos and aquariums list job postings at their Web sites. A few zoos and aquariums have job lines. People in the profession often learn about openings by word of mouth.

Working on a part-time or volunteer basis at an animal facility could provide an excellent opportunity to improve eligibility for higher level jobs in later years.

Moving up from supervisory keeper positions to curator and director positions usually involves moving to another institution, often in another city or state.

Today's zoo and aquarium directors are often people who began their careers in education, marketing, business, research, and academia as well as animal management.

WHERE CAN I GO FROM HERE?

Curatorial positions are often the top rung of the career ladder for many zoo and aquarium professionals. Curators do not necessarily wish to become zoo or aquarium directors, although the next step for specialized curators is to advance to the position of general curator. Those who are willing to forego direct involvement with animal management altogether and complete the transition to the business of running a zoo or aquarium will set the position of zoo or aquarium director as their ultimate goal. Curators and directors who work for a small facility may aspire to a position with greater responsibilities and a commensurate increase in pay at a larger zoo or aquarium. Although some directors may move around, the majority remain at the same institution, reflecting the strong identification of the director with the institution that he or she leads.

Advancing to executive positions requires a combination of experience and

Facts About the Georgia Aquarium

- The aquarium was founded in 2003.

- It is the world's largest aquarium, with 8 million gallons of water.

- The aquarium has the largest collection of aquatic animals in the world. It has 60 exhibits, 500 species, and 80,000 specimens.

- There were 3.6 million guest visits in the aquarium's first year of operation.

- Approximately 430 employees and more than 1,100 volunteers work at the aquarium.

- The aquarium has received many awards during its short history, including being ranked second in *Parents* magazine's "10 Best Aquariums for Kids" list and named as one of top 10 U.S. attractions by TripAdvisor.com.

Source: Georgia Aquarium

education. General curators and zoo directors often have graduate degrees in zoology or in business or finance. Continuing professional education, such as AZA's courses in applied zoo and aquarium biology, conservation education, institutional record keeping, population management, and professional management, can be helpful. Attending workshops and conferences sponsored by professional groups or related organizations and making presentations are other means of networking with colleagues from other institutions and professions and becoming better known within the zoo world.

WHAT ARE THE SALARY RANGES?

Salaries of zoo and aquarium curators and directors vary widely depending on factors including the size and location of the institution, whether it is privately or publicly owned, the size of its endowments and budget, and job responsibilities, educational background, and experience. Generally, zoos and aquariums in metropolitan areas pay higher salaries.

Yearly salaries for curators range from as low as $20,000 to $80,000 or more for general curators in major metropolitan areas; average earnings are about $55,000. Directors tend to be the highest-paid employees at zoos and aquariums; the range of their salary is also broad, from $30,000 to more than $100,000 per year, with some directors at major institutions earning considerably more than $150,000. Given the scope of their responsibilities, salaries are not very high.

Most zoos and aquariums provide benefits packages that include medical insurance, paid vacation and sick leave, and generous retirement benefits. As salaried employees, curators are not eligible for overtime pay, but they may get compensatory time for extra hours worked. Larger institutions may also offer coverage for prescription drugs, dental and vision insurance, mental health plans, and retirement savings plans. Private corporate zoos may offer better benefits, including profit sharing.

WHAT IS THE JOB OUTLOOK?

There are only about 215 professionally operated zoos, aquariums, wildlife parks, and oceanariums in North America. Considering the number of people interested in animal careers, this is not a large number. Therefore, it is expected that competition for jobs as curators and directors (as well as for most zoo and aquarium jobs) will continue to be very strong. However, one area with greater growth potential than conventional zoos and aquariums is privately funded conservation centers.

Zookeepers

SUMMARY

Definition
Zookeepers provide daily care for animals in zoological parks.

Alternative Job Titles
Animal care technicians
Animal care workers
Animal caretakers
Animal keepers
Zoo technicians

Salary Range
$15,140 to $30,000 to $75,000

Educational Requirements
Bachelor's degree

Certification or Licensing
None available

Employment Outlook
More slowly than the average

High School Subjects
Biology
Speech

Personal Interests
Animals
Science
Wildlife

"My favorite animals to work with are species that I have encountered in the wild," says Shane Good, an animal keeper at Cleveland Metroparks Zoo. "For example, I spend a lot of time camping and hiking in bear country. Seeing a bear in the wild helps you develop an even greater respect for the species, because you have greater insight into their wild behaviors, habitat, and any threats that may exist to the species. Returning to the zoo, I am better prepared to share that information with zoo visitors. Additional knowledge of the species and its wild habitat also results in better exhibits, enrichment programs, and animal husbandry, and allows a keeper to better understand certain behaviors like aggres-sion, reproductive displays, and other interactions between animals within an exhibit."

WHAT DOES A ZOOKEEPER DO?

Zookeepers provide the basic care required to keep animals healthy in zoos. Daily tasks include preparing food by chop-ping or grinding meat, fish, vegetables, or fruit; mixing prepared commercial feeds; and unbaling forage grasses. Zookeepers may administer vitamins or medications when necessary. In addition, zookeepers fill water containers in the cages. They clean animal quarters by hosing, scrub-bing, raking, and disinfecting.

Zookeepers must safely move animals from one location to another (if one living area needs to be cleaned or for other reasons). They maintain exhibits (for example, by planting grass or putting in new bars) and modify them to enhance the visitors' experience. They also provide enrichment devices for the animals, such as ropes for monkeys to swing on, ice-covered treats that provide a challenge to eat, or scratching areas for big cats. They regulate environmental factors by monitoring temperature and humidity or water quality controls and maintain an inventory of supplies and equipment. They may bathe and groom animals.

Zookeepers must become experts on the species—and the individuals—in their care. They must observe and understand all types of animal behaviors, including feeding, aggression, sociality, moving, sleeping, courtship, mating, and even urination and defecation. Zookeepers must be able to detect even small changes in an animal's appearance or behavior. They must maintain careful records of these observations in a logbook and file daily written or electronic reports. Often, they make recommendations regarding diet or modification of habitats and implement those changes. In addition, they assist the veterinarian in providing treatment to sick animals and may be called upon to feed and help raise infants. Zookeepers may capture or transport animals. When an animal is transferred to another institution, a keeper may accompany it to aid in its adjustment to its new home.

The professional zookeeper works closely with zoo staff on research, conservation, and animal reproduction. Many keepers conduct research projects, presenting their findings in papers or professional journals or at workshops or conferences. Some keepers participate in regional or national conservation plans or conduct field research in the United States and abroad.

Keepers may assist an animal trainer or instructor in presenting animal shows or lectures to the public. Depending on the species, keepers may train animals to shift or to move in a certain way to facilitate routine husbandry or veterinary care. *Elephant keepers*, for example, train their charges to respond to commands to lift their feet so that they may provide proper foot care, including footpad and toenail trims.

Zookeepers must be able to interact with zoo visitors and answer questions in a friendly, professional manner. Keepers may participate in formal presentations for the general public or for special groups. This involves being knowledgeable about the animals in one's care, the animals' natural habitat and habits, and the role zoos play in wildlife conservation.

Keepers must carefully monitor activity around the animals to discourage visitors from teasing or harming them. They must be able to remove harmful objects that are sometimes thrown into an exhibit and tactfully explain the "no feeding" policy to zoo visitors.

Taking care of animals is hard work. About 85 percent of the job involves custodial and maintenance tasks, which can be physically demanding and dirty. Some of the work may involve lifting

To Be a Successful Zookeeper, You Should...

- have love and compassion for animals

- be willing to work nights and weekends

- have good interpersonal skills

- be an excellent communicator

- be able to follow instructions

- be detail-oriented

- know a lot about the habits and behaviors of animals

- be able to work both independently and as a member of a team

- be in good physical shape

- not mind getting dirty as you do your job

heavy supplies such as bales of hay. The cleaning of an animal's enclosure may be unpleasant and smelly. These tasks must be done both indoors and outdoors, in all types of weather.

The zookeeper may be exposed to bites, kicks, zoonotic diseases, and possible fatal injury from the animals he or she attends. He or she must practice constant caution because working with animals presents the potential for danger. Even though an animal may have been held in captivity for years or even since birth, it can be frightened, become stressed because of illness, or otherwise revert to its wild behavior. The keeper must know the physical and mental abilities of an animal, whether it be the strength of an ape, the reaching ability of a large cat, the intelligence of an elephant, or the sharp teeth and claws of a small animal. In addition, keepers must develop a healthy relationship with the animals in their care by respecting them as individuals and always being careful to observe safety procedures.

Cleaning, feeding, and providing general care to the animals are a necessity seven days a week. Zookeepers must be prepared for a varied schedule that may include working weekends and holidays. Sick animals may need round-the-clock care. Zookeepers may also be called upon to work special events outside their normal working hours. A large portion of the job involves routine chores for animals that will not express appreciation for the keeper's efforts.

In large zoological parks keepers often work with a limited collection of animals. They may be assigned to work specifically with one taxonomy, such as primates, large cats, or birds, or with different types of animals from a specific ecogeographic area, such as the tropical rainforest or Africa. In smaller zoos, keepers may have more variety and care for a wider range of species.

Many keepers believe that the advantages of this job outweigh the disadvantages. A chief advantage is the personal gratification of successfully maintaining wild animals, especially rare or endangered species. A healthy, well-adjusted animal collection provides a keeper with a deep sense of satisfaction.

WHAT IS IT LIKE TO BE A ZOOKEEPER?

Shane Good has worked as an animal keeper at the Cleveland Metroparks Zoo (http://www.clemetzoo.com) for 17 years. "I decided to enter this field," he says, "because I wanted a career that combined hands-on animal care, the conservation of endangered species, and the chance to work closely with exotic animals. My main duties include feeding, cleaning, behavioral observations and enrichment, administering medications, interacting with the public through educational programs, and maintaining exhibits. My secondary duties include some maintenance, participation in research and/or conservation projects, working with the veterinary staff, pest control, and renovation of animal exhibits. The work environment can be hot in summer, cold in winter, or dusty. Zookeepers may be exposed to allergens or zoonotic diseases—although safety is always a priority for zookeepers."

Shane says that the pros of working as a zookeeper include the "opportunity to work closely with exotic animals, to make a difference in the quality of their lives on a daily basis, and to directly and indirectly have a positive impact on the conservation of endangered species through our conservation, research, and animal husbandry programs." Although there are many positives to this career, Shane stresses that zookeeping is difficult work. "It requires a combination of manual labor, scientific background, an ability to work with people, and attention to

The Benefits of Association Membership

Shane Good, president of the American Association of Zoo Keepers (AAZK), details the benefits of becoming a member of a professional association:

Professional associations like the American Association of Zoo Keepers serve as the hub of activity in a profession. Membership provides information on all of the new scientific research through journals, conferences, and our Web site. Professional development opportunities, including classes and workshops, are available through the association. Finally, the AAZK provides a forum for its members to network, share information, and problem solve in an effort to advance the profession of animal care.

detail. Additionally, zookeepers are very passionate about their work, but receive relatively low pay."

Shane has also served as president of the American Association of Zoo Keepers and the International Congress of Zookeepers. These leadership positions have provided him with opportunities to visit zoos and work with animals in both captive and wild habitats around the world.

DO I HAVE WHAT IT TAKES TO BE A ZOOKEEPER?

Zookeepers must first and foremost have empathy and love for animals. Work as a zookeeper is not glamorous. It takes dedication and commitment to provide care to captive animals that require attention 24 hours a day, 365 days a year.

Zookeepers should have strong interpersonal skills to work together and to interact with visitors and volunteers. Excellent oral and written communication skills are also required. Zookeepers should be detail-oriented and not mind doing paperwork and keeping records.

Zookeepers must also have the ability to work as a member of a team, but they should be able to work independently if necessary. Keepers rely on each other to get their jobs done safely. A calm, stable nature, maturity, good judgment, and the ability to adhere to established animal handling and/or safety procedures is essential.

Keepers must have keen powers of observation to be able to identify subtle changes in animal behavior or habits that may signal illness or another issue.

Due to the physical demands of the job, keepers must be physically fit. Psychological fitness is important, too. Zookeepers have to be able to handle the emotional impact when animals with which they have built a relationship go to another institution or die. They can't be squeamish about handling body wastes or live food items or dealing with sick animals.

Some zoos require aspiring zookeepers to pass written aptitude tests or oral exams. Applicants must pass a physical exam, as keepers must be able to do such demanding work as lifting heavy sacks of feed or moving sick or injured animals.

Union membership is more common at publicly operated zoos, but it is on the rise in privately run institutions as well. There is no single zookeepers' union, and a variety of different unions represent the employees at various zoos and aquariums.

HOW DO I BECOME A ZOOKEEPER?
Education
High School

To prepare for a career in zookeeping, take as many science classes as possible. A broad-based science education, including courses in biology, ecology, chemistry, physics, and botany, coupled with mathematics and computer science, will be helpful. Courses in English and speech will help you develop your vocabulary and hone your public speaking skills.

Postsecondary Training

Although practical experience may sometimes be substituted for formal education, most entry-level positions require a four-year college degree. Animal management has become a highly technical and specialized field. Zookeepers do much more than care for animals' bodily comforts: Many of today's zookeepers are trained zoologists. They must be able to perform detailed behavioral observations, record keeping, nutrition studies, and health care. Their increased responsibilities make their role an essential one in maintaining a healthy animal collection.

Degrees in animal science, zoology, marine biology, conservation biology, wildlife management, and animal behavior are preferred. Electives are just as important, particularly writing, public speaking, computer science, education, and even foreign languages. Applicants with interdisciplinary training sometimes have an advantage. A few colleges and junior colleges offer a specialized curriculum for zookeepers. Those seeking advancement to curatorial, research, or conservation positions may need a master's degree. Animal care experience, such as time spent volunteering at a zoo, or working at a farm, ranch, or veterinary hospital, is a must.

Smaller zoos may hire keeper trainees, who receive on-the-job training to learn the responsibilities of the zookeeper. Several major zoos offer formal keeper training courses, as well as on-the-job training programs, to students who are studying areas related to animal science and care.

Certification or Licensing

No certification or licensing is available for this profession.

Internships and Volunteerships

Many institutions offer unpaid internships for high school and college students interested in exploring a career in animal care. Internships may involve food preparation, hands-on experience with the animal collection, interpretive services for the public, exhibit design and construction, or the collection and analysis of data. The length of the internships varies. The minimum age for most of these programs is 18.

College students can also participate in internships. Contact the Association

> ### That's a Lot of Animals!
>
> Zoos and aquariums that are accredited by the Association of Zoos and Aquariums have:
>
> - 339,195 fish
> - 239,925 invertebrates (organisms that do not have a spine)
> - 57,115 birds
> - 53,189 mammals
> - 29,573 reptiles
> - 14,916 amphibians
> - 1,260 marine mammals
>
> Source: Association of Zoos and Aquariums

of Zoos and Aquariums (AZA) for information about which schools and animal facilities are involved in internship programs. Such programs could lead to full-time positions. The American Association of Zoo Keepers also offers internship and job listings at its Web site (http://www.aazk.org/job_listings.php).

Many zoos offer volunteer opportunities for teens, such as Explorers or Junior Zookeeper programs, which are similar to programs for adult volunteers but with closer supervision. Most volunteer programs require a specific time commitment. Opportunities vary between institutions and run the gamut from cleaning enclosures, to preparing food, to handling domesticated animals, to

Facts About Polar Bears

- Polar bears can be up to 12 feet tall.

- Males can weigh 770 to 1,430 pounds or more.

- Polar bears live 25 to 30 years in the wild.

- Polar bears can smell prey from up to 30 miles away.

- In the wild they eat ringed seals, bearded seals, beluga whales, walruses, fish, sea birds, carcasses of marine mammals, berries, and vegetation.

- In zoos they eat fish (herring, trout, blue gill, crappie), omnivore biscuits, carrots, and bread.

- Approximately 20,000 to 25,000 polar bears live in the wild.

Sources: Brookfield Zoo, *National Geographic*

conducting tours or giving educational presentations.

Prospective zookeepers can volunteer or work part time at animal shelters, boarding kennels, wildlife rehabilitation facilities, stables, or animal hospitals. They may get a feel for working with animals by seeking employment on a farm or ranch during the summer. Joining a 4-H club also gives a person hands-on experience with animals. Experience with animals is invaluable when seeking a job and provides opportunities to learn about the realities of work in this field.

WHO WILL HIRE ME?

Despite the low pay and challenging working conditions, competition for jobs at zoos is intense. There are many more candidates than available positions. Most zookeepers enjoy their work, and turnover is low. The majority of new jobs result from the need to replace workers who leave the field. A limited number of jobs are created when new zoos open. Entry-level applicants may find it easier to start out in small zoos in smaller communities, where the pay is usually low, and then move on once they have gained some experience. There are many such small-town zoos in the Midwest.

Part-time work, summer jobs, or volunteering at a zoo increases an applicant's chances of getting full-time employment. Many zoos fill new positions by promoting current employees. An entry-level position, even if it does not involve working directly with animals, is a means of making contacts and learning about an institution's hiring practices.

Zoos that are municipally operated accept applications through municipal civil service offices. At other zoos, applications are accepted at the zoo office.

Occasionally zoos advertise for personnel in the local newspapers. Better sources of employment opportunities are trade journals such as AZA's *CONNECT* or the American Association of Zoo Keepers (AAZK) Inc.'s *Animal Keepers' Forum*, the Web sites of specific institutions and professional associations (such as the AZA and AAZK), or special-focus periodicals. A few zoos even have job lines.

Most zoos have internal job postings. People in the profession often learn about openings by word of mouth. Membership in a professional organization can be helpful when conducting a job search.

WHERE CAN I GO FROM HERE?

Job advancement in zoos is possible, but the career path is more limited than in some other professions requiring a college degree. The possibility for advancement varies according to a zoo's size and operating policies and an employee's qualifications.

It is important for zookeepers to pursue continuing professional education throughout their careers in order to stay current regarding developments in animal husbandry, veterinary care, and technology, and in order to advance. The AZA offers formal professional courses in applied zoo and aquarium biology, conservation education, elephant management, institutional record keeping, population management, professional management, and studbook keeping. Attending workshops and conferences sponsored by professional groups or related organizations, such as universities or conservation organizations, is another means of sharing information with colleagues from other institutions and professions.

Most zoos have different levels of animal management staff. The most common avenue for job promotion is from keeper to senior keeper to head keeper, then possibly to area supervisor or assistant curator, and then curator. On rare occasions, the next step will be to zoo director. Moving up from the senior keeper level to middle and upper management usually involves moving to another institution, often in another city or state.

In addition to participating in daily animal care, the senior keeper manages a particular building on the zoo grounds and is responsible for supervising the keepers working in that facility. An *area supervisor* or *assistant curator* works directly with the curators and is responsible for supervising, scheduling, and training the entire keeper force. In major zoological parks, there are head keepers for each curatorial department.

Facts About the Cleveland Metroparks Zoo

- The Cleveland Metroparks Zoo is the seventh oldest zoo in the United States.
- It houses more than 3,000 animals from 600 species.
- The zoo features animals from six of the seven continents.
- It runs successful breeding programs for dozens of endangered species, including black rhinos.

Source: Cleveland Metroparks Zoo

The *curator* is responsible for managing a specific department or section within the zoo, either defined by taxonomy, such as mammals, birds, or reptiles, or by habitat or ecogeography, such as the forest edge or African savannah. The *curator of mammals*, for example, is in charge of all mammals in the collection and supervises all staff that work with mammals. Usually, an advanced degree in zoology and research experience is required to become a curator, as well as experience working as a zookeeper and in zoo management.

Many zookeepers eschew advancement and prefer to remain where they have the most direct interaction with and impact on the animals.

WHAT ARE THE SALARY RANGES?

Most people who choose a career as a zookeeper do not do so for the money. They just love working with animals!

Salaries for zookeepers vary widely among zoological parks and depend on the size and location of the institution, whether it is publicly or privately owned, the size of its endowments and budget, and whether the zookeepers belong to a union. Generally, the highest salaries are paid to zookeepers who work in large urban areas, have many years of experience in the field, and have advanced degrees. Salaries for zookeepers can range from slightly above minimum wage to more than $40,000 a year, depending on the keeper's background, grade, and tenure, and the zoo's location. Zoos in certain areas of the country pay higher wages, reflecting the higher cost of living there. City-run institutions, where keepers are lumped into a job category with less-skilled workers, pay less. On average, aquarists earn slightly more than zookeepers.

Salaries for nonfarm animal caretakers (a career category that includes zookeepers) ranged from less than $15,140 to $31,590 or more in 2008, according to the U.S. Department of Labor. In 2009 Simplyhired.com reported an average salary of $29,000 annually for zookeepers.

A salary survey by the American Association of Zoo Keepers in the early 2000s reported that the average salary for zookeepers was $24,925. Those with a college degree fared better, earning an average of $26,715. However, salaries as low as $15,000 and as high as $50,000 to $75,000 were also reported.

Most zoos provide benefits packages that include medical insurance, paid vacation and sick leave, and generous retirement benefits. Keepers at larger institutions may also have coverage for prescription drugs, dental and vision insurance, mental health plans, and 401(k) accounts. Those who work on holidays may receive overtime pay or comp time. A few institutions offer awards, research grants, and unpaid sabbaticals. Private corporate zoos may offer better benefits, including profit sharing.

WHAT IS THE JOB OUTLOOK?

Zoos hire more animal keepers than any other classification. But this is still a very small field. For this reason, employment should grow more slowly than the average for all careers through 2016, according to the U.S. Department of Labor. Each year, there are many more applicants than positions available. Competition for jobs is stiff at the approximately 215 AZA-accredited zoological parks, aquariums, and wildlife parks in North America. Opportunities arise mainly through attrition, which is lower than in many other professions, or the startup of a new facility. "Zookeeping is a very competitive field, despite relatively low pay," says Shane Good. "Prospective zookeepers need a combination of a college degree in one of the sciences, and hands-on experience with exotic animals. Internships are a common way for students to get into the occupation."

As the preservation of animal species becomes more complicated, there will be a continuing need for zoo staff to work to preserve endangered wildlife and educate the public about conservation. The demand will increase for well-educated personnel who will be responsible for much more than simply feeding the animals and cleaning their enclosures. Zookeepers will need more knowledge as zoos expand and become more specialized. The amount of knowledge and effort necessary to maintain and reproduce a healthy animal collection will keep zookeepers in the front line of animal care.

Pursuing a job in this area is well worth the effort for those who are dedicated to providing care for rapidly diminishing animal species and educating the public about the fate of endangered animals and the need to preserve their natural habitats.

Zoologists

SUMMARY

Definition
Zoologists are biologists who study animals. They often select a particular type of animal to study, and they may study an entire animal, one part or aspect of an animal, or a whole animal society.

Alternative Job Titles
(Note: The following jobs are a small sampling of career specialties for zoologists.)

Embryologists
Entomologists
Herpetologists
Ichthyologists
Mammalogists
Ornithologists

Salary Range
$33,550 to $55,290 to $90,850+

Educational Requirements
Bachelor's degree; master's degree required for top positions

Certification or Licensing
None available

Employment Outlook
About as fast as the average

High School Subjects
Biology
Chemistry
English

Personal Interests
Animals
Science
Wildlife

"Every time I wake up in the beautiful rain-dripping glow of southeast Alaska sunrises or take my pack off after hiking up a mountain to gaze at a beautiful ridgeline, I am rewarded!" says Natalie Dawson, a staff scientist at the Center for Biological Diversity. "I think it is also really rewarding to take others into the field with me. A few years ago, we had a new graduate student from Uruguay join my field crew for the summer. He had never been in an area as remote as southeast Alaska and had never really done any hiking. He absolutely loved the experience. He became an advocate for conserving a place that he may never have otherwise known existed. Watching people connect with the natural world, each in his or her own individual way, with enthusiasm and childlike wonder, is by far the most amazing and gratifying component of the work that I do."

WHAT DOES A ZOOLOGIST DO?

Although zoology is a single specialty within the field of biology, it is a vast specialty that includes many major subspecialties. Some *zoologists* study a single animal or a category of animals, whereas others may specialize in a particular part of an animal's anatomy or study a process that takes place in many kinds of animals. A zoologist might study single-cell organisms, a particular variety of fish, or the behavior of groups of animals such as elephants or bees.

Many zoologists are classified according to the animals they study. For example, *entomologists* are experts on insects, *mammalogists* focus on mammals, *ichthyologists* study fish, *herpetologists* specialize in the study of reptiles and amphibians, and *ornithologists* study birds. *Embryologists*, however, are classified according to the process that they study. They examine the ways in which animal embryos form and develop from conception to birth.

There is a wide range of subspecialties within each primary area of specialization. An ichthyologist, for example, might focus on the physiology, or physical structure and functioning, of a particular fish; on a biochemical phenomenon such as bioluminescence in deep-sea species; on the discovery and classification of fish; on variations within a single species in different parts of the world; or on the ways in which one type of fish interacts with other species in a specific environment. Others may specialize in the effects of pollution on fish or in finding ways to grow fish effectively in controlled environments in order to increase the supply of healthy fish available for human consumption.

Some zoologists work primarily as teachers, while others spend most of their time performing original research in the field. Teaching jobs in universities and other facilities are probably the most secure positions available, but zoologists who wish to do extensive research may find such positions restrictive. Even zoologists whose primary function is research, however, often need to do some teaching in the course of their work, and almost everyone in the field has to deal with the public at one time or another.

It is a common misconception that zoological scientists spend most of their time in the field collecting specimens and observing animals. In fact, most researchers spend no more than two to eight weeks in the field annually. Zoologists spend much of their time at a computer or talking on the telephone with other researchers. Junior scientists often spend more time in the field than senior scientists, who study specimens and data collected in the field by their younger colleagues. Senior scientists spend much of their time coordinating research, directing younger scientists and technicians, and writing grant proposals or soliciting funds in other ways.

Raising money is an extremely important activity for zoologists who are not employed by government agencies or major universities. The process of obtaining money for research can be time consuming and difficult. Good development skills can also give scientists a flexibility that government-funded scientists do not have. Government grants are sometimes available only for research in narrowly defined areas that a scientist may not wish to study. A zoologist who wants to study a particular area may seek his or her own funding in order to bypass government restrictions.

There is much variation in the conditions under which zoologists work. *Professors of zoology* may teach exclusively during the school year or may both teach and

---

To Be a Successful Zoologist, You Should…

- be dedicated and have a passion for your specialty
- be willing to work in all types of weather if you conduct field research
- have patience
- have excellent research skills
- be willing to continue to learn throughout your career
- enjoy reading and writing

---

conduct research. Many professors whose school year consists of teaching spend their summers conducting research. *Research scientists* spend some time in the field, but most of their work is done in the laboratory. There are zoologists who spend most of their time in the field, but they are the exceptions to the rule.

Zoologists who do field work may encounter difficult conditions. A gorilla expert may have to spend her time in the forests of Rwanda; a mammalogist may spend his time in windy, dusty conditions in Mongolia; a shark expert may need to observe his subjects from a shark cage while wearing a wetsuit to protect himself from the frigid waters of the ocean. For most people in the field, however, that aspect of the work is particularly interesting and satisfying.

Zoologists spend much of their time corresponding with others in their field,

studying the latest literature, reviewing articles written by their peers, and corresponding via email or telephone. They also log many hours working with computers, using computer modeling, performing statistical analyses, recording the results of their research, or writing articles and grant proposals.

No zoologist works in a vacuum. Even those who spend much time in the field have to keep up with developments within their specialty. In most cases, zoologists deal with many different kinds of people, including students, mentors, the public, colleagues, representatives of granting agencies, private or corporate donors, reporters, and science writers. For this reason, the most successful members of the profession tend to develop good communication skills.

WHAT IS IT LIKE TO BE A ZOOLOGIST?

Natalie Dawson is a staff scientist at the Center for Biological Diversity (http://www.biologicaldiversity.org), a nonprofit organization that seeks to protect threatened and endangered species. She is based in Anchorage, Alaska. Natalie has worked for the center for approximately two months, after having received her Ph.D. in biology from the University of New Mexico. "My main job duties," she says, "include research and outreach education on endangered and threatened species in Alaska and other Arctic and subarctic regions. I also help with our projects in the lower 48 states in my areas of expertise, which include terrestrial mammals. Secondary job duties include attending scientific meetings and visits to local communities."

Natalie says that one of the biggest challenges of her new job is that it is not field-based. "I spent the last five years as a research associate while going through graduate school," she says, "and had the time and funding to spend many weeks in the field collecting data. I enjoy spending long hours in the rainforests in southeast Alaska, or the tundra benches in Denali, and on the Alaska Peninsula. It has been hard to transition from a primarily field-based lifestyle to a lifestyle where I spend many hours in front of a computer."

Natalie says that there are many pros that offset her time in front of a computer. "This is incredibly challenging work," she explains. "Instead of working on one species of animal or plant, I work on many species, all at once, and am expected to be an expert in many ways. I also have the opportunity to be directly involved in the conservation community in Alaska, which is wonderful, and it is a refreshing change from an academic lifestyle. I have the opportunity to work for a mission-driven organization with similar views to my own, and the people in the environmental community are incredibly passionate and enthusiastic for what they do. Being able to work on projects, species, and issues that I care about is infinitely rewarding!"

Dr. Michael Mares is a professor of zoology, professor and curator of mammalogy, and director of the Sam Noble Oklahoma Museum of Natural History (http://www.snomnh.ou.edu) at the University of Oklahoma. He is also the president of the American Society of Mammalogists and the Natural Science Collections Alliance. He says that the best part of his job is discovering new species. "I love doing field work in new places and revisiting old places as well. I have discovered perhaps three-dozen new species of mammals and over the last decade most of my research has been dedicated to finding species that are unknown to science."

In addition to working as a professor, Dr. Mares has spent his career conducting field biological research, especially in Latin America, where he has worked for almost 40 years. "My Ph.D. research involved a study of whether or not faunas of desert mammals converge on one another in their evolutionary adaptive characteristics," he recalls. "I compared the fauna of the Monte Desert of Argentina with the Sonoran Desert of North America (especially in the Tucson area). This led to further comparisons with other deserts and, over the years, I worked in arid and semi-arid areas of Brazil, Venezuela, Mexico, the United States, the entire country of Argentina, Iran, India, and Namibia, becoming an authority on desert mammals and their evolution. I published a book of the research and 'adventures' called *A Desert Calling: Life in a Forbidding Landscape*, with Harvard University Press. It tells the hows and whys of field research and my own personal story of doing field research around the world."

Dr. Mares says that one of the most rewarding aspects of his career has been his work at the Sam Noble Oklahoma Museum of Natural History. "Although I am a research biologist," he says, "I was selected to lead a very impoverished natural history museum. Through my efforts, I was able to lead that institution into a new state-of-the-art facility, increase the staff

Facts About African Elephants

- African elephants can weigh 7,000 to 14,000 pounds and reach 14 feet in height. They are the largest land animals on Earth.

- They eat only plants, including grasses, twigs, roots, bark, leaves, fruits, and vegetables.

- African elephants use their long trunks to gather food, drink, bathe, and to interact socially with other elephants. Their smelling apparatus is located in their trunk, and their sense of smell is hundreds of times better than that of dogs.

- They have the largest brain of any mammal and are considered one of the most intelligent land animals.

- African elephants are found in 37 countries in Africa. They are currently listed as threatened because of loss of habitat, poaching, and other factors.

Source: The Maryland Zoo in Baltimore

from seven people to 120, and develop perhaps the preeminent university natural history museum in the world. The people of the state have benefited enormously from this facility and the skilled museum professionals who work there. Without my efforts this museum would not be there today, and I can take a special feeling of accomplishment knowing that I played an important role in the project.

"Beyond that," he continues, "I am always glad to hear that a course I taught or a paper or book that I published changed a life. One of the leading paleontologists in the world told me that my first paper published after my Ph.D. degree had led him to pursue his life's calling. Those kinds of things are always the best kind of reward for a professor."

Theresa Nietfeld is a senior biologist at the Georgia Aquarium (http://www.georgiaaquarium.org) in Atlanta, Georgia. It is the largest aquarium in the world. "I have worked in the aquarium field for about 10 years," she says. "I became interested in fish, especially sharks, when as a young child I would visit aquariums with my grandparents. My typical day includes diving into the exhibits for maintenance, feeding the animals, and training sessions working with the animals. The aquarium field is a unique and rewarding career, but it is not without some sacrifice. This is a job of love and hard work, not one that is financially extravagant."

One of Theresa's most interesting and rewarding experiences in the field came when she traveled to Taiwan with the Georgia Aquarium to work with whale sharks. "I was able to travel to a place I would not have been able to go on my own and work with animals that I never even thought I would see in my lifetime," she recalls. "Despite all of the challenges that are required to get into the field of animal care, I would not change any of my decisions that have led me to this career path."

DO I HAVE WHAT IT TAKES TO BE A ZOOLOGIST?

Dr. Mares says that "intelligence, tenacity, diligence, dedication, and passion for one's profession are the most important qualities for zoologists. One must be able to overcome the many difficulties that will surely be encountered over a career, whether personal or professional, and persevere," he says. "Almost anyone can have a good short career, but few can continue working over the decades and contribute to their discipline in a meaningful manner without that singular dedication."

Success in zoology requires tremendous effort. People who want to work an eight-hour day should probably avoid entering this field because hard work and long hours (sometimes 60 to 80 hours per week) are the norm. "A strong work ethic is necessary for this kind of career," says Natalie Dawson. "Self-discipline and self-motivation have been invaluable while in graduate school, as well as while in my new job as a biologist. It is important to be able to motivate yourself to get out of the tent in the morning when it is cold and rainy, and find a positive spin on what the day is going to bring."

Also, although some top scientists are paid well, the field does not provide a rapid route to riches. A successful zoologist finds satisfaction in work, not in a paycheck. The personal rewards, however, can be tremendous. The typical zoologist finds his or her work satisfying on many levels. "I think it is important to love what you do if you are in my field," says Natalie. "Passion and enthusiasm for this work is the only way to be truly successful, as with any career. I always encourage students to find what you love, and then do that thing, and do it the best that you can do it."

Successful zoologists are patient, flexible, and able to multitask. A person who cannot juggle various tasks will have a difficult time in a job that requires doing research,

teaching students, writing articles, dealing with the public, soliciting funds, and staying up to date with the latest publications in the field. Flexibility also comes into play when funding for a particular area of study ends or is unavailable. A zoologist whose range of expertise is too narrowly focused will be at a disadvantage when there are no opportunities in that particular area. A flexible approach and a willingness to explore various areas can be crucial in such situations, and a too-rigid attitude may lead a zoologist to avoid studies that he or she would have found rewarding.

An aptitude for reading and writing is a must for any zoologist. "It is important to be a good writer, both in field notes and in summary statements, when working in the office," says Natalie. A person who does not enjoy reading will find it difficult to keep up with the literature in the field. Those who cannot write or dislike writing would be unable to write effective articles

Advice for Young People

Dr. Michael Mares, a professor of zoology at the University of Oklahoma, offers the following advice to young people who are interested in pursuing careers in zoology:

Read books! Find a museum or university where you can volunteer to assist a scientist doing real research in the field and the lab. Learn the basics. Learn to read, write, and speak English correctly. Learn the basics of math. Facility with language, the ability to write and communicate, and the ability to learn from the Web and, especially, books, are the primary materials for a successful career.

and books. Publishing is an important part of zoological work, especially for those who conduct research.

Natalie also says that "it is important to keep a positive attitude and be self-confident in situations where others may lose their heads. It is important to also be strong in uncomfortable surroundings. For example, often on environmental issues my organization is the first to take a strong stance regarding a particular endangered species or environmental concern. I may be in disagreement with everyone in the room. So, it is important for me to support my conclusion with scientific facts and remain levelheaded about my decision. Often people will agree to disagree, but continue to treat me as a respected colleague."

HOW DO I BECOME A ZOOLOGIST?

Education

"My passion and desire to become a biologist started when I was in high school and took a fantastic biology class in my junior year," Natalie Dawson recalls. "This passion was then fueled by summer research experiences while I was in college. I spent a summer in Colorado on a trail crew. I worked for the U.S. Geologic Survey for a summer in Wyoming, hiking up mountains and looking for bears. I spent a summer in Alaska trapping wolves and lynx. All these experiences brought me closer to figuring out what I wanted to do when I got out of college, and in my case, drove me to pursue a career in research in graduate school. Furthermore, these experiences enhanced my conservation values for land

stewardship and wildlife protection, which has led me into my current position, where my job is to be a scientifically supported land steward and advocate for fish, wildlife, and plant species in peril."

High School

Aspiring zoologists should pursue a well-rounded high school education. Biology and chemistry courses are very important, but you should remember that facility in English will also be invaluable. Writing monographs and articles, communicating with colleagues both orally and in writing, and writing persuasive fund-raising proposals are all activities at which scientists need to excel. You should also read widely, not merely relying on books on science or other subjects that are required by school. The scientist-in-training should search the library for magazines and journals dealing with areas that are of personal interest. Developing the habit of reading will help prepare you for the massive amounts of reading involved in research and keeping up with the latest developments in the field. It is important to develop good computer skills since most zoologists not only use the computer for writing, communication, and research, but they also use various software packages to perform statistical analyses.

Postsecondary Training

A bachelor's degree is the minimum requirement to work as a zoologist. Though it is possible to find work with a bachelor's degree, it is likely that you will need an advanced degree. Competition for higher paying, high-level jobs among those with doctoral degrees is very strong; as a result, it is often easier to break into the field with a master's degree than it is with a Ph.D. Many zoologists with a master's degree seek a mid-level job and work toward a Ph.D. part time.

Certification or Licensing

No licensing or certification is available for this profession.

Internships and Volunteerships

Try to become an intern or a volunteer at an organization that is involved in an area that you find interesting. Many organizations offer internships, and if you search with determination you are likely to find one. "Students interested in pursuing a career as a professional biologist should 'get outside and get dirty,'" advises Natalie. "Go volunteer in the summers, or the winters, whenever possible, and collect deer pellets, count seedlings, trap mice, track wolves, hike up mountains, walk down streams! The best way to become a field biologist is to be in the field."

WHO WILL HIRE ME?

Zoologists can find employment opportunities at a wide variety of institutions, not just zoos. Many zoologists teach at universities and other facilities, where they may teach during the school year while spending their summers doing research. Many zoologists work as researchers. They may work for nonprofit organizations (requiring grants to fund their work), scientific institutions, or the government. Of course, there are many zoologists who are employed by zoos, aquariums, and museums. While jobs for zoologists are available throughout the country, large cities that

---

Did You Know?

- Up to 99 percent of animals are invertebrates. This means that they do not have a backbone. Examples of invertebrates include worms, snails, crabs, and insects.

- Animals that are vertebrates (have a backbone) include amphibians, birds, fish, mammals, and reptiles.

- There are approximately 9 to 10 million species of animals on earth.

Source: St. Louis Zoo

---

have universities, zoos, and museums will provide far more opportunities for zoologists than rural areas.

You will have an advantage over other job applicants if you have made contacts as an intern or as a member of a professional organization. It is an excellent idea to attend the meetings of professional organizations, which generally welcome students. At those meetings, introduce yourself to the scientists you admire and ask for their help and advice.

Don't be shy, but be sure to treat people with respect. Ultimately, it's the way you relate to other people that determines how your career will develop.

WHERE CAN I GO FROM HERE?

Higher education and publishing are two of the most important means of advancing in the field of zoology. The holder of a Ph.D. will make more money and have a higher status than the holder of a bachelor's or master's degree. The publication of articles and books is important for both research scientists and professors of zoology. A young professor who does not publish cannot expect to become a full professor with tenure, and a research scientist who does not publish the results of his or her research will not become known as an authority in the field. In addition, the publication of a significant work lets everyone in the field know that the author has worked hard and accomplished something worthwhile.

Because zoology is not a career in which people typically move from job to job, people generally move up within an organization. An associate professor may become a full professor; a research scientist may become known as an expert in the field or may become the head of a department, division, or institution; a zoologist employed by an aquarium or a zoo may become an administrator or head curator. In some cases, however, scientists may not want what appears to be a more prestigious position. A zoologist who loves to conduct and coordinate research, for example, may not want to become an administrator who is responsible for budgeting, hiring and firing, and other tasks that have nothing to do with research.

WHAT ARE THE SALARY RANGES?

New graduates with bachelor's degrees in the biological and life sciences earned average starting salaries of $34,953 in 2007, according to the National Association of Colleges and Employers.

The median annual wage for zoologists was $55,290 in 2008, according to the U.S. Department of Labor. Salaries ranged from less than $33,550 to $90,850 or more. Zoologists employed by the federal government had mean annual earnings of $72,330 in 2008.

It is possible for the best and brightest of zoologists to make higher salaries. Occasionally, a newly graduated Ph.D. who has a top reputation may be offered a position that pays $100,000 or more per year, but only a few people begin their careers at such a high level.

The benefits that zoologists receive as part of their employment vary widely. Employees of the federal government or top universities tend to have extensive benefit packages, but the benefits offered by private industry range from extremely generous to almost nonexistent.

WHAT IS THE JOB OUTLOOK?

Employment for biological scientists is expected to grow about as fast as the average for all careers through 2016, according to the *Occupational Outlook Handbook*. There will be demand for zoologists, but competition for good positions—especially research positions—is strong. High-level jobs are further limited when federal and state governments cut budgets. Employment growth in the biological sciences should continue during the next decade, spurred partly by the need to analyze and offset the effects of pollution on the environment.

SECTION 3

Do It Yourself

Just because you're a teenager doesn't mean that you can't begin learning about animal-related careers right now. In fact, there are many opportunities available that will fuel your passion for animals and interest in their continued care and conservation. You can take field trips, visit a museum, surf the Internet, volunteer your time and energy, or even tap into your entrepreneurial potential. The following sections provide more information and suggestions on how you can explore animal-related careers.

❏ CONTACT ASSOCIATIONS AND ORGANIZATIONS

One of the best ways to obtain information about animal careers is by contacting professional associations and government agencies. For example, the Association of Zoos and Aquariums offers a wealth of information at its Web site (http://www.aza.org). You can learn about career options in the field, get the scoop on its conservation efforts, read publications, and find a zoo or aquarium near you. This is just one example of a professional association for students who are interested in animal careers. See "Look to the Pros" in Section 4, What Can I Do Right Now?, for a comprehensive list of animal-related associations.

❏ SURF THE WEB

You probably already use the Internet for research and to communicate with friends—and you may even have a page on MySpace or Facebook. But did you know that the Web also offers countless resources for those who are interested in animals? You can surf the Web to find animal-related blogs, photographs, videos, competitions, college programs, glossaries, information on employers (such as zoos and aquariums), worker profiles and interviews, and the list goes on and on. So surf the Web, and begin learning about animals! To help get you started, we've prepared a list of what we think are the best animal-related sites on the Web. For more information, check out "Surf the Web" in Section 4, What Can I Do Right Now?

❏ READ BOOKS AND PERIODICALS ABOUT ANIMALS

Looking for detailed information about animals? If so, your high school or local library is a great place to start. There you'll find books and periodicals about every type of animal-related topic imaginable, such as the eating habits of kangaroos; endangered species like the hawksbill sea turtle; famous scientists (such as Jane Goodall); competitions (like the Canon Envirothon); career options (such as animal trainer, veterinarian, or zoologist); and almost any other topic imaginable. For a great list of books and periodicals about animals and the environment, explore "Read a Book" in Section 4, What Can I Do Right Now?

❏ WATCH MOVIES ABOUT NATURE AND ANIMALS

If you can't make it to a zoo or aquarium or volunteer at a veterinarian's office, try watching a movie or two about animals. There are countless animal documentaries, such as *March of the Penguins* (2004) and *Winged Migration* (2001). You can catch many of these on television or cable stations, or you can rent them. There are also many feature films that focus on environmental threats and attempts by dedicated scientists to save wildlife. For example, *Gorillas In The Mist* (1988) is the story of Dian Fossey (played by Sigourney Weaver), the famed naturalist who spent her life studying primates, especially the mountain gorillas of Rwanda. She fought against the practice of poaching, the killing of gorillas and other animals to sell their hands, heads, skin, and other body parts. Her fight against poaching and the Rwandan government's apathy toward stopping this practice led, many believe, to Fossey's murder.

❑ TAKE HIGH SCHOOL CLASSES THAT FOCUS ON ANIMALS, THE ENVIRONMENT, AND SCIENCE

Make sure your class schedule includes courses that will help you prepare for careers in the field. Take the usual introductory courses—biology, mathematics, science, ecology, environmental science—as well as other higher level classes that are available.

For example, New Trier High School in Winnetka, Illinois, offers specialized courses for students interested in animal careers. One popular elective, zoology, teaches students the diversity of animals

and their environments, and existing patterns of biodiversity. The final project for this class includes "creating" an animal, complete with a description of the habitat best suited for its needs. Students can also take a marine biology elective. In this class, students are introduced to marine ecosystems in a controlled laboratory environment. Other topics covered include ocean profiles and species, the evolution of marine life, and environmental issues affecting ocean organisms.

It's a good idea to meet with your high school counselor before signing up for any electives. Tell your counselor about your career plans so he or she can steer you toward the proper sequence of classes.

❑ VISIT A ZOO, AQUARIUM, OR NATURE CENTER

You can learn more about animals by visiting your local zoo, aquarium, or nature center. Not only will you spend a fun-filled day surrounded by bobcats, bears, bats, and other animals, you'll get to observe the professionals that keep these animals healthy and the facilities running smoothly.

Have you ever stopped to think how much work it takes to care for the animals and exhibits at just one zoo? The Phoenix Zoo (http://www.phoenixzoo.org) in Arizona is one of the most popular zoos in the United States. It houses more than 1,200 animals within its 125-acre compound. The zoo is composed of four theme areas, each with its own collection of distinct creatures and habitats. The Arizona Trail features the wildlife found in the Arizona desert—such as coyotes, Mexican grey wolves, and turkey vultures. The African Trail boasts animals such as cheetahs, African lions, and African wild dogs. The Tropics Trail is home to Asian elephants, anteaters, and black jaguars. The animals are a little tamer, yet no less interesting, in the Children's Trail. Visitors to this area can see porcupines, raccoons, and various farm animals. Besides its exhibits, the Phoenix Zoo is known for its animal conservation efforts, including a captive breeding program that has been successful in helping bring the Arabian oryx back from near extinction. Other breeding programs work with thick-billed parrots, cheetahs, and California condors.

It's no secret that the success of the Phoenix Zoo is due largely to its staff. Each department is responsible for different areas of operation—veterinarians, zoologists, animal trainers, and animal technicians are just a few of the animal specialists that help make the zoo a success. The Phoenix Zoo is also known for its large corps of volunteers, including the Zooteen program for children ages 13 to 17.

Looking for a zoo or aquarium near you? If so, visit http://www.aza.org/FindZooAquarium for a searchable database of facilities in your town or city.

❏ BECOME A MEMBER!

Membership in a professional association or animal care organization is another way to learn about the field. Member benefits often include magazine subscriptions, discounts on products, job shad-owing opportunities, and the chance to attend conferences and seminars. See "Get Involved" in Section 4 for a list of animal-related organizations and environmental organizations that offer membership to teens.

❏ VISIT A NATURAL HISTORY MUSEUM

Museum visits are a good way to learn more about your favorite animals, as well as learn more about animal curators and other professionals. The Las Vegas Natural History Museum (http://www.lvnhm.org), for example, is a nonprofit museum dedicated to educating the public about the natural sciences, past and present. The museum offers many exhibits and collections of the world's wildlife, ecosystems, and cultures. Exhibits include the Marine Life Gallery, a 3,000-gallon exhibit that is home to sharks, stingrays, and eels, and the Wild Nevada Gallery, which shows small animals, such as pocket mice and catclaws, and large animals, such as elk. Plants indigenous to Nevada are also represented in this exhibit. The museum also offers a hands-on exhibit where guests can practice their skills in animal tracking, observe a paleontology lab, and learn more about animal senses.

❏ GET TO CLASS OR CAMP ON YOUR SUMMER VACATION

Another good way to learn more about animals and animal science is to participate in summer enrichment programs at colleges and universities. This will give you the opportunity to meet other young people who are interested in the field and interact with educators and other professionals. Summer programs usually consist of workshops, seminars, and outdoor activities that introduce you to the field. Some offer college credit. Many require you to live on campus, although some provide commuter options. Summer programs are covered in depth in "Get Involved" in Section 4.

❏ VOLUNTEER TO BE A DOCENT

Docents are volunteers who lead tours or work special exhibits at museums and educational institutions, including zoos and aquariums. While many docents are adults, some institutions have teen docent programs. For example, the Reid Park Zoo (http://www.tucsonzoo.org) in Tucson, Arizona, has a team of teen docents that work throughout the zoo. Docents do not work directly with animals, but instead take a behind-the-scenes role. As a teen docent, you may be asked to supervise a craft or activity table for visiting children, lead a story time activity or slide show, or work at the zoo's information booth. Docents should have good knowledge of their exhibit or station in order to present correct information and field questions.

Competition for docent positions—especially those for teens—is strong. Qualifications at Reid Park Zoo include an age minimum of 13 years, successful completion of a training course and examination, and a six-month work commitment. How do you find docent opportunities for your age group? Simply contact a local zoo or aquarium and inquire about such programs. If they don't have one in place, you should see if they'll start one!

To find opportunities near you, visit http://www.aza.org/FindZooAquarium, where you will find a database of zoos and aquariums that is searchable by state.

You should also check out "Get Involved" in Section 4 for a detailed list of opportunities—including additional volunteer positions at professional animal rights and humane associations.

❏ LAND A PART-TIME JOB

A part-time job is a great way to explore the field of animal care, and get paid at the same time! Visit local pet stores, veterinary clinics, or grooming salons to inquire about positions. At pet stores you may be assigned to stock retail items, clean cages and tanks, feed the animals, operate the cash register, or help customers locate pet food or supplies. Veterinary clinics often hire part-timers to help answer phones, file charts, assist with the animals, or run errands for the staff. Part-time duties at a grooming salon may entail checking pets in for their appointments, assisting in small grooming tasks, restocking shampoos and soaps, or cleaning the tubs and grooming tools.

It pays to work hard in these jobs. Your employer may notice your effort and commitment and consider you for a full-time position if one becomes available.

CONDUCT AN INFORMATION INTERVIEW OR JOB SHADOW AN ANIMAL PROFESSIONAL

Information interviews and job shadowing are two great ways to learn about animal careers. Not only will you learn more about different careers, you'll get a chance to make valuable industry contacts. Information interviews consist of a phone or in-person conversation with a worker about his or her job. You can learn more about why they chose their specialty, their daily tasks, the tools and other equipment they use to do their job, what skills are required, and how best to prepare for the field. Job shadowing simply means observing someone at their job as they go about their duties.

Do you have any family members or know any friends' parents who are zoologists, animal shelter workers, or zoo curators? Ask them if they could take time out for an information interview—whether face to face or via telephone. You can also contact your local veterinary clinic, animal shelter, or grooming salon to ask if someone might be willing to participate in an interview. If you are interested in a career as a zookeeper, curator, director, or aquarist, you may want to contact the public relations manager of the nearest zoo or aquarium. He or she may be able to connect you with one of the facility's employees for an interview or shadowing opportunity. Imagine spending the day shadowing a few zookeepers! You'll observe them as they perform their daily duties, which may include feeding and grooming the animals, recording data, renovating exhibits, and participating in conservation projects.

If you are lucky enough to have the opportunity to participate in an information interview or job shadowing experience, be prepared. Create a list of questions to ask about the individual's educational path, job duties, work schedule, and career goals. It's a good idea to write these questions down, and even carry a notebook or small recorder to record their responses and take notes on your experiences. Dress according to the job at hand—if you are going to follow a zookeeper for a day, you may want to reconsider those high heels. Khaki pants, shirt, and hiking boots or sneakers are probably a safer bet. Some facilities may even provide you with a lab coat or official work shirt to wear during your shadowing appointment.

Don't forget to send a thank-you note to everyone who helped you. People like to be appreciated, and your simple thank-you note may prompt them to remember you when it comes time to hire interns or full-time employees.

❏ START A PET-CARE BUSINESS

Are you interested in both animals and business? If so, you should consider starting your own pet-care business. The first step to any successful business is creating a business plan. Make a list of different services you want to offer—pet grooming and pet sitting are some options. Identify your place of service, any supplies that need to be purchased, and advertising costs. This will help you determine what you should charge customers. If you plan on making your home your "corporate headquarters," you may want to ask your parents' permission first. Perhaps you could use a portion of the laundry room or a corner of your garage as your office or work area.

Design and print advertising flyers and pass them out around your neighborhood. Keep in mind that walking one dog is fine, but you'll earn more by exercising multiple dogs at the same time. If possible, try to schedule your appointments to maximize your earning potential. For pet sitting, have an appointment book handy that lists all feeding schedules, additional chores, and emergency contact information for each client. Grooming pets could include bathing, brushing, and applying flea powders. Keep a list of supplies used so you can charge accordingly. When it comes time to bill your customers, use your computer to create professional-looking statements. It is also a handy way to keep your invoices organized.

Word of mouth is priceless advertising. Ask your customers to recommend your services to their friends. Who knows . . . you may be on your way to building a pet care empire!

SECTION 4

What Can I Do Right Now?

Get Involved: A Directory of Camps, Programs, Competitions, and Other Opportunities

Now that you've read about some of the different animal-related careers, you may be anxious to experience this line of work for yourself, to find out what it's really like. Or perhaps you already feel certain that this is the career path for you and want to get started on it right away. Whichever is the case, this section is for you! There are plenty of things you can do right now to learn about animal-related careers while gaining valuable experience. Just as important, you'll get to meet new friends and see new places, too.

In the following pages you will find programs designed to pique your interest in animals and start preparing you for a career. You already know that this field is complex, and that to work in it you need a solid education. Since the first step toward an animal-related career will be gaining that education, we've found nearly 50 organizations that provide programs that will start you on your way. Some are camps or special introductory sessions, others are actual college courses—one of them may be right for you. Take time to read over the listings and see how each compares to your situation: how committed you are to an animal-related field, how much of your money and free time you're willing to devote to it, and how the program will help you after high school. These listings are divided into categories,

with the type of program printed right after its name or the name of the sponsoring organization.

❏ THE CATEGORIES

Camps

When you see an activity that is classified as a camp, don't automatically start packing your tent and mosquito repellent. Where academic study is involved, the term "camp" often simply means a residential program including both educational and recreational activities. It's sometimes hard to differentiate between such camps and other study programs, but if the sponsoring organization calls it a camp, so do we! Visit the following Web sites for an extended list of camps: http://www.kidscamps.com and http://find.acacamps.org/finding_a_camp.php.

College Courses/Summer Study

These terms are linked because most college courses offered to students your age must take place in the summer, when you are out of school. At the same time, many summer study programs are sponsored by colleges and universities that want to attract future students and give them a head start in higher education. Summer study of almost any type is a good idea because it keeps your mind and your study skills sharp over the long vacation. Summer study at a college offers any number of additional benefits, including giving you the tools to make a well-informed decision about your future academic career.

Competitions

Competitions are fairly self-explanatory, but you should know that there are only a few in this book because animal-related competitions on a regional or national level are relatively rare. What this means, however, is that if you are interested in entering a competition, you shouldn't have much trouble finding one yourself. Your school counselor or science teacher can help you start searching in your area.

Conferences

Conferences for high school students are usually difficult to track down because most are for professionals in the field who gather to share new information and ideas with each other. Don't be discouraged, though. A number of professional organizations have student branches or membership options for those who are simply interested in the field offer conferences. Some student branches even run their own conferences. This is an option worth pursuing because conferences focus on some of the most current information available and also give you the chance to meet professionals who can answer your questions and even offer advice.

Employment and Internship Opportunities

As you may already know from experience, employment opportunities for teenagers can be very limited—especially for jobs that require a bachelor's, graduate, or doctor of veterinary medicine degree. On the other hand, you can get started in jobs such as pet sitting or pet grooming by just getting a few supplies and letting it be known that you offer these services. If you can't land an animal-related job you may just have to earn your money by working at a mall or restaurant and get your experience in an unpaid position elsewhere. Bear in mind that if you do a good enough job and the group you work for has the funding, this summer's volunteer position could be next summer's job.

Basically, an internship combines the responsibilities of a job (strict schedules, pressing duties, and usually written evaluations by your supervisor) with the uncertainties of a volunteer position [no wages (or only very seldom), no fringe benefits, no guarantee of future employment]. That may not sound very enticing, but completing an internship is a great way to prove your maturity, your commitment to an animal-related career, and your knowledge and skills to colleges, potential employers, and yourself. Some internships here are just formalized volunteer positions; others offer unique responsibilities and opportunities. Choose the kind that works best for you!

Field Experience

This is something of a catch-all category for activities that don't exactly fit the other descriptions, but anything called a field experience in this book is always a good opportunity to get out and explore the work of animal professionals.

Membership

When an organization (such as a professional association or an environmental activist organization such as the Sierra Club) is in this category, it simply means that you are welcome to pay your dues and become a card-carrying member. Formally joining any organization brings the benefits of meeting others who share your interests, finding opportunities to get involved, and keeping up with current events. Depending on how active you are, the contacts you make and the experiences you gain may help when the time comes to apply to colleges or look for a job.

In some organizations, you pay a special student rate and receive benefits similar to regular members. Many organizations, however, are now starting student branches with their own benefits and publications. As in any field, make sure you understand exactly what the benefits of membership are before you join.

Finally, don't let membership dues discourage you from making contact with these organizations. Some charge dues as low as $25 because they know that students are perpetually short of funds. When the annual dues are higher, think of the money as an investment in your future and then consider if it is too much to pay.

Seminars

Like conferences, seminars are often classes or informative gatherings for those already working in the field, and are generally sponsored by professional organizations. This means that there aren't all that many seminars for young people. But also like conferences, they are often open to affiliated members. Check with various organizations to see what kind of seminars they offer and if there is some way you can attend.

Volunteer Programs

Volunteerism is now enjoying great popularity, particularly among young people. Whether you're volunteering to meet your school's community service requirements or simply to help others and support a worthy cause, you can use the experience to explore animal-related careers. Caring for wildlife, campaigning to protect endangered or abused animals, and preserving the wilderness are just a few common volunteer activities—the listings in this book and your own ingenuity can lead to many more. Depending on your needs and interests, volunteering can be a long- or short-term commitment, perhaps part time during the school year or full time during the summer. This is an option that is flexible and broad enough for almost everyone.

If you are interested in volunteering with a federal government agency that focuses on natural and cultural resources protection, you should visit http://www.volunteer.gov/gov. This Web site allows you to search for a volunteer activity by keyword, state, zip code, agency, and opportunity type.

❑ PROGRAM DESCRIPTIONS

Once you've started to look at the individual listings themselves, you'll find that they contain a lot of information. Naturally, there is a general description of each program, but wherever possible we have also included the following details.

Application Information

Each listing notes how far in advance you'll need to apply for the program or position, but the simple rule is to apply as far in advance as possible. This ensures that you won't miss out on a great opportunity simply because other people got there ahead of you. It also means that you will get a timely decision on your application, so you'll still have some time to apply elsewhere if you are not accepted. As for the things that make up your application—essays, recommendations, etc.— we've tried to tell you what's involved, but be sure to contact the program about specific requirements before you submit anything.

Background Information

This includes such information as the date the program or organization was established, the name of the organization that is sponsoring it financially, and the faculty and staff who will be there for you. This can help you—and your family—gauge the quality and reliability of the program.

Classes and Activities

Classes and activities change from year to year, depending on popularity, availability of instructors, and many other factors. Nevertheless, colleges and universities quite consistently offer the same or similar classes, even in their summer sessions.

Courses like Introduction to Veterinary Science and Biology 101, for example, are simply indispensable. So you can look through the listings and see which programs offer foundational courses like these and which offer courses on more variable topics. As for activities, we note when you have access to recreational facilities on campus, and it's usually a given that special social and cultural activities will be arranged for most programs.

Contact Information

Wherever possible, we have given the title of the person whom you should contact instead of the name because people change jobs so frequently. If no title is given and you are telephoning an organization, simply tell the person who answers the phone the name of the program that interests you and he or she will forward your call. If you are writing, include the line "Attention: Summer Study Program" (or whatever is appropriate after "Attention") somewhere on the envelope. This will help to ensure that your letter goes to the person in charge of that program.

Credit

Where academic programs are concerned, we sometimes note that high school or college credit is available to those who have completed them. This means that the program can count toward your high school diploma or a future college degree just like a regular course. Obviously this can be very useful, but it's important to note that rules about accepting such credit vary from school to school. Before you commit to a program offering high school credit, check with your guidance counselor to see if it is acceptable to your school. As for programs offering college credit, check with your chosen college (if you have one) to see if they will accept it.

Eligibility and Qualifications

The main eligibility requirement to be concerned about is age or grade in school. A term frequently used in relation to grade level is "rising," as in "rising senior" (someone who will be a senior when the next school year begins). This is especially important where summer programs are concerned. A number of university-based programs make admissions decisions partly in consideration of GPA, class rank, and standardized test scores. This is mentioned in the listings, but you must contact the program for specific numbers. If you are worried that your GPA or your ACT scores, for example, aren't good enough, don't let them stop you from applying to programs that consider such things in the admissions process. Often, a fine essay or even an example of your dedication and eagerness can compensate for statistical weaknesses.

Facilities

We tell you where you'll be living, studying, eating, and having fun during these programs, but there isn't enough room to go into all the details. Some of those details can be important: what is and isn't accessible for people with disabilities, whether the site of a summer program has air-conditioning, and how modern the laboratory and computer equipment are. You can expect most program brochures

and application materials to address these concerns, but if you still have questions about the facilities, just call the program's administration and ask.

Financial Details

While a few of the programs listed here are fully underwritten by collegiate and corporate sponsors, most of them rely on you for at least some of their funding. The 2009 prices and fees are given here, but you should bear in mind that costs rise slightly almost every year. You and your parents must take costs into consideration when choosing a program. We always try to note where financial aid is available, but really, most programs will do their best to ensure that a shortage of funds does not prevent you from taking part.

Residential vs. Commuter Options

Simply put, some programs prefer that participating students live with other participants and staff members, others do not, and still others leave the decision entirely to the students themselves. As a rule, residential programs are suitable for young people who live out of town or even out of state, as well as for local residents. They generally provide a better overview of college life than programs in which you're only on campus for a few hours a day, and they're a way to test how well you cope with living away from home. Commuter programs may be viable only if you live near the program site or if you can stay with relatives who do. Bear in mind that for residential programs especially, the travel between your home and the location of the activity is almost always your responsibility and can significantly increase the cost of participation.

❑ FINALLY . . .

Ultimately, there are three important things to bear in mind concerning all of the programs listed in this volume. The first is that things change. Staff members come and go, funding is added or withdrawn, and supply and demand determine which programs continue and which terminate. Dates, times, and costs vary widely because of a number of factors. Because of this, the information we give you, although as current and detailed as possible, is just not enough on which to base your final decision. If you are interested in a program, you simply must contact the organization concerned to get the latest and most complete information available, or visit its Web site. This has the added benefit of putting you in touch with someone who can deal with your individual questions and problems.

Another important point to keep in mind when considering these programs is that the people who run them provided the information printed here. The editors of this book haven't attended the programs and don't endorse them: We simply give you the information with which to begin your own research. And after all, we can't pass judgment because you're the only one who can decide which programs are right for you.

The final thing to bear in mind is that the programs listed here are just the tip of the iceberg. No book can possibly cover all of the opportunities that are available to you—partly because they are so numerous and are constantly coming and going, but partly because some are waiting to be discovered. For instance, you may be very interested in taking a college course but don't see the college that interests you in the listings. Call its admissions office! Even if the college doesn't have a special program for high school students, it might be able to make some kind of arrangements for you to visit or sit in on a class. Use the ideas behind these listings and take the initiative to turn them into opportunities!

❑ THE PROGRAMS

American Association of Equine Practitioners

Field Experience

The association offers the Shadow a Veterinarian program for students of all ages who are interested in learning more about equine veterinary medicine. Participants accompany veterinarians on farm calls or spend a day observing them as they work in a clinic. Contact the student programs administrator for more information.

American Association of Equine Practitioners
Attn: Student Programs Administrator
4075 Iron Works Parkway
Lexington, KY 40511-8483
859-233-0147
aaepoffice@aaep.org
http://www.aaep.org/index.php

American Association of Zoo Keepers

Membership/Conferences

The association offers membership for college students and affiliate membership for "those interested in the profession but not associated with a zoo or aquarium." Membership benefits for affiliate members include a subscription to *Animal Keepers' Forum*, members-only access to the association's Web site, and discount rates on conferences, publications, and products.

> **American Association of Zoo Keepers**
> 3601 29th Street, SW, Suite 133
> Topeka, KS 66614-2054
> 785-273-9149
> http://www.aazk.org

American Society for the Prevention of Cruelty to Animals (ASPCA)

Membership/Volunteer Programs

The society offers membership to people who support the humane treatment of animals. Members receive a publication that features expert advice on caring for animals and stories about animals from members.

Volunteer opportunities are also available at the society's New York City headquarters. Volunteers "assist in the care and placement of the animals, educate the public, and provide support for administrative programs." Volunteers must be at least 16 years of age and willing to work a minimum of eight hours per month for six months. Some of the specific volunteer opportunities that are available include: volunteer adoptions counselor (volunteers must be 18 years of age and older), administrative assistant (16+), animal care technician (18+), cat volunteer (16+), children's bibliography reviewer (18+), dog volunteer (18+), foster caretaker (18+), humane educator (21+), mobile clinic assistant (18+), public relations assistant (18+), veterinary assistant (18+), and workplace giving event volunteer (18+).

> **American Society for the Prevention of Cruelty to Animals**
> 424 East 92nd Street
> New York, NY 10128-6804
> 800-628-0028
> http://www.aspca.org

American Society of Limnology and Oceanography Minority Student Directory

Employment and Internship Opportunities

Minority high school (junior and senior years) and undergraduate and graduate students can post information about their educational backgrounds and aquatic science interests in the Minority Student Directory, which is available at the society's Web site. Listings include your name, current student status, an overview of your interests in the field, and a statement detailing your background and goals. Participating in the directory will help you meet other people in the field, as well as possibly obtain internships and employment.

American Society of Limnology and Oceanography

5400 Bosque Boulevard, Suite 680
Waco, TX 76710-4446
800-929-2756
http://www.aslo.org/mas/directory.
html

Animal and Plant Health Inspection Service

Employment and Internship Opportunities/Volunteer Programs

Paid internships are available for students at the high school through graduate school levels as part of the USDA's Summer Intern Program. Participants work as assistants in professional, scientific, and technical fields. Internships begin in May and end when the participant returns to school in the fall. Summer volunteer opportunities are also available for recent high school graduates and college students as part of the Federal Student Volunteer Program. These are available at the USDA's Washington, D.C., headquarters and at USDA satellite offices throughout the United States.

Animal and Plant Health Inspection Service

U.S. Department of Agriculture (USDA)
1400 Independence Avenue, SW
Washington, DC 20250-0002
APHIS.Web@aphis.usda.gov
http://www.usda.gov/da/employ/
intern.htm
http://www.studentjobs.gov/
agencies/agency-doa-people.asp

Aquatic Sciences Adventure Camp at Southwest Texas State University, San Marcos

Camps

The Aquatic Sciences Adventure Camp is run by the Edwards Aquifer Research and Data Center at Southwest Texas State University, San Marcos. It offers students ages nine to 15 the chance to explore and conduct research on various bodies of water, from artesian wells, to ponds, to rivers. During the weeklong residential camp, your days start early (around 6:45 A.M.) and include snorkeling and scuba lessons, lectures, videos, and evening recreational activities (including cave tours, swimming and tubing in the San Marcos River, swimming in a spring-fed pool, a raft trip on the Guadalupe River, and a trip to Sea-World). Each session costs about $450, which includes room, board, equipment, and field trips. Students are accepted into each session on a first-come, first-served basis. All participants should be accustomed to moderate physical activity and be comfortable around water, and preferably have the ability to swim.

Aquatic Sciences Adventure Camp

Southwest Texas State University, San Marcos
248 Freeman Building
San Marcos, TX 78666-4616
512-245-2329
aqscicamp@txstate.edu
http://www.eardc.txstate.edu/about camp.html

Association of Zoos and Aquariums (AZA)

Membership/Volunteer Programs/Conferences

The association offers an associate membership category "for zoo and aquarium professionals, as well as other interested parties, who want to support and forward the mission, vision, and goals of AZA." Members receive a subscription to *CONNECT*, the association's monthly magazine; free and discounted admission to AZA-accredited zoos and aquariums; and discounts on conferences.

The AZA does not offer volunteer opportunities, but it does offer links to its member organizations that do. Visit http://www.aza.org/Education/KidsAndFamilies/detail.as px?id=278 to find volunteer opportunities at a zoo or aquarium near you. Volunteering at a zoo or aquarium is a good way to learn about careers in the field. Volunteers learn about zoos and aquariums via classroom activities and hands-on work in animal care, conservation education, conservation and research, and visitor services. In addition to learning firsthand how zoos and aquariums work, there are other benefits to volunteering. Volunteers often receive discounts on admission and membership, get to participate in field trips and other activities, make valuable contacts with zoo and aquarium professionals, and meet new friends.

Association of Zoos and Aquariums (AZA)

8403 Colesville Road, Suite 710
Silver Spring, MD 20910-3314
301-562-0777
http://www.aza.org

Bureau of Land Management Volunteer Opportunities/Student Educational Employment Program

Employment and Internship Opportunities/Volunteer Programs

The Bureau of Land Management (BLM) is the division of the U.S. Department of the Interior responsible for managing the land and resources of more than 258 million acres of public-owned property. It offers volunteer opportunities to people of all ages and skill levels. As a volunteer, you can take part in research projects, help monitor wilderness areas, perform office work, or participate in any number of activities designed to conserve and preserve the land's natural and historic resources. Depending on your interests and the BLM's needs, you can work alone or in a group, on a prearranged project or on one of your own devising, for a few hours or every day, just once, or on a continuing basis. (Note: Information on volunteer opportunities with other federal environmental agencies—including the Bureau of Reclamation, Fish & Wildlife Service, Forest Service, National Park Service, Natural Resources Conservation Service, U.S. Army Corps of Engineers, and U.S. Geological Survey—can be found at http://www.volunteer.gov/gov.)

Additionally, you can participate in the federal government's Student Educational Employment Program (SEEP). High school students in SEEP are employed in entry-level positions with the BLM and other federal agencies that match their interests and career goals. Applicants must be U.S. citizens or residents of American Samoa or Swains Islands. Successful completion of SEEP may lead to permanent opportunities in federal service upon completion of other educational requirements (namely, a college degree). College students at the undergraduate and graduate levels are also eligible to participate in SEEP. For further information, visit http://www.opm.gov/employ/students.

Bureau of Land Management
U.S. Department of the Interior
1849 C Street, NW, Room 5665
Washington, DC 20240-0001
http://www.blm.gov/wo/st/en/res/
Volunteer.3.html

Canon Envirothon
Competitions
The Envirothon is a series of competitions, established in 1979, for ninth- through 12th-graders who want to increase their knowledge of the natural sciences and environmental issues. Progressing from local to state/provincial/territorial to national competitions, teams of five students perform experiments and activities and then work together to answer the questions they are given. Competition questions come from five subjects: Soils and Land Use, Aquatic Ecology, Forestry, Wildlife, and a current wildlife issue that changes each year. State/provincial/territorial competitions feature questions about the local environment, regulations, and concerns in addition to general knowledge questions. While the goal of the Envirothon is to develop knowledgeable, environmentally active adults, the program is also designed to be fun for all participants. Teams are headed by high school teachers or other youth leaders and may draw members from schools or from other organizations and associations. At the national level, the Envirothon is sponsored by Canon USA; at the regional levels, usually by state environmental protection agencies, forest services, and game and parks commissions. More than $100,000 in scholarships and prizes is awarded at the national competition. For information about the Envirothon program in your area, contact relevant state agencies, or speak to your science teacher or guidance counselor. You may also contact the national executive director at the address below.

Canon Envirothon
Attn: National Executive Director
PO Box 855
League City, TX 77574-0855
800-825-5547
http://www.envirothon.org

Carolina Raptor Center
Volunteer Programs
The Carolina Raptor Center (CRC) has been working since 1981 to care for injured and orphaned birds of prey (raptors) while running an environmental education program for visitors to the center and for local schoolchildren. Volunteers are largely responsible for the continuing success and growth enjoyed by the CRC, and high school students who are at least 16 years of age are encouraged to donate their time. (Note: Those who are between the ages of 10 and 15 can become junior volunteers.) Opportunities are available in the educational, animal care, administrative, and fundraising areas of operation. Work may

include training birds, preparing exhibits at the center, maintaining the center's nature trail and its aviaries, or working in the office or gift shop. All volunteers, but especially those working directly with the raptors, receive comprehensive training from experienced staff members. Contact the director of volunteer services for more information, or visit the center to find out more about its work.

Carolina Raptor Center

Attn: Director of Volunteer Services
PO Box 16443
Charlotte, NC 28297-6443
704-875-6521, ext. 128
volunteer@carolinaraptorcenter.org
http://www.carolinaraptorcenter.org

Catalina Sea Camp
Camps/Field Experience

Catalina Sea Camp is located on Catalina Island, a 26-mile-long island off the coast of Southern California. You must be between the ages of 12 and 17 to attend. (Note: A Junior Sea Camp is available for those between the ages of eight and 11.) Campers become certified scuba divers during the three-week course. In addition to scuba certification, you also learn the basics of marine biology, oceanography, and island ecology. You explore tide pools and marine life of the Catalina Island system—sharks, skaters, rays, and other marine mammals. A typical day consists of scuba diving in the morning and two-and-a-half hours of labs and instruction in the afternoon. Catalina Island campers partake of island life in their spare time. You can learn to sail, sea kayak, snorkel, and rock climb. During the camp session,

everyone takes a day hike to the beach located on the other side of the island. All instructors at the Catalina Sea Camp have at least a bachelor's degree in science or a related field, and scuba diving instructors are fully certified. Applicants for this program are taken on a first-come, first-served basis. You must prove that you are in good physical health, as scuba diving is a rigorous activity. Teacher recommendations are required for first-time applicants. The cost of the summer camp is $3,500. Financial aid is available. There is no deadline, but camp enrollment is limited and usually fills up every year. Catalina Sea Camp offers two different sessions every summer. To receive a brochure and application, contact Guided Discoveries.

Guided Discoveries Inc.

Catalina Sea Camp
PO Box 1360
Claremont, CA 91711-1360
909-625-6194
http://www.catalinaseacamp.org/
    catalinaseacamp.html

The Center for Excellence in Education USA Biology Olympiad/ Research Science Institute
Competitions/Field Experience

The goal of the Center for Excellence in Education (CEE) is to nurture future leaders in science, technology, and business. And it won't cost you a dime: All of CEE's programs are free (except for transportation costs).

All high school students are eligible to participate in the USA Biology Olympiad (USABO). To participate, you must be nominated by your teacher. If you score well on a multiple-choice exam, and then subsequently excel on another exam, you will make the group of 20 finalists who are eligible to compete at the USABO National Finals at a leading university. The National Finals consist of two weeks of intensive practical and theoretical tutorials where you will get the opportunity to work with leading biologists in the United States. At the end of the two weeks, you will take a theoretical and practical exam to compete for one of the four positions on the U.S. team that will compete in the International Biology Olympiad.

Since 1984 the CEE has sponsored the Research Science Institute, a six-week residential summer program held at the Massachusetts Institute of Technology. Seventy-five rising high school seniors with scientific and technological promise are chosen from a field of more than 700 applicants to participate in the program, conducting projects with scientists and researchers. You can read more about specific research projects online.

The Center for Excellence in Education
8201 Greensboro Drive, Suite 215
McLean, VA 22102-3813
703-448-9062
cee@cee.org
http://www.cee.org

Delta Society
Membership/Volunteer Programs
The Delta Society "is dedicated to improving human health through therapy and service animals." It offers membership to anyone who supports its goals. Members receive a subscription to *Interactions*,

which covers research, trends, and stories about the healing bond between animals and humans.

Additionally, there are two types of volunteer opportunities available. People who live in or near Bellevue, Washington; Seattle, Washington; or Portland, Oregon, may choose to help out at the society's offices in these cities. Volunteers will do filing, prepare mailings, conduct event planning, write articles, conduct research, and perform database work, as well as be assigned other duties that match their skill set. You can help out in a Delta Society office or become a member of a Pet Partners Team. Pet Partners Team volunteers are trained to take their animal to hospitals, nursing homes, classrooms, and other facilities to help improve people's health. The following animals can be used in this program: dogs, cats, guinea pigs, rabbits, domesticated rats, horses, goats, llamas, donkeys, potbellied pigs, miniature pigs, cockatoos, African gray parrots, and chickens. Volunteers must be at least 16 years of age (or age 10 to 16 with guardian participation). Contact the society for more information.

Delta Society
875 124th Avenue, NE, Suite 101
Bellevue, WA 98005-2531
425-679-5500
info@deltasociety.org
http://www.deltasociety.org

Earthwatch Institute
Conferences/Field Experience/ Employment and Internship Opportunities/Membership
Earthwatch Institute is an organization for people whose spirit of adventure is as

great as their commitment to the earth's well-being. A nonprofit membership organization founded in 1971, Earthwatch's major activity is linking volunteers with scientific research expeditions that need them. There are about 130 different expeditions every year, covering all continents but Antarctica, each lasting anywhere from five days to almost three weeks. If you are 16 or 17, you can join a Teen Team and participate in an expedition researching Costa Rican caterpillars, for example, or Australia's fossil forests. Whichever expedition you choose, you work with five to 10 other people under the guidance of a research scientist (often a university professor working in his or her field of expertise).

Living and working conditions vary widely among the expeditions; you might stay in a hotel or a tent, remain at one site or hike to several locations while carrying a heavy backpack. Expenses also vary widely, from about $199 to $4,000, depending on travel, accommodation and eating arrangements, and other necessary provisions. Earthwatch reminds potential volunteers, however, that your payment of expenses (along with the donation of your time) is really an investment in environmental research. Of course, you're also investing in your own future. With so many expeditions to choose from, you'll be able to gain experience in career fields from ecology to national park service, and from natural history to wildlife preservation. Contact Earthwatch for its annual catalog listing all the details.

Even if you're not up for one of their demanding expeditions, Earthwatch invites you to become a member at the standard rate of $35 per year. You can also attend Earthwatch's annual conference or apply for an internship at its offices in Oxford, England; Melbourne, Australia; or Tokyo, Japan. Contact the institute for more information.

Earthwatch Institute
Three Clock Tower Place, Suite 100
PO Box 75
Maynard, MA 01754-2549
800-776-0188
info@earthwatch.org
http://www.earthwatch.org

Environmental Field Studies Abroad Program at The School for Field Studies

College Courses/Summer Study/Field Experience

The School for Field Studies (SFS) offers summer programs in locations around the world for students who are at least 16 years of age and have completed at least their junior year in high school. You spend one month on location pursuing the four main tenets of the SFS curriculum: an interdisciplinary, "case studies" approach; problem solving through fieldwork; involvement in the local community; and a proactive role in your own education. You can choose one of the following SFS programs based on your scientific and environmental interests: Community Wildlife Management in Kenya; Community Wildlife Management in Tanzania; Marine Protected Areas: Management Techniques and Policies in the Turks and Caicos Islands; Natural Resource Management and Rainforest Research Field Techniques in Australia; Tropical Rainforest Studies in New Zealand; Sustaining Tropical Ecosystems: Biodiversity, Conservation, and Development in Costa Rica; and Coastal Diversity and Threatened Marine Turtles in Mexico. There is also a program on public health and the environment available in Kenya. Each program focuses on a genuine environmental problem facing local inhabitants, and your research and suggestions become part of SFS's solution to that problem. All programs are physically demanding and, because there are academic lectures as well as field expeditions, you have virtually no free time. Meals are included in the tuition fee, which ranges from $3,720 to $5,800, depending on the location. Extensive financial aid is available. You have to provide some of your own personal backpacking gear and transportation to and from your departure point. The SFS, established in 1981, is fully accredited by Boston University, so participants can earn college credit via the summer program. The SFS staff consists largely of trained academics, including many Ph.D.s, with years of field research experience behind them.

The School for Field Studies also offers semester-long programs in the fall and spring for students who have completed at least one semester of college credit and one college-level biology or ecology course. All correspondence should be directed to the SFS Admissions Office.

Environmental Studies Program
The School for Field Studies
Admissions Office
10 Federal Street, Suite 24
Salem, MA 01970-3876

800-989-4418
admissions@fieldstudies.org
http://www.fieldstudies.org

Environmental Studies Summer Youth Institute at Hobart and William Smith Colleges
College Courses/Summer Study
Hobart and William Smith Colleges sponsor the Environmental Studies Summer Youth Institute (ESSYI) for rising high school juniors and seniors. Academically talented students are invited to participate in this examination of environmental issues from scientific, social, and humanistic perspectives. Running for two full weeks in July, the ESSYI comprises classroom courses, laboratory procedures, outdoor explorations, and plenty of time to discuss and think about integrating these many approaches to understanding the environment. Lectures encompass ecology, philosophy, geology, literature, topography, and art, among other areas of study, and are conducted by professors from Hobart and William Smith Colleges. Your study of the environment and how humans relate to it also includes field trips to such places as quaking bogs, organic farms, the Adirondack Mountains, and Native American historical sites. Participants also make use of the *HMS William F. Scandling*, the colleges' 65-foot research vessel, as they explore the ecology of nearby Seneca Lake. ESSYI students live on campus and have access to all the colleges' recreational facilities. Those who complete this intellectually and physically challenging program are awarded college credit. The fee for the program is $2,200. Contact the institute

director for information on financial aid and application procedures.

Environmental Studies Summer Youth Institute

Hobart and William Smith Colleges
Attn: Director
Geneva, NY 14456-3397
315-781-4401
essyi@hws.edu
http://academic.hws.edu/enviro

Explore-a-College at Earlham College

College Courses/Summer Study

Rising high school freshmen, sophomores, and juniors can participate in Explore-a-College, a two-week college experience program that offers 10 classes. Students take one class for college credit and learn how to develop their time-management, research, and discussion skills. Students interested in animal careers can take Animals Inside and Out, which "explores the anatomy, physiology, ecology, and natural history of domestic and wild animals (and humans) in the east central Indiana area." You will study the anatomy of a variety of animals, study local animal diseases and parasites in a laboratory, conduct physiology experiments, and visit an animal shelter, a veterinary hospital, farms, and local nature preserves and natural areas. Classes are typically held in late June; the application deadline is June 1. Students stay in residence halls on campus. Tuition is $1,600 (which includes room and board). Very limited financial aid is available. Contact the program director for more information.

Earlham College

Explore-a-College
Attn: Program Director
801 National Road West
Richmond, IN 47374-4095
800-327-5426
http://www.earlham.edu/~eac

Friends of the Earth

Membership

This international organization is made up of people working to protect the earth's well-being. If you're interested in joining its ranks, you can simply pay your dues ($25 annually). Members receive a subscription to the organization's magazine, voting rights at its annual meeting, and the opportunity to participate in Friends of the Earth initiatives. You can also join the Friends of the Earth Action Network by registering at its Web site. Members of the Action Network receive action alerts and a biweekly newsletter by email. Additionally, all site visitors can use organization email templates to lobby members of Congress about environmental issues.

Friends of the Earth

1717 Massachusetts Avenue,
  Suite 600
Washington, DC 20036-2008
202-783-7400
http://www.foe.org

Global Response Environmental Action and Education Network

Employment and Internship Opportunities/Membership

Global Response is an international action and education network that works with environmental, indigenous, peace, and justice groups. Its mission is to help these groups develop strategies to raise public awareness and create public pressure to address specific environmental emergencies. Every month, Global Response issues an Action Alert to its members. *Eco-Club Actions* is the monthly bulletin specifically for high school students and youth environmental clubs. It describes an environmental emergency, gives background information, recommends points to be made in a letter, and provides the names, addresses, fax numbers, and email addresses of people who are in a position to make positive changes. Then it's up to you to write your own letter requesting that action be taken (or use a template provided at its Web site). The idea is for small groups of students, perhaps getting together to share a pizza, to sit down and write these letters. This simple approach is highly effective. Global Response played a major role in creating a wetlands park in South Africa and stopping the dredge mining within it. It also saved 900,000 acres on Honduras's Mosquito Coast from clear cutting by a lumber company, and protected a fishery in Russia from development by the oil industry. The organization has youth members in more than 35 countries. The student membership fee is $30. Internships and employment opportunities are also available. Contact Global Response for more information and the latest *Eco-Club Actions* newsletter.

Global Response
PO Box 7490
Boulder, CO 80306-7490
303-444-0306
action@globalresponse.org
http://www.globalresponse.org

High School Field Ecology Program at the Teton Science School

College Courses/Summer Study/Field Experience

The Teton Science School operates an intense High School Field Ecology summer program for rising high school juniors and seniors. The program lasts four weeks and, while based in Jackson Hole, Wyoming, includes time at Yellowstone and Grand Teton National Parks. In the program, you "learn field ecology by doing field ecology," and are expected to maintain a high level of physical activity while conducting research (such as studying coyote ecology, red-tailed hawk habitat, or bat habitat preference) and exploring ecosystems. Working with instructors, scientists, and representatives of federal agencies, you learn proper field investigation techniques as well as how to keep a field journal, read and make maps, and explore the wilderness without harming the environment. The program culminates with a major independent research project that addresses a current conservation issue. Each participant is formally assigned a grade and given a written evaluation for his or her work in the program, so this is a suitable source of high school credit. You live in log cabin–style dormitories with modern facilities, except during a backpacking trip through the mountains. Most outdoor gear and all meals are covered by the tuition fee, which is around $3,600; some financial assistance is available. You must have completed a biology class and received favorable teacher recommendations to be considered. The Teton Science School also runs a Middle School Field Ecology program; a Field Natural History program for rising high school freshmen, sophomores, and juniors; and various programs for adults and teachers. All correspondence should be directed to the registrar.

High School Field Ecology Program

Attn: Registrar
Teton Science School
700 Coyote Canyon Road
Jackson, WY 83001-8501
307-733-1313
info@tetonscience.org
http://www.tetonscience.org

Humane Society of the United States

Employment and Internship Opportunities/Membership

The Humane Society of the United States advocates for animals, the earth, and the environment. It offers employment and internship opportunities; visit its Web site for a list of current positions. Membership is available to anyone who supports the society's goals. Members receive *All Animals*, an attractive, quarterly publication.

Humane Society of the United States

2100 L Street, NW
Washington, DC 20037-1525
202-452-1100
http://www.hsus.org

International Association of Canine Professionals

Conferences/Membership

The association offers a membership category for those who have "an active interest in making a career within the canine profession, but do not yet have the experience to qualify for acceptance" at professional membership levels. Members receive a newsletter, receive access to seminars and educational materials, and can attend the association's conference.

International Association of Canine Professionals

877-843-4227
iacpadmin@mindspring.com
http://www.dogpro.org

International Marine Animal Trainers' Association (IMATA)

Conferences/Membership

The association offers membership to college students and a Web membership to anyone who is interested in and supports its objectives. Web members receive an online edition of *Soundings* magazine, access to the member's area of the IMATA Web site, and discounted registration at its annual conference.

International Marine Animal Trainers' Association

1200 South Lake Shore Drive
Chicago, IL 60605-2490
312-692-3193
info@imata.org
http://www.imata.org

Intern Exchange International
Employment and Internship Opportunities

High school students ages 16 to 18 (including graduating seniors) who are interested in gaining real-life experience in veterinary medicine can participate in a month-long summer internship in the United Kingdom. Participants work as veterinary assistants in animal clinics. The cost of the program is approximately $7,335 plus airfare; this fee includes tuition, housing (students live in residence halls at the University of London), breakfast and dinner daily, housekeeping service, linens and towels, special dinner events, weekend trips and excursions, group activities including scheduled theatre outings, and a Tube Pass. Contact Intern Exchange International for more information.

Intern Exchange International, Ltd.
2606 Bridgewood Circle
Boca Raton, FL 33434-4118
561-477-2434
info@internexchange.com
http://www.internexchange.com

Internship Connection
Employment and Internship Opportunities

Internship Connection provides summer or "gap year" internships to high school and college students in Boston, New York City, and Washington, D.C. For students interested in animal careers, internships are available in veterinary medical settings. As part of the program, participants learn how to create a resume, participate in a job interview, and develop commu-nication and personal skills that are key to success in the work world. They also get the chance to make valuable contacts during their internships that may help them land a job once they complete college. The program fee for interns in New York or Washington is $3,000, and $2,500 for those in Boston. Contact Internship Connection for more information.

Internship Connection
17 Countryside Road
Newton, MA 02459-2915
617-796-9283
carole@internshipconnection.com
http://www.internshipconnection.com

Marine Science Institute
Camps

Students entering grades nine through 12 can participate in Project Discovery, a weeklong summer exploration program where they get the opportunity to study the San Francisco Bay. You will use scientific equipment to study fish, invertebrates, plankton, and water. You will also get a chance to kayak and spend a day aboard the institute's research vessel, the *R/V Robert G. Brownlee*. The cost for the commuter program is $599 (which includes lunch). Financial aid is available. (Note: The institute also offers programs for students in kindergarten through eighth grade.) Contact the institute for more information.

Marine Science Institute
500 Discovery Parkway
Redwood City, CA 94063-4715
650-364-2760
julie@sfbaymsi.org
http://sfbaymsi.org/marinecamp.html

National Association of Professional Pet Sitters
Conferences/Membership

The association offers a membership category for "those who are interested in the pet-sitting profession, but are not currently active in the industry." Members receive publications, access to a virtual library, the opportunity to attend the association's annual conference, and other benefits.

National Association of Professional Pet Sitters
15000 Commerce Parkway, Suite C
Mt. Laurel, NJ 08054-2212
856-439-0324
napps@ahint.com
http://www.petsitters.org

National Audubon Society
Employment and Internship Opportunities/Membership/Volunteer Programs

This membership organization for people and organizations that are committed to "conserving and restoring natural ecosystems, focusing on birds, other wildlife, and their habitats for the benefit of humanity and the earth's biological diversity" offers internships and volunteer and employment opportunities.

Anyone who supports the society's goals can join. Members receive *Audubon* magazine, the opportunity to visit Audubon sanctuaries and nature centers, access to workshops and ecology camps, discounts on products, and more. The society also offers several programs for kids in grades three through eight.

The society, in cooperation with Toyota, offers the TogetherGreen volunteer program that seeks to connect people from all over the United States to complete environment-related projects. Visit http://www.togethergreen.org/Volunteer/VolunteerEvents.aspx for more information.

National Audubon Society
225 Varick Street, 7th Floor
New York, NY 10014-4396
212-979-3000
http://www.audubon.org

National Dairy Shrine (NDS)
Employment and Internship Opportunities/Membership

The NDS is a membership organization for people interested in the dairy industry—from children and teens to college students and scientists. Members receive a newsletter, a membership certificate, and a lapel pin. The organization also offers a list of internships available from other organizations at its Web site.

National Dairy Shrine
PO Box 1
Maribel, WI 54227-0001
920-863-6333
info@dairyshrine.org
http://www.dairyshrine.org

National 4-H Council
Camps/Competitions/Membership

4-H Clubs teach young people about science, engineering, technology, healthy living, and citizenship via clubs, camps, competitions, and other activities. It has

6 million members in the United States. Students ages eight through 18 can join the organization. Visit the 4-H national organization's Web site for information on a chapter near you and programs it offers.

National 4-H Council
7100 Connecticut Avenue
Chevy Chase, MD 20815-4934
301-961-2800
info@fourhcouncil.edu
http://4-h.org

National Oceanic and Atmospheric Administration
Employment and Internship Opportunities

The National Oceanic and Atmospheric Administration offers a variety of summer programs and paid internships for young people. Examples of opportunities for high school students include an employment and internship program for students with disabilities; an apprenticeship program in Florida that allows students to gain experience at the Atlantic Oceanographic and Meteorological Laboratory and Southeast Fisheries Science Center; and an engineering and science career orientation summer program for students in the Washington, D.C., area. Contact the administration for more information on these and other programs.

National Oceanic and Atmospheric Administration
1401 Constitution Avenue, NW, Room 5128
Washington, DC 20230-0001

http://www.oesd.noaa.gov/noaa_student_opps.html

National Park Service Student Educational Employment
Program/Youth Programs/Volunteers-in-Parks Employment and Internship Opportunities/Field Experience/ Volunteer Programs

The federal government's Student Educational Employment Program is available to high school, college, and professional degree students. Participants are paid a salary and gain valuable work experience while attending school, which may lead to future employment with the National Park Service (NPS) or other federal agencies after graduation. Applicants must be U.S. citizens or residents of American Samoa or Swains Islands. For further information, visit http://www.opm.gov/employ/students.

The NPS offers more than 25 programs for people between the ages of five and 24. The programs, such as the Youth Conservation Corps and Public Land Corps, will help educate you about the environment while you work with conservation workers to improve national parks. Visit the NPS Web site to learn about the wide range of available programs and to view photos of past projects.

You can also protect and preserve America's natural and cultural heritage by becoming a park volunteer. You might work as a volunteer at a visitor center in Acadia National Park, a horse center volunteer at Rock Creek Park, help out in the office at Big Cypress National Preserve, or perform a variety of other tasks. Visit the NPS Web site to search for volunteer opportunities by state and national park.

National Park Service
U.S. Department of the Interior
1849 C Street, NW
Washington, DC 20240-0001
202-208-6843
http://www.nps.gov/gettinginvolved

National Science Bowl for High School Students
Competitions

The National Science Bowl, which is sponsored by the U.S. Department of Energy, is an academic competition that tests your knowledge of science and math fields, including astronomy, biology, chemistry, earth science, general science, mathematics, and physics. Teams of students are quizzed using a style that is similar to the television show *Jeopardy*. High school and middle school students may participate. Contact the U.S. Department of Energy for more information about this annual competition.

U.S. Department of Energy
http://www.scied.science.doe.gov/nsb

The Nature Conservancy
Employment and Internship Opportunities/Membership/Volunteer Programs

People of any age can join the conservancy, which has protected more than 119 million acres of land and 5,000 miles of rivers throughout the world. Members receive four issues of *Nature Conservancy* magazine and invitations to participate in field trips, events at conservancy preserves, and local chapter outings.

If you care about the environment and want to make a difference, The Nature Conservancy needs your help as a volunteer. Opportunities are available in all 50 states. Visit its Web site for more information.

The conservancy's New York office offers The Internship Program for City Youth, which seeks to help city youth explore nature and learn about college and career opportunities. The summer internships are paid and last four weeks. Visit http://www.nature.org/wherewework/northamerica/states/newyork for more information.

The Nature Conservancy
4245 North Fairfax Drive, Suite 100
Arlington, VA 22203-1606
800-628-6860
http://nature.org

Opportunities at Zoos and Aquariums
Camps/College Courses/Summer Study/Employment and Internship Opportunities/Field Experience/Membership/Seminars/Volunteer Programs

Zoos and aquariums provide a wealth of exploration opportunities for students interested in pursuing careers as animal caretakers, aquarists, curators, directors, veterinarians, veterinary technicians, zookeepers, and zoologists, among other careers. Approximately 215 zoos and aquariums are accredited by the Association of Zoos and Aquariums (AZA). To find a program near you, visit http://

www.aza.org/FindZooAquarium for a searchable database of facilities in your town or city.

Association of Zoos and Aquariums

8403 Colesville Road, Suite 710
Silver Spring, MD 20910-3314
301-562-0777
http://www.aza.org

The Peregrine Fund at the World Center for Birds of Prey

Volunteer Programs

The Peregrine Fund has worked nationally and internationally to promote conservation and environmental education since 1970, "focusing on birds to conserve nature." The fund is headquartered at the World Center for Birds of Prey, which houses more than 100 birds and releases their young into the wild. The Velma Morrison Interpretive Center at the headquarters provides opportunities for the public to learn more about birds of prey by encountering live birds and viewing multimedia presentations and exhibits. Volunteers are needed to make presentations and lead tours of the Interpretive Center. Other volunteer opportunities include working as a chamber cleaner, office assistant, and bird sitter. Volunteers must be at least 15 years old, willing to participate in training sessions, and able to commit to working a set number of hours per month. Continuing education programs are offered to all volunteers who want to learn more about birds of prey and general conservation work. Training classes are scheduled annually, but applications are accepted year-round and individual training is also available. For more information about volunteer opportunities, contact the volunteer coordinator.

Peregrine Fund at the World Center for Birds of Prey

Velma Morrison Interpretive Center
Attn: Volunteer Coordinator
5668 West Flying Hawk Lane
Boise, ID 83709-7289
208-362-3716
tpf@peregrinefund.org
http://www.peregrinefund.org

Pet Care Services Association

Conferences/Membership

This professional membership association for pet boarders, sitters, groomers, animal trainers, and pet suppliers offers a membership category for any "individual who is interested in the pet care industry, but who does not presently operate a non-veterinary pet care business." Members receive access to association publications, discussion groups, and networking, as well as discounts on products, education programs, and conventions.

Pet Care Services Association

1702 East Pikes Peak Avenue
Colorado Springs, CO 80909-5717
877-570-7788
http://www.petcareservices.org

Rainforest Action Network

Membership

The Rainforest Action Network (RAN) is a 30,000-member grassroots organization that "runs hard-hitting campaigns to break America's oil addiction, reduce our reliance on coal, protect endangered forests and Indigenous rights, and stop destructive investments through education, grassroots organizing, and nonviolent direct action." You can become involved with RAN on an individual basis by simply visiting its Web site frequently and responding to "Action Alerts." Or you can join RAN Youth Sustaining the Earth, the organization's youth branch. RANs, as they're called (or RYSEs, RAN Youth Sustaining the Earth), are community or student groups of concerned people. They work through direct action, letter writing, protests, and by pressuring corporations and politicians. If you decide to start your own group, RAN will provide information, advice, event notification, ideas for activities, a quarterly report, and a bimonthly newsletter. Visit the Rainforest Action Network on the Web or write for more information.

Rainforest Action Network

221 Pine Street, 5th Floor
San Francisco, CA 94104-2705
415-398-4404
answers@ran.org
http://www.ran.org

SEACAMP San Diego

Camps/College Courses/Summer Study

SEACAMP, founded in 1987, offers summer camps for students ages 12 to 18, using the Pacific Ocean as a classroom for marine science education. Campuses are fully equipped with modern residential facilities as well as an aquarium room and laboratory. Staff members have degrees in marine science and are trained in safety and first aid. SEACAMP I is offered as a residential or day program and includes labs and workshops in marine biology and ecology, oceanography, and a study of career opportunities. Field trips, tidepooling, snorkeling, and an introduction to scuba diving round out the curriculum. SEACAMP II is a residential program for those who have completed SEACAMP I and want to tackle a more in-depth marine-science research project and improve their scuba and snorkeling capabilities. SEACAMP III is an advanced version of SEACAMP II. Participants will get even more opportunities to develop their in-water skills and field research and observation techniques. The camps are offered several times each summer. SEACAMP I is a six-day program, SEACAMP II lasts a week, and SEACAMP III is eight days in length. The number of places available in all programs is limited. The tuition fees are all-inclusive and average about $790 for SEACAMP I, $1,300 for SEACAMP II, and $1,550 for SEACAMP III. There is a special offer for students who take SEACAMP I and SEACAMP II back-to-back.

SEACAMP also offers programs for visiting classes during the school year, traveling programs for area schools, and programs for adults.

SEACAMP San Diego

1380 Garnet Avenue, PMB E6
San Diego, CA 92109-3013
800-SEACAMP
seacamp@seacamp.com
http://www.seacamp.com

Secondary Student Training Program/Life Science Summer Program at the University of Iowa

College Courses/Summer Study

The University of Iowa offers two interesting youth programs for those who are interested in science: the Secondary Student Training Program and the Life Science Summer Program.

Those who have completed grade 10 or 11 can apply to the Secondary Student Training Program (SSTP). The program allows students to explore a particular area of science, such as biology, while conducting scientific research. Participants study and conduct research projects for approximately 40 hours per week with university faculty in one of the many laboratories on campus. At the end of the program, which usually runs from late June to early August, you present your project to a formal gathering of faculty, staff, and fellow SSTP participants. Throughout the program you also take part in various seminars on career choices and the scientific profession, and a variety of recreational activities designed especially for SSTP participants. Students live in University of Iowa dormitories and use many of the facilities on campus. The admissions process is highly competitive and is based on an essay, transcript, and recommendations. Those who complete the program have the option of receiving college credit from the University of Iowa. Applications are due in March, and applicants will be notified of the decisions by mid May. Tuition fees, room, and board generally total around $2,360; spending money and transportation to and from the university are not included. Financial aid is available. For an application form, financial aid information, and to discuss possible research projects, contact the Secondary Student Training Program.

Rising high school freshmen and sophomores who are interested in biology can participate in the Life Science Summer Program. The program, which is sponsored by The Center for Diversity & Enrichment (CDE), is held for two weeks each July. Applicants must demonstrate an aptitude for and interest in biology. In the program, you will "participate in hands-on laboratory training and classroom instruction covering a wide range of topics in the area of developmental biology." Participants live on campus in air-conditioned residence halls. The cost for the program is $25 plus transportation costs to and from the university. Contact the CDE for more information about the program.

Secondary Student Training Program
Attn: Will Swain
University of Iowa
E203 Seashore Hall
Iowa City, IA 52242
319-335-3876
william-swain@uiowa.edu
http://www.continuetolearn.uiowa.edu/SSTP

Life Science Summer Program
University of Iowa
The Center for Diversity & Enrichment
24 Phillips Hall

Iowa City, IA 52242
319-335-3555
cde@uiowa.edu
http://cde.uiowa.edu/index.php/
   life-science-summer-program.html

Sierra Student Coalition
**College Courses/Summer Study/
Employment and Internship
Opportunities/Membership**

The Sierra Student Coalition (SSC) was founded by a high school student in 1991 as the student-run arm of the Sierra Club, America's oldest and largest environmental organization. Those between the ages of 14 and 30 are welcome to join the SSC as individuals or as part of a group (such as an ecology club or scouting troop). Student dues are $25 a year. The SSC develops grassroots campaigns on environmental issues, working largely through a network of activists and coordinators who organize campaigns at all levels. As a member, you receive an e-newsletter full of action opportunities, organizing advice, and articles on student activism. Each semester, the SSC runs major national campaigns and local projects that you can work on or even lead. The SSC is also a great resource if you're already part of an existing club. The e-newsletter should give you great ideas and boost your enthusiasm for ongoing projects. Members can also link up with the Sierra Club's speakers and get help in capturing media attention for local campaigns.

All SSC members entering the ninth through 12th grades may take part in its High School Environmental Leadership Training Program. The program is held in several locations throughout the United States each summer. Each session runs for a week, during which experienced student activists help you learn how and when to take action and how to recruit others to support your cause. Each session includes seminars on specific topics such as Effective Public Speaking, Creative Fund-Raising, and How to Make a Group More Effective. Because both sessions of the Leadership Training Program are held in rustic settings with woodsy or rural surroundings, a good deal of time is also devoted to the exploration and appreciation of the natural world. Room and board, entertainment expenses, and local transportation to and from the site are all included in the program fee, which ranges from $150 to $200. Scholarships are available for those who otherwise could not attend due to financial limitations. Applications are accepted on a rolling basis, but because space is limited you are encouraged to apply earlier. You may apply to both sessions to increase your chances of securing a place, but you may attend only one. The SSC also offers a variety of internships. For further information, contact the SSC.

Sierra Student Coalition
600 14th Street, NW, Suite 750
Washington, DC 20005-2088
888-JOIN-SSC
info@ssc.org
http://www.ssc.org

Student Conservation Association National Crew/Community Programs
Field Experience/Volunteer Programs

Students between the ages of 15 and 19 can participate in summer trail crew opportunities at state and national parks throughout the United States. You will be responsible for building hiking trails, protecting threatened ecosystems, and performing a variety of other tasks. Crew assignments last anywhere from 15 to 35 days. Crew members work about eight hours a day and sleep outdoors in tents. Past crew members have worked in natural areas ranging from Denali National Park, to Indiana Dunes National Lakeshore, to Great Sand Dunes National Monument and Preserve. Other than a $25 application fee, there is no charge for this exciting program.

If you are interested in conservation, making new friends, and live in Baltimore, Maryland; the San Francisco Bay Area; Boston, Massachusetts; Dallas, Texas; Houston, Texas; Jacksonville, Florida; Manchester, New Hampshire; Milwaukee, Wisconsin; Pittsburgh, Pennsylvania; Seattle, Washington; Stamford, Connecticut; or Washington, D.C., you can participate in one or more of the SCA's Community Programs. If you participate in the Conservation Leadership Corps, for example, you'll work every weekend during the school year to "build trails, restore river and lakefront environments, and conserve habitats; learn about your environment through field trips, weekend camping excursions; and give back to your community through service projects." If you join a Summer Commuter Crew, you'll "complete trail maintenance and site restoration projects in national, regional, and state parks; learn about your local environment through field trips; and plan and go on a recreational camping trip where you will learn outdoor skills,

and visit local parks." Community Programs last for six to seven weeks.

In addition to the aforementioned programs, the SCA also offers internships for students who are 18 and older.

Student Conservation Association

689 River Road
PO Box 550
Charlestown, NH 03603-0550
603-543-1700, ext. 496
admissions@thesca.org
http://www.thesca.org/
conservation_crews

Summer College Programs for High School Students at Cornell University

College Courses/Summer Study

Rising high school juniors and seniors can take two veterinary science-related programs: Veterinary Medicine: Fertilization and Veterinary Medicine: Raptors. The for-credit programs are run by the College of Veterinary Medicine. In these programs, students learn about the job responsibilities of veterinarians and learn about specialties and disciplines such as zoo animal medicine, marine mammal medicine, animal behavior, anatomy of domestic species, emergency medicine, and pathology. They also get "hands-on opportunities to work with live animals such as production animals (cows, sheep, or goats), athletes (horses), companion animals (dogs and cats), raptors, and everything in between." Students will interact closely with professors, veterinarians, and fellow students. You must bear in mind that these are regular undergraduate courses condensed into a very short time span, so they are especially challenging and demanding. Students can also explore veterinary science through a noncredit Career Explorations Program. Program participants live in residence halls on campus and get to take advantage of campus facilities. The cost for each three-week program is $5,310 (which includes room and board). Applications are due in early May, although Cornell advises that you submit them well in advance of the deadline; those applying for financial aid must submit their applications by April 1. Further information and details about the application procedure are available from the Summer College office.

Cornell University Summer College for High School Students

B20 Day Hall
Ithaca, NY 14853-2801
607-255-6203
http://www.sce.cornell.edu/sc

Summer Program in Marine Studies at the Acadia Institute of Oceanography

College Courses/Summer Study

The Acadia Institute of Oceanography, which has offered educational programming since 1975, offers residential marine science programs every summer. Introductory sessions (ages 10 to 12, $995, one week in length), intermediate sessions (ages 12 to 15, $2,100, two weeks in length), and advanced sessions (ages 15 to 19, $2,100, two weeks in length) are available. Participants at the intermediate level receive a solid natural his-

tory approach to oceanography, learning basic marine concepts and becoming acquainted with the methods and materials of laboratory research. Students in advanced sessions must have completed at least one year of high school biology or chemistry. These sessions are more analytical in nature, and students must prepare regular laboratory reports and analyses of their work. Sessions are primarily academic (although there is some recreation time each day), but no one is expected to have any previous training in oceanography. Students live at the Acadia Institute on Mount Desert Island in Seal Harbor, Maine. Transportation to and from the mainland, room, board, and virtually all other expenses are included in the tuition fee. Exemplary students who complete the advanced session may be eligible for a special winter course in marine science.

Additionally, the institute offers the Florida Career Seminar, which gives students age 14 and older the chance to interact with marine biologists at SeaWorld in Orlando, Homassasa Springs Wildlife Refuge, and the Everglades National Park. A nine-day program in tropical marine ecology for alumni of advanced sessions is also available in Belize.

Summer Program in Marine Studies

Acadia Institute of Oceanography
PO Box 8308
Ann Arbor, MI 48107-8308
800-375-0058
info@acadiainstitute.com
http://www.acadiainstitute.com

Summer Youth Explorations at Michigan Technological University
College Courses/Summer Study

Michigan Technological University (MTU) offers the Summer Youth Explorations program for students in grades six through 12. Participants attend one of five weeklong sessions, choosing either to commute or live on campus. Students undertake an Exploration in one of many career fields through laboratory work, field trips, and discussions with MTU faculty and other professionals. Past Explorations include Aquatic Ecology, Blacksmithing, Entrepreneurship: Start a Business While in High School, Field Geology, Genetic Engineering and Biotechnology, Wildlife Ecology, and Wolf Ecology. The cost of the Summer Youth Program is $650 for the residential option and $395 for commuters. Applications are accepted up to one week before the Exploration begins.

> **Summer Youth Explorations**
> Michigan Technological University
> Youth Programs Office,
>   Alumni House
> 1400 Townsend Drive
> Houghton, MI 49931-1295
> 906-487-2219
> http://youthprograms.mtu.edu/syp

U.S. Fish & Wildlife Service
Volunteer Programs

Volunteers of all ages are welcomed by the U.S. Fish & Wildlife Service. Volunteers may be tasked with conducting wildlife population surveys, leading tours, helping with laboratory work, banding ducks at a National Wildlife Refuge, restoring wildlife habitat, performing clerical tasks, and photographing natural and cultural resources. Contact the U.S. Fish &Wildlife Service for more information.

> **U.S. Fish & Wildlife Service**
> U.S. Department of the Interior
> Division of Human Resources
> 4401 North Fairfax Drive,
>   Mailstop: 2000
> Arlington, VA 22203-1610
> 800-344-9453
> http://www.fws.gov/volunteers and
> http://volunteer.gov/gov

The Wildlife Society
Membership

The society offers membership to anyone who is interested in wildlife conservation and management. Members receive *The Wildlifer* newsletter and *The Wildlife Professional* magazine. The cost of membership is $69 a year. Membership ($35) is also available for college students. Contact the society for more information.

> **The Wildlife Society**
> 5410 Grosvenor Lane, Suite 200
> Bethesda, MD 20814-2144
> 301-897-9770
> tws@wildlife.org
> http://www.wildlife.org

Yosemite Institute
Camps/Field Experience/College Courses/Summer Study

The Yosemite Institute, established in 1971, works in cooperation with the

National Park Service to offer several programs for young people. Overnight Wilderness Backpacking Trips are one- to three-night camping adventures that encourage young people to "appropriately challenge themselves while exploring the wilderness and practicing Leave No Trace ethics." Led by professional naturalist guides, you explore Yosemite's high peaks, deep canyons, alpine lakes, and other features rarely seen by other visitors. You learn about the area's abundant wildlife and unique cultural and natural history while hiking four to six miles per day at elevations of 6,000 to 10,000 feet. Only 12 participants are accepted for each Overnight Wilderness Backpacking Trip. The program fee includes meals and group overnight gear (tents, cooking pots, etc.). You must provide your own personal gear, however, including a sleeping bag, water bottle, and utensils.

Teens who participate in the institute's two-week Field Research Course can earn college credit by creating their own ecology research project. You will learn "wilderness survival and backpacking skills; Sierra Nevada natural history and ecology; how to record field observations and identify patterns; how to generate answerable questions and hypotheses; how to collect data that will answer your question; and how to analyze and present your data to other scientists." To participate, you must be at least 16 years old and have completed at least one year of high school biology. The cost of the program is $1,900 for California residents and $2,400 for out-of-state participants. Participants will receive three college credits when they complete the program.

Additionally, young women between the ages of 15 and 18 can participate in the Armstrong Scholars Program, which "seeks to inspire young women to reach their highest potential and develop a stronger sense of self and community and a stronger connection to nature." The nine-day program costs $150 (the remaining costs are covered by a scholarship).

The Yosemite Institute also offers environmental workshops for teachers, and various programs throughout the year. Contact the institute for further information and for details on available scholarship funds.

Yosemite Backcountry Adventure

Yosemite Institute
PO Box 487
Yosemite, CA 95389-0487
209-379-9511
http://www.yni.org/yi

Zoological Association of America
Membership

The association "promotes conservation, preservation, and propagation of animals in both private and public domains." It offers a membership category for those who support its goals. The membership fee is $40. Members receive access to the members-only section of the association's Web site.

Zoological Association of America

PO Box 511275
Punta Gorda, FL 33951-1275
813-449-4356
info@zaa.org
http://www.zaa.org

Read a Book

When it comes to finding out about animals, don't overlook a book. (You're reading one now, after all.) What follows is a short, annotated list of books and periodicals related to animal careers. The books range from personal accounts and biographies of the greats to career-oriented publications. Don't be afraid to check out the professional journals, either. The technical stuff may be way above your head right now, but if you take the time to become familiar with one or two, you're bound to pick up some of what is important to professionals, not to mention begin to feel like a part of their world, which is what you're interested in, right?

We've tried to include recent materials as well as old favorites. Always check for the most recent editions, and, if you find an author you like, ask your librarian to help you find more. Keep reading good books!

❏ BOOKS

Barr, Nevada. *Endangered Species.* Reprint ed. New York: Berkley Books, 2008. One in a series of ecological mysteries featuring Anna Pigeon, park ranger. In the Cumberland Island National Seashore in Georgia, in a world of loggerhead turtles and wild ponies, Anna finds herself embroiled in a plot involving espionage, airplane crashes, eccentric islanders, and many twists and turns of plot before she can unravel the mystery.

Brazaitis, Peter. *You Belong in a Zoo!: Tales from a Lifetime Spent with Cobras, Crocs, and Other Extraordinary Creatures.* New York: Villard, 2004. A funny and engaging look back at a long career in zoos from the former superintendent of reptiles at the Bronx Zoo and curator of the Central Park Zoo.

DeGalan, Julie. *Great Jobs for Environmental Studies Majors.* 2d ed. New York: McGraw-Hill, 2008. This book will help environmental science majors develop winning job-search strategies and explore career options in the field.

Fisher, Lester E. *Dr. Fisher's Life on the Ark: Green Alligators, Bushman, and Other "Hare-Raising" Tales from America's Most Popular Zoo and Around the World.* Ashland, Ohio: Racom Communications, 2004. Fascinating memoir from the former director of Chicago's Lincoln Park Zoo.

Goodall, Jane. *My Life with the Chimpanzees.* Rev. ed. New York: Aladdin, 1996. The world-famous conservationist and scientist details her decades studying and protecting chimpanzees in Africa.

Hawthorne, Mark. *Striking at the Roots: A Practical Guide to Animal Activism.* Ropley, U.K.: O Books, 2008. This primer for animal activists provides advice on becoming an effective advocate for animals and features interviews with activists from around the world.

Hayhurst, Chris. *Cool Careers Without College for Animal Lovers.* New York: Rosen Publishing Group, 2002. Provides information on 12 careers that do not require a college degree, including assistance-dog trainer, wildlife control and relocation specialist, wrangler, animal photographer, and pet groomer. Information is provided on job duties, a typical day on the job, education and training, and employment outlook.

Heitzman, Ray. *Opportunities in Marine Science and Maritime Careers.* Rev. ed. New York: McGraw-Hill, 2006. This book provides an overview of educational requirements, earnings, and career options for a variety of marine science and maritime careers.

Herriot, James. *Every Living Thing.* London, U.K.: Pan Macmillan, 2006. A veterinarian in rural Yorkshire, England, after World War II discusses the engaging people and animals he meets during his career.

Heyerdahl, Thor. *Green Was the Earth on the Seventh Day.* New York: Random House, 1996. Warm, spirited, and amusing memoir of Heyerdahl's youth, setting out with his new wife to discover the natural and unspoiled world of the South Pacific. This was the first of many journeys and expeditions that would lead to his distinguished career as a naturalist and adventurer.

Hollow, Michele C., and William P. Rives. *The Everything Guide to Working with Animals: From Dog Groomer to Wildlife Rescuer—Tons of Great Jobs for Animal Lovers.* Cincinnati, Ohio: Adams Media Corporation, 2009. Provides an overview of careers for people who love and care about animals, including animal acupuncturist, wildlife rehabilitator, veterinarian, zoo designer, veterinary technician, animal trainer for the entertainment industry, beekeeper, and guide dog trainer.

Hosey, Geoff, Vicky Melfi, and Sheila Pankhurst. *Zoo Animals: Behaviour, Management and Welfare.* New York: Oxford University Press, 2009. This textbook provides a comprehensive overview of the science and management of zoos and aquariums.

Hunter, Malcolm L., David Lindenmayer, and Aram Calhoun. *Saving the Earth as a Career: Advice on Becoming a Conservation Professional.* Hoboken, N.J.: Wiley-Blackwell, 2007. Professionals provide advice on choosing and landing a career in conservation biology.

Irwin, Terri. *Steve & Me.* New York: Simon Spotlight Entertainment, 2008. The wife of much-beloved naturalist Steve Irwin, better known as The Crocodile Hunter, recalls his life and career.

Kaplan, Eugene H. *Sensuous Seas: Tales of a Marine Biologist.* Princeton, N.J.: Princeton University Press, 2006. These wonderful essays by a Hofstra University educator serve as an excellent introduction to the beauty, mysteries, and science of the sea.

Klass, David. *California Blue.* New York: Scholastic Paperbacks, 1996. When 17-year-old John Rodgers discovers a new subspecies of butterfly that may necessitate closing the lumber mill where his dying father works, he and his father find themselves on opposite sides of the environmental conflict. A gripping novel that brings to life the heated emotions on both sides of an environmental issue.

Lee, Mary Price. *Opportunities in Animal and Pet Careers.* 2d ed. New York: McGraw-Hill, 2008. Features information on career options, job duties, educational requirements, earnings, and more.

Leigh, Diane, and Marilee Geyer. *One at a Time: A Week in an American Animal Shelter.* 3d ed. Santa Cruz, Calif.: No Voice Unheard, 2005. This moving, thought-provoking book tells the story of 75 animals that passed through an animal shelter in Northern California in one week.

Lopez, Barry. *Arctic Dreams.* New York: Vintage Books, 2001. The renowned nature writer describes the flora and fauna of the Canadian Arctic, including polar bears, beluga whales, musk oxen, narwhals, and caribou. Winner of the National Book Award.

Lowman, Margaret D., Edward Burgess, and James Burgess. *It's A Jungle Up There: More Tales from the Treetops.* New Haven, Conn.: Yale University Press, 2008. A rainforest biologist, nicknamed "Canopy Meg" because she often climbs to the top of the rainforest to conduct research, details the rewards of working in rainforests in Peru, India, and Samoa alongside her sons. (Note: For more information on Canopy Meg, visit http://www.canopymeg.com.)

Mackay, Richard. *The Atlas of Endangered Species.* Berkeley, Calif.: University of California Press, 2008. This illustrated guide to the world's endangered species provides an overview of the major threats to biodiversity (loss of habitat, war, hunting, global warming) and the steps conservation scientists are taking to slow the destruction of wildlife.

Mares, Michael A. *A Desert Calling: Life in a Forbidding Landscape.* Cambridge, Mass.: Harvard University Press, 2002. A zoologist offers fascinating stories of his adventures studying the amazing creatures of the deserts of the world. (Note: See the profile of Mr. Mares in the Zoologists article for more information on his work and career.)

McBride, Douglas F., and Miriam and Harvey Austrin. *Learning Veterinary Terminology.* 2d ed. St. Louis: Mosby, 2001. This student workbook features a listing of terms for veterinary procedures and specialties, anatomical drawings, lists of commonly used abbreviations, and answers to frequently asked questions.

McGavin, George C. *Endangered: Wildlife on the Brink of Extinction.* Richmond Hill, O.N.: Firefly Books, 2006. Provides an overview of endangered species, why they are at risk, and what we can do to save them. Includes more than 400 photographs.

Miller, Louise. *Careers for Animal Lovers and Other Zoological Types.* 3d ed. New York: McGraw-Hill, 2007. Provides an overview of career options, including animal trainer, zoo curator, pet sitter, animal attendant, ornithologist, veterinarian, aquarist, and animal transporter.

Moran, Patti J. *Pet Sitting for Profit.* 3d ed. Indianapolis, Ind.: Howell Book House, 2006. This key resource for pet sitters provides information on starting and running a business, attracting clients, customer service, animal management, and other topics.

Nigro, Joseph. *101 Best Businesses for Pet Lovers.* Naperville, Ill.: Sphinx Publishing, 2007. Provides comprehensive information on a diverse range of careers, such as dog-fashions designer, gourmet treat maker, dog walker, pet groomer, pet-party organizer, pet-grief counselor, and veterinary technician.

Nyhuis, Allen W., and Jon Wassner. *America's Best Zoos: A Travel Guide for Fans & Families.* Branford, Conn.: The Intrepid Traveler, 2008. Provides detailed overviews of the best 97 zoos in the United States, as well as details on why zoos play such an important role in wildlife conservation.

Poulsen, Else, and Stephen Herrero. *Smiling Bears: A Zookeeper Explores the Behaviour and Emotional Life of Bears.* Vancouver, B.C., Canada: Greystone Books, 2009. A veteran zoo professional and bear management consultant takes an in-depth look at the lives of bears.

Quammen, David. *Wild Thoughts from Wild Places.* New York: Scribner, 1999. Fascinating, and often funny, essays about the natural world.

Ritter, Christie. *Animal Rights.* Edina, Minn.: Abdo Publishing Company, 2008. Provides an easy-to-understand overview of animal rights topics.

Robinson, Phillip T. *Life at the Zoo: Behind the Scenes with the Animal Doctors.* New York: Columbia University Press, 2007. The former director of veterinary services at the San Diego Zoo takes readers inside the world of zoos—from the design of exhibits, to the care of animals, to conservation issues.

Samansky, Terry S. *Starting Your Career as a Marine Mammal Trainer.* 2d ed. Napa, Calif.: Dolphintrainer.com, 2002. Covers typical job duties, educational and training requirements, job-search techniques, and more.

Schaller, George B. *A Naturalist and Other Beasts: Tales from a Life in the Field.* San Francisco: Sierra Club Books, 2007. Noted naturalist Schaller presents short essays on his adventures and discoveries during more than 50 years studying wildlife.

Schueler, Don. *A Handmade Wilderness.* Boston, Mass.: Mariner Books, 1997. Suspenseful, funny, and deeply moving account of two men, one white and one black, who in 1968 purchased 80 acres in Mississippi to bring back the native plant and animal life, creating a wilderness area that contained every ecosystem in the region.

Shenk, Ellen. *Careers with Animals: Exploring Occupations Involving Dogs, Horses, Cats, Birds, Wildlife, and Exotics.* Mechanicsburg, Pa.: Stackpole Books, 2005. Includes profiles of workers in the field and information on job duties, educational requirements, earnings, and job outlooks for a wealth of animal careers, including cat breeder, veterinarian, zookeeper, dog show judge, and animal chiropractor.

Spelman, Lucy H., and Ted Y. Mashima. *The Rhino with Glue-On Shoes and Other Surprising True Stories of Zoo Vets and their Patients.* New York: Delacorte Press, 2008. This book takes the reader inside the wild world of zoo veterinary medicine via essays from 28 wildlife veterinarians.

Stephens, Lester D., and Dale R. Calder. *Seafaring Scientist: Alfred Goldsborough Mayor, Pioneer in Marine Biology.* Columbia, S.C.: University of South Carolina Press, 2006. This biography details the fascinating life of the Harvard-trained scientist who founded the first tropical marine biology laboratory in the Western hemisphere.

Stewart, Liz. *Vault Career Guide to Veterinary and Animal Careers.* New York: Vault Inc., 2008. Provides a comprehensive overview of career opportunities in the field.

Sutherland, Amy. *Kicked, Bitten, and Scratched: Life and Lessons at the World's Premier School for Exotic Animal Trainers.* New York: Viking Adult, 2006. The author chronicles the year she spent working with educators and animal trainers at the Exotic Animal Training and Management Program at Moorpark College, the only program in the United States that teaches people how to train baboons, tortoises, camels, cougars, wolves, snakes, rats, and other exotic animals.

Trout, Nick. *Tell Me Where It Hurts: A Day of Humor, Healing and Hope in My Life as an Animal Surgeon.* New York: Broadway Books, 2009. A staff surgeon at a veterinary medical center provides a fascinating look at the rewards and challenges he has faced on the job.

University of California Press. *The Atlas of Endangered Species.* Berkeley, Calif.: University of California Press, 2008. This book uses photographs, maps, graphics, and text to spotlight the severe threat that many of our world's plants and animals face as a result of pollution, deforestation, development, hunting, and other factors.

Van Tuyl, Christine. *Zoos and Animal Welfare.* Farmington Hills, Mich.: Greenhaven Press, 2007. Covers major animal rights issues at zoos.

Wells, Jeff. *All My Patients Have Tales: Favorite Stories from a Vet's Practice.* New York: St. Martin's Press, 2009. A veterinarian details his experiences as a veterinary student and young practitioner.

Wilde, Nicole. *So You Want to Be a Dog Trainer.* 2d ed. Santa Clarita, Calif.: Phantom Publishing, 2006. Details the ins and outs of entering this rewarding career.

❏ PERIODICALS

All Animals. Published quarterly by the Humane Society of the United States (2100 L Street, NW, Washington, DC 20037-1525, 202-452-1100, http://www.hsus.org). This attractive magazine is available to members of the society and provides information on animal safety, animal activism, and society activities, as well as answers to frequently asked pet care questions and profiles of celebrity pet owners.

Animal Keepers' Forum. Published monthly by the American Association of Zoo Keepers (3601 29th Street, SW, Suite 133, Topeka, KS 66614-2054, 785-273-9149, http://www.aazk.org/animalKeepersForum), this resource offers useful articles about professional issues, association news, conservation/legislative updates, and book reviews.

Animal Sheltering. Published bimonthly by the Humane Society of the United States (2100 L Street, NW, Washington, DC 20037-1525, 202-452-1100), this magazine provides useful articles for shelter professionals. Visit http://www.animalsheltering.org/publications/magazine to read sample articles.

Association of Pet Dog Trainers Chronicle of the Dog. Published six times annually by the Association of Pet Dog Trainers (150 Executive Center Drive, Box 35, Greenville, SC 29615-4505, 800-738-3647) for members of the association. It features articles about pet dog training techniques. Visit http://www.apdt.com/po/chronicle to read a sample issue.

Audubon. Published bimonthly by the National Audubon Society (225 Varick Street, 7th Floor, New York, NY 10014-4396, 212-979-3000). This attractive magazine is available to members of the society, which seeks to "conserve and restore natural ecosystems." Visit http://audubonmagazine.org to read sample articles.

CONNECT. Published monthly by the Association of Zoos and Aquariums (8403 Colesville Road, Suite 710, Silver Spring, MD 20910-3314, 301-562-0777). This publication for association members features articles about new exhibits, conservation developments, and other topics. Recent articles include "Latino Outreach at The Phoenix Zoo," "Saving the Critically Endangered Mississippi Gopher Frog," "Not a Laughing Matter: Conservation Effects of Media Portrayals," and "Significant Efforts in Conservation Exhibits." Visit http://www.aza.org/AZAPublications to read sample articles.

Earthwatch Journal. Member publication of the Earthwatch Institute (Three Clock Tower Place, Suite 100, Box 75, Maynard, MA 01754-2549, 800-776-0188, info@earthwatch.org, http://www.earthwatch.org/newsandevents/publications). Topics discussed range from acid rain to endangered species.

Endangered Species Bulletin. Published by the U.S. Fish & Wildlife Service (4401 North Fairfax Drive, Mailstop: 2000, Arlington, VA 22203-1610, 703-358-1735, esb@fws.gov). *Endangered Species Bulletin* is published online three times annually; a highlights edition is also published. It provides fascinating stories about endangered species and efforts to save them. Recent stories include "Chiricahua Leopard Frog Inches Toward Recovery," "Jump Starting a Rabbit's Recovery," and "Fisheries and Habitat Conservation." Issues are available for free at http://www.fws.gov/endangered/bulletin.html.

Environmental Career Opportunities. Published bimonthly by Environmental Career Opportunities Inc. (700 Graves

Street, Charlottesville, VA 22902-5722, 866-750-9777, ecosubscriptions@mind-spring.com, http://ecojobs.com). This newsletter provides job listings in a variety of environmental fields, including environmental science and engineering, renewable energy, law, and natural resources and conservation.

Friends of the Earth Newsmagazine. Quarterly resource from Friends of the Earth (1717 Massachusetts Avenue, Suite 600, Washington, DC 20036-2008, 202-783-7400), an organization that focus on environmental justice and activism. Issues cover organization events, environmental hot topics, and leaders in the field. Visit http://www.foe.org to read a sample issue.

Groomer to Groomer. Published nine times annually by Barkleigh Productions Inc. (970 West Trindle Road, Mechanicsburg, PA 17055-4071, 717-691-3388, info@barkleigh.com, https://www.barkleigh.com/gtg.html), this magazine provides tips and advice for pet groomers. Visit http://www.groomertogroomer.com to read a sample issue. Print and online editions are available.

Grooming Business. Published monthly by Macfadden Communications Group (333 Seventh Avenue, 11th Floor, New York, NY 10001-5004, 847-763-8107). This professional resource for pet groomers covers a wide variety of topics in the field and features product reviews and editorial commentary. Recent articles include "Grooming Goes Green," "Breaking Into Show Grooming," and "Groomers in Cyberspace." Visit http://www.groomingbusiness.com to read sample articles.

Journal of the American Veterinary Medical Association. Published 24 times annually by the American Veterinary Medical Association (1931 North Meacham Road, Suite 100, Schaumburg, IL 60173-4360, 847-925-8070). This resource for veterinarians and other veterinary professionals provides peer-reviewed articles, editorials, and association news. Visit http://www.avma.org/onlnews to read sample articles.

Journal of Zoo & Wildlife Medicine. Published quarterly by the American Association of Zoo Veterinarians (581705 White Oak Road, Yulee, FL 32097-2169, 904-225-3275, http://www.aazv.org). The journal covers cutting-edge topics in zoo and wildlife veterinary medicine.

Limnology and Oceanography. Published bimonthly by the American Society of Limnology and Oceanography (5400 Bosque Boulevard, Suite 680, Waco, TX 76710-4446, 800-929-2756, business@aslo.org, http://www.aslo.org/publications.html). This professional journal features original articles about limnology and oceanography and seeks to promote an understanding of aquatic ecosystems.

The National Association of Veterinary Technicians in America Journal. Published quarterly by the National Association of Veterinary Technicians in America (50 South Pickett Street, Suite 110, Alexandria, VA 22304-7206, 703-740-8737, http://www.navta.net), this publication is a professional practice resource for association members. It features articles on association news, career planning and management, and educational opportunities.

National Geographic. Published monthly by the National Geographic Society (PO Box 63002, Tampa, FL 33663-3002, 800-647-5463), this attractive and informative magazine provides a wealth of stories and features about environmental issues, plants and animals, and historical and cultural topics. Visit http://www.nationalgeographic.com to read sample articles.

National Parks. Published quarterly by the National Parks Conservation Association (1300 19th Street, NW, Suite 300, Washington, DC 20036-1628, http://www.npca.org). This attractive publication for the general public includes information about national parks and reserves in the United States and the conservation of natural resources. Visit http://www.npca.org/magazine to read sample articles.

National Wildlife. Published six times annually by the National Wildlife Federation (11100 Wildlife Center Drive, Reston, VA 2019-5361, 800-822-9919). A popular magazine devoted to wildlife conservation issues. Visit http://www.nwf.org/nationalwildlife to read sample articles.

Nature Conservancy. Quarterly publication of The Nature Conservancy (4245 North Fairfax Drive, Suite 100, Arlington, VA 22203-1606, 800-628-6860), a "conservation organization working around the world to protect ecologically important lands and waters for nature and people." Visit http://www.nature.org/magazine to read sample articles.

Oceanography. Published four times annually by The Oceanography Society (PO Box 1931, Rockville, MD 20849-1931, 301-251-7708, magazine@tos.org, http://www.tos.org/oceanography). Discusses current issues involving ocean science worldwide.

Off Lead & Animal Behavior. Published quarterly by Barkleigh Productions Inc. (970 West Trindle Road, Mechanicsburg, PA 17055-4071, 717-691-3388, info@barkleigh.com), this magazine is a professional resource for dog trainers, instructors, exhibitors, behavior therapists, groomers, kennel operators, and other pet care workers. Recent articles include "Hot Topic: Choke Chains—A Look at the Pros and Cons," "Simple Skills for Successful Training," "An Interview with Two Influential Trainers," and "Inside the Mind of an Off Lead Dog." Visit http://www.off-lead.com to read a sample issue.

Pet Age. Published monthly by H. H. Backer Associates Inc. (18 South Michigan Avenue, Suite 1100, Chicago, IL 60603-3233, 312-578-1818, petage@hhbacker.com), this magazine offers information for pet store owners and suppliers. Recent articles include "Tracking Your Store's 'Vital Signs,'" "Catering to Upmarket Customers," and "National Python Ban Proposed." Visit http://www.petage.com to read sample articles.

Pet Business. Published monthly by Macfadden Communications Group (333

Seventh Avenue, 11th Floor, New York, NY 10001-5004), this magazine for pet retailers provides articles on industry trends, advice on operating a business, and profiles of pet retail store owners. Recent articles include "Dealing with 'Adolescent' Parrots," "Trends in Small Animal Nutrition," "Battling Parasites," "Cage Cleaning 101," and "The Dirty Truth About Turtles." Visit http://www.petbusiness.com to read sample articles.

The Rural Vet. Published quarterly by the Academy of Rural Veterinarians (90 State Street, Suite 1009, Albany, NY 12207-1710, 877-362-1150), this newsletter offers updates about academy activities and practice issues. Recent articles included "Rural Vet Reflects on Applying to Vet School" and "Rural Veterinary Practice in North America: Why Veterinarians Enter and Leave Rural Veterinary Practice." Visit http://www.ruralvets.com to read a sample issue.

Sierra. Published bimonthly by the Sierra Club (85 Second Street, 2nd Floor, San Francisco, CA 94105-3456, 415-977-5500, sierra.magazine@sierraclub.org). Fascinating consumer publication that focuses on environmental protection and conservation of natural resources. Visit http://www.sierraclub.org/sierra to read sample articles.

Veterinary Technician. Published 12 times annually by Veterinary Learning Systems (780 Township Line Road, Yardley, PA 19067-4200, 800-426-9119, info@vetlearn.com, http://www.vetlearn.com). This peer-reviewed resource for veterinary technicians, practice managers, and veterinary assistants features current clinical information, case studies, and practice management information.

Whalewatcher. Published by the American Cetacean Society (PO Box 1391, San Pedro, CA 90733-1391, http://www.acsonline.org/publications/whalewatcher), this magazine is available to members of the society. This general-interest publication offers articles by marine scientists, book reviews, updates on society activities, human-interest stories, and information on world events.

The Wildlife Professional. Published quarterly by The Wildlife Society (5410 Grosvenor Lane, Suite 200, Bethesda, MD 20814-2144, 301-897-9770, http://joomla.wildlife.org). Provides information for professionals in wildlife management and conservation.

The WORLD of Professional Pet Sitting. Published bimonthly by Pet Sitters International (201 East King Street, King, NC 27021-9161, 336-983-9222, http://www.petsit.com), this magazine features articles about pet-care needs, animal health, marketing and managing a pet-sitting business, products, and employment trends.

Surf the Web

You must use the Internet to do research, to find out, to explore. The Internet is the closest you'll get to what's happening now all around the world. This chapter gets you started with an annotated list of Web sites related to animal careers. Try a few. Follow the links. Maybe even venture as far as asking questions in a chat room. The more you read about and interact with animal professionals, the better prepared you'll be when you're old enough to participate as a professional.

One caveat: You probably already know that URLs change all the time. If a Web address listed below is out of date, try searching on the site's name or other keywords. Chances are, if it's still out there, you'll find it. If it's not, maybe you'll find something better!

❏ THE LIST

Animal Corner
http://www.animalcorner.co.uk

Use this Web site as an online encyclopedia to learn more about animals. Information is provided on each animal's physical characteristics, habitat, behavior, and reproduction habits. A photograph of each animal is also provided. There is even a section devoted to endangered animals.

Classification of animals at this site is less than scientific; rather, they are separated into groupings such as farm animals, marine wildlife, reptiles, venomous animals, British wildlife, and world wildlife. One interesting section is the link to Biomes—check out this link to learn out more about the different ecosystems of the world, and where they are located.

Animal Diversity Web
http://animaldiversity.ummz.umich.edu

This Web site is actually an online encyclopedia of animal natural history, classification, distribution, and conservation biology that has been compiled by the University of Michigan. Browse by animal name or classification, and learn. Each page provides important information about the animals, as well as photographs and the occasional sound bite. Professional biologists prepare all information about the animal's phyla, class, and order. However, other sections of the site feature contributions from student users, including species accounts, photos, and audio.

Animal Fact Guide
http://www.animalfactguide.com

Did you know that puffins are called clowns of the sea? Koalas love to feast on eucalyptus leaves? Or that cabybaras eat their own droppings?! Log on to this Web site to learn other fun facts and trivia. The section Wildlife Blog is not a blog at all, but rather a collection of press releases, photos, and videos of animal news from around the world. This site is recommended for a younger audience or those who are looking for basic information on different animals.

Animal Planet
http://animal.discovery.com

There's a lot to discover on this Web site operated by Discovery Communications LLC, the owner of several educational cable channels. You can preview new cable shows, many of them with an animal or animal career interest, and play interactive games tied to the theme of the show. For the reality show *Groomer Has It*, for example, you can groom your own virtual pet, and see how your grooming stacks up against the pros!

Don't miss the link for R.O.A.R. (Reach Out. Act. Respond) designed specifically for young people. You can learn more about endangered animals of the world, get suggestions on how to be proactive about worldwide animal conservation, and obtain information on the steps you must take to adopt a pet.

British Broadcasting Corporation: Science & Nature
http://www.bbc.co.uk/nature

There's so much information presented at this Web site that it's hard to figure out where to begin! What about links to many of adventurer Steve Fry's travels to remote places in search of some pretty rare animals? Or perhaps you'd be interested in a news story and video on an African albino elephant? What about a 360-degree video giving you an idea of a deep-sea diving expedition? Our favorite link is the Last Chance To See Map. Simply click on symbols placed on a map of the world to search and learn more about animals on the verge of extinction.

CanopyMeg.com
http://www.canopymeg.com

Who is Canopy Meg, you ask? She's Dr. Meg Lowman, a pioneer of *canopy ecology*, the study of wildlife and plant life found within the layers of a group of mature tree crowns. Browse her Web site to get a glimpse of her many travels and studies—from the Amazon rain forest to the tropical ecosystems of Panama. One of the most interesting sections is Photos & Multimedia. Here you can really get a feel for Meg's work and how it has affected people around the world. You'll see pictures ranging from a treetop camp held in New York, to a photo and blog from a middle school student's history project on Canopy Meg.

Careers in Forestry & Natural Resources
http://www.forestrycareers.org

This site, which is sponsored by the National Science Foundation, provides a wealth of information about careers in the following subdisciplines in the field: Fish & Wildlife Management; Parks, Recreation, and Tourism; Management and Conservation; Policy and Planning; Forestry & Natural Resources Sciences; Environmental Science and Technology; Wood and Paper Science; and Genetics and Biotechnology.

Each section offers a list of possible careers, brief interviews with forestry and natural resources workers in the field, photographs of workers in the field, and links to other Web sites. There is also a useful Education section (which features information on schools that offer degrees in forestry or natural resources) and a Diversity section that encourages people of color to enter the field.

Cool Works.com
http://www.coolworks.com

Can you picture yourself saddling up burros at the Grand Canyon or working as a tour guide at Mount Rushmore this summer? Cool Works quickly links you up to a wealth of information about seasonal employment at dozens of national and state parks, preserves, monuments, and wilderness areas. There are also listings of jobs and volunteer opportunities at ski areas, private resorts, cruise ships, and summer camps. Most of the national and state jobs require that applicants be 18 years or older. Most national and state parks listed here have seasonal positions available in similar departments. Specific job descriptions can also be accessed by searching a pull-down menu of U.S. states and regions or international locations. While only some jobs allow you to apply directly online, many have downloadable application forms.

DolphinTrainer.com: A Career Guide to Marine Mammal Care and Training
http://www.dolphintrainer.com/career_guide.htm

Are you interested in training dolphins? Sea lions? Or perhaps a "killer whale?" If so, this is a good place to begin. Created by marine mammal professionals, this Web site contains basic information on different careers and what it takes to get to the top. A cool feature is the photo and video link, which features video of a dolphin birth and other animal wonders.

EE-Link: Environmental Education on the Internet
http://eelink.net/pages/EE-Link+ Introduction

Sponsored by the North American Association for Environmental Education, EE-Link aims to provide online educational resources for students and teachers interested in the environment. At this site, you'll find more than 5,800 links to environmental organizations, foundations, schools, and current projects that are on the Internet. Search headings include Endangered Species, K–12 Students, EE Jobs, and Higher Ed.

The Encyclopedia of Earth
http://www.eoearth.org

The Encyclopedia of Earth is written by environmental scholars, professionals, educators, and experts. The articles, which are peer-reviewed, are written in nontechnical language for students and the general public. There are thousands of detailed entries on a variety of topics and well-known individuals in the field, including the Endangered Species Act, the Exxon Valdez oil spill, the Ocean Dumping Act, Rachel Carson, species diversity, and the Yapen rain forests. There are also news articles on the latest environmental developments and a forum where you can comment on issues ranging from man-made chemicals in drinking water to the ecological impacts of climate change.

Environmental Career Opportunities
http://ecojobs.com

This Web site lists environmental internships and careers in a wide range of fields, including natural resources and conservation, environmental science, advocacy, renewable energy, education, policy, and law. There is also information on environmental degree programs, such as the Environmental Studies Program at the University of Colorado at Boulder and the master's program in environmental sciences and policy at Johns Hopkins University. You can also sign up for an email listserv that will send you announcements of new job listings in selected environmental fields.

Environmental News Network
http://www.enn.com

The Environmental News Network publishes information from a variety of sources to "help people understand and communicate the environmental issues and solutions that face us and hopefully inspire them to get involved." This site is loaded with timely articles on environmental issues. Subject areas include wildlife, agriculture, ecosystems, energy, business, climate, pollution, green building, science/technology, and lifestyle. This is an excellent clearinghouse of environmental articles and a great place

to start learning more about environmental issues.

GradSchools.com
http://www.gradschools.com

This site, while somewhat rough around the edges, offers listings of graduate schools searchable by country. From the home page, use the drop-down menu to choose the concentration of your interest, such as Agricultural, Animal, and Food Science; Biological Science; or Earth Science. Listings include program info, degrees offered, school Web site, and email contact.

How Stuff Works
http://www.howstuffworks.com

If you spend a lot of time wondering how stuff you use or see every day actually works, then this site should be on your short list of Web sites to explore. It covers how "stuff," as varied and timely as tsunamis, identity theft, and satellite radio, works. Complex concepts are carefully broken down and examined, including photos and links to current and past news items about the subject. Topics of interest to those interested in animals include How Lion Taming Works, How Animal Camouflage Works, and more.

The Humane Society of the United States: A Closer Look at Wildlife
http://www.hsus.org/wildlife/a_closer_look_at_wildlife

Are you a little curious or perhaps spooked by some of the critters in your backyard? If so, check out this Web site—quick! This site gives a detailed overview of each animal, the problems they cause in peoples' backyards (and homes), and solutions to humanely solve these problems. Take the case of bats. The site says that if a bat gets in your house it's important to remain calm and keep all interior doors closed, but provide an exit for your unwanted friend. You may have to use leather gloves (cotton gloves won't protect you from the bat's teeth) to gently pick up the bat and release it outside. Each animal section also includes myths and facts regarding any potential health or environmental concerns.

The Humane Society of the United States: Animal Channel
http://video.hsus.org

These stories previously appeared on the Animal Channel as original film, documentaries, or commentaries, and are assembled together on the Humane Society's Web site. They tell sad, often horrific, stories of animal abuse and neglect, many of which occurred in the United States. Stories posted include mutilating show horses for a better perception of performance, lack of fur labeling in high-fashion clothing, and mistreatment of animals at some research laboratories. Not all stories tell of abuse; the site also features informative documentaries such as a film on a nightly assembly of thousands of crows en route to their winter roost.

Insectclopedia
http://www.insectclopedia.com

Insectclopedia is a portal to different links on insects. Links include an alphabetical database of insect species, entomological associations, and insect identification. Our vote for the strangest link, though rather entertaining, goes to the one for insect cuisine. Browse through bug-centered recipes, join a bug-eating association, or find your closest fluker farm.

The Jane Goodall Institute
http://www.janegoodall.org

Founded by the famed primatologist and ethnologist Jane Goodall, this Web site contains a wealth of information regarding chimpanzees, which happen to be Dr. Goodall's specialty. You can read about their physical characteristics, behaviors, and habitats. A career section is provided, but it offers little more than links to associations and homepages for information on a career as a primatologist.

A better choice would be the link to Roots and Shoots—a program run by the institute that offers information about how kids, their parents, and educators can learn about issues facing the environment and how they can help make positive changes in their community.

Minnesota Zoo
http://www.mnzoo.com

Visit this site to learn what it takes to keep one of the nation's busiest zoos in tiptop shape. You can "shadow" various staff members as they go through their daily routines—including zookeepers, animal health professionals, and animal managers. Behind-the-scenes workers—such as education and outreach workers and special events planners—are also profiled. Slide shows and video clips complete each career profile.

Don't leave the site without checking out the conservation link. Browse this section to learn more about the zoo's conservation agendas, such as its Home of the Tiger Species Survival Plan.

Monterey Bay Aquarium: Science Careers
http://www.montereybayaquarium. org/lc/kids_place/kidseq_careers.asp

This site provides an overview of some of the career specialties at the Monterey Bay Aquarium, including aquarist, education specialist, exhibits coordinator, exhibits designer, research biologist, and science writer. Each staff profile features details on job duties, education and training required, and the pros and cons of the job. There are also photographs of each worker, and some profiles even have audio clips.

National Oceanic and Atmospheric Administration
http://www.noaa.gov

The Web site of the National Oceanic and Atmospheric Administration is typical of most government-sponsored Web sites—it's a bit dry, with no fancy graphics or gimmicks. What it does deliver is good information on how to develop a career in the industry—including those in animal-related fields. Check out the Student Opportunities (http://www.oesd.noaa. gov/noaa_student_opps.html) section to find summer programs and paid internships designed for your age group. Some opportunities recently listed include apprenticeship programs at the Southeast Fisheries Science Center, onsite research positions supporting sustainable harvests, and high-tech internships designed for students with disabilities.

National Park Service: Nature and Science: Views of the National Parks
http://www.nature.nps.gov

Views of the National Parks is a multimedia program that "presents the natural, historical, and cultural wonders associated with national parks." Users can learn about parks in the system (such as the Badlands, Devil's Tower, and the Grand Canyon), listen to interviews about the parks and their features, and view photos of the parks.

Natural Resources Conservation Service: Backyard Conservation
http://www.nrcs.usda.gov/feature/ backyard

Soil and water conservation practices are key to the success of farms across the country. But did you know that you can conserve and protect natural resources in your own backyard? This Web site lists 10 things you can do in your backyard to protect the environment and make your backyard more beautiful. Topics include Backyard Pond, Backyard Wetland, Composting, Mulching, Nutrient Management, Pest Management, Terracing, Tree Planting, Water Conservation, and Wildlife Habitat.

Oakland Zoo: Animals
http://www.oaklandzoo.org/animals

There's more to this Web site than information about the Oakland Zoo and the animals within its facility (although you will find detailed information about birds, amphibians, arthropods, reptiles, and mammals, too). Browse the Conservation section to learn about how to participate in animal welfare programs throughout the world and help animals ranging from butterflies and hornbills to elephants and western pond turtles. Check out the Education section for unique opportunities to learn more about your favorite animals, including scout programs, a zoo-mobile, overnights at the facility, and a summer camp program.

Peterson's Summer Camps and Programs
http://www.petersons.com/summer op/code/ssector.asp

This Web site offers great information about academic and career-focused summer programs. Finding a camp that suits your interests is easy enough at this site; just search Peterson's database by activity (Academics, Arts, Sports, Wilderness/Outdoors, Special Interests), geographic region, category (Day Programs in the U.S., Residential Programs in the U.S., Travel in the U.S. and to Other Countries, Special Needs Accommodations), keyword, or alphabetically. By conducting a keyword search using the word "environment," you'll find a list of links to hundreds of programs. Click on a specific program or camp for a quick overview description. In some instances you'll get a more in-depth description, along with photographs, applications, and online brochures.

Public Broadcasting Service: American Field Guide
http://www.pbs.org/americanfield guide

This fascinating Web site features more than 1,400 videos in the following environmental categories: Animals, Ecosystems, Human History, Livelihoods, Earth & Space, Plants, Public Policy, and Recreation. For example, under Animals you can view videos of sandhill cranes in Nebraska, the Kemp's ridley sea turtle in Texas, and the training of search-and-rescue dogs in Maryland. This is an excellent place to learn more about animals and the environment.

Rainforest Action Network (RAN)
http://www.ran.org

The Rainforest Action Network has a Web site that you don't merely visit: You make a statement while you're there. This dynamic, colorful home page draws you in with its sense of urgency to tackle the network's signature issues: forests, global warming, human rights, energy, and sustainable economies. The Take Action section allows visitors to read about pressing environmental issues (such as protecting tropical ecosystems) and send an email to legislators right from the site, using RAN's sample letters or emails. The Our Campaigns section describes ongoing campaigns such as the Rainforest Agribusiness Campaign or the Old Growth Campaign. This is a great educational resource regarding the serious environmental challenges that we face. It will inspire you to get involved and do your part to save the earth and the plants and animals that live on it.

Sea Grant Marine Careers
http://www.marinecareers.net

Interested in a career as a marine biologist, oceanographer, or ocean engineer? If so, you've come to the right place. Sea Grant Marine Careers provides detailed information about careers, educational requirements, typical work settings, earnings, and much more. There are also profiles of workers in the field (such as marine biologists, marine biotechnologists, aquatic chemists, fisheries ecologists, baykeepers, and biological oceanographers), answers to frequently asked questions, and photographs of marine science professionals at work.

SeaWorld: Animals
http://www.seaworld.org

This Web site offers a wealth of information about SeaWorld facilities and programs. You'll find tons of information about marine animals—from mammals to cnidarians (jellyfish, sea anemones, and corals)—by reading the short informational Animal Bytes and checking out other sections of the site.

If you are interested in further exploration, you'll want to check out the link to educational programs and camps offered at SeaWorld facilities throughout the United States. One educational program, offered at Busch Gardens, involves work and training as an assistant zookeeper. Another program, at SeaWorld, is a training camp that allows students to get hands-on experience feeding, inter-acting, and caring for beluga whales or dolphins. Each program and camp is designed and closely supervised by trained professionals.

Shedd Aquarium
http://www.sheddaquarium.org

Do you want to visit Shedd Aquarium, but have no immediate plans to visit the city of Chicago? Don't worry—this Web site is the next best thing to actually being there! You can learn about the 1,500 species of animals housed at this award-winning aquarium—including beluga whales, penguins, sharks, river otters, and more. Information on each animal includes details on their appearance, behavior, and habitat, as well as photographs. You can also "tour" the aquarium via an online exploration of different exhibits such as the Oceanarium, Caribbean Reef, or the Waters of the World. You'll learn how each environment changes depending on the season, and how animals must adapt. Keep the audio of your computer on—the sounds of the surf will only add to your experience!

Don't forget to check out the Education section, which provides great ideas for activities tailored for family or school trips, as well as listings of available internships and summer programs.

U.S. Fish & Wildlife Service Students' Page
http://www.fws.gov/educators/students.html

This site provides links to information on a variety of environmental resources—from birds and fish, to habitat and endangered species, to plants and wildlife. There is also an FAQ section and links to the service's photo and video libraries.

Yahoo: Environment & Nature
http://dir.yahoo.com/Society_and_
Culture/Environment_and_Nature?sk
w=%22Environment%22

It might seem odd to include the popular search engine Yahoo among a list of environmental- and animal-oriented Web sites, but it won't seem so after you've visited it. If you're hungry for more after visiting the sites listed in this appendix, pull up a chair at Yahoo's feast. Yahoo has done a tremendous amount of legwork for you. For example, if you're interested in environmental organizations, then scan through the more than 4,000 sites currently included here. Water resources posts an impressive 654 sites, conservation has 276 entries, and global change yields

382 links. Even environmental crime offers 10 sites you probably wouldn't have known to look for otherwise.

ZooToo
http://www.zootoo.com

At first glance, zootoo.com may appear to be simply a social networking site for animal lovers where you can join pet owner groups, find pet-centric events in your neighborhood, or engage in pet wars (my cute pet photo vs. your cute pet photo).

But if you dig deeper there is a lot of information available, including answers to important questions about pet/animal topics ranging from grooming and breeding to behavior and training. There are also pet news stories and classified ads. This is a good place to get the lowdown on the world of pets and interact with others who share your interests.

Ask for Money

By the time most students get around to thinking about applying for scholarships, grants, and other financial aid, they have already extolled their personal, academic, and creative virtues to such lengths in essays and interviews for college applications that even their own grandmothers wouldn't recognize them. The thought of filling out yet another application fills students with dread. And why bother? Won't the same five or six kids who have been competing for academic honors for years walk away with all the really good scholarships?

The truth is that most of the scholarships available to high school and college students are being offered because an organization wants to promote interest in a particular field, encourage more students to become qualified to enter it, and finally, to help those students afford an education. Certainly, having a great grade point average is a valuable asset. More often than not, however, grade point averages aren't even mentioned; the focus is on the area of interest and what a student has done to distinguish himself or herself in that area. In fact, sometimes the only requirement is that the scholarship applicant must be studying in a particular area.

❑ GUIDELINES

When applying for scholarships there are a few simple guidelines that can help ease the process considerably.

Plan Ahead

The absolute worst thing you can do is wait until the last minute. For one thing, obtaining recommendations or other supporting data in time to meet an application deadline is incredibly difficult. For another, no one does his or her best thinking or writing under the gun. So get off to a good start by reviewing scholarship applications as early as possible—months, even a year, in advance. If the current scholarship information isn't available, ask for a copy of last year's version. Once you have the scholarship information or application in hand, give it a thorough read. Try to determine how your experience or situation best fits into the scholarship, or if it even fits at all. Don't waste your time applying for a scholarship in literature if you couldn't finish *Great Expectations*.

If possible, research the award or scholarship, including past recipients and, where applicable, the person in whose name the scholarship is offered. Often, scholarships are established to memorialize an individual who majored in zoology, animal science, or a related field, for example, but in other cases the scholarship is to memorialize the *work* of an individual. In those cases, try to get a feel for the spirit of the person's work. If you have any similar interests, experiences, or abilities, don't hesitate to mention them.

Talk to others who received the scholarship, or to students currently studying in the same area or field of interest in which the scholarship is offered, and try to gain insight into possible applications or work related to that field. When you're working on the essay asking why you want this scholarship, you'll have informed answers: "I would benefit from receiving this scholarship because studying zoology will help me become a better advocate for saving endangered species in the American Southwest."

Take your time writing the essays. Make sure that you are answering the question or questions on the application and not merely restating facts about yourself. Don't be afraid to get creative; try to imagine what you would think of if you had to sift through hundreds of applications: What would you want to know about the candidate? What would convince you that someone was deserving of the scholarship? Work through several drafts and have someone whose advice you respect—a parent, teacher, or guidance counselor—review the essay for grammar and content.

Finally, if you know in advance which scholarships you want to apply for, there might still be time to stack the deck in your favor by getting an internship, volunteering, or working part time. Bottom line: The more you know about a scholarship and the sooner you learn it, the better.

Follow Directions

Think of it this way: Many of the organizations that offer scholarships devote 99.9 percent of their time to something other than the scholarship for which you are applying. Don't make a nuisance of yourself

by pestering them for information. Simply follow the directions as they are presented to you. If the scholarship application specifies that you should write for further information, then write for it—don't call.

Pay close attention to whether you're applying for a grant, a loan, an award, a prize, or a scholarship. Often these words are used interchangeably, but just as often they have different meanings. A loan is financial aid that must be paid back. A grant is a type of financial aid that does not require repayment. An award or prize is usually given for something you have done: built a park or helped distribute meals to the elderly; or something you have created: a musical composition, a design, an essay, a short film, a screenplay, or an invention. On the other hand, a scholarship is frequently a renewable sum of money that is given to a person to help defray the costs of college. Scholarships are given to candidates who meet the necessary criteria based on essays, eligibility, grades, or sometimes all three. They do not have to be paid back.

Supply all the necessary documents, information, and fees, and make the deadlines. You won't win any scholarships by forgetting to include a recommendation from a teacher or failing to postmark the application by the deadline. Bottom line: Get it right the first time, on time.

Apply Early

Once you have the application in hand, don't dawdle. If you've requested it far enough in advance, there shouldn't be any reason for you not to turn it in well in advance of the deadline. You never know, if it comes down to two candidates, your timeliness just might be the deciding factor. Bottom line: Don't wait, don't hesitate.

Be Yourself

Don't make promises you can't keep. There are plenty of hefty scholarships available, but if they all require you to study something that you don't enjoy, you'll be miserable in college. And the side effects from switching majors after you've accepted a scholarship could be even worse. Bottom line: Be yourself.

Don't Limit Yourself

There are many sources for scholarships, beginning with your guidance counselor and ending with the Internet. All of the search engines have education categories. Start there and search by keywords, such as "financial aid," "scholarship," and "award." But don't be limited to the scholarships listed in these pages.

If you know of an organization related to or involved with the field of your choice, write a letter asking if they offer scholarships. If they don't offer scholarships, don't stop there. Write them another letter, or better yet, schedule a meeting with the executive director, education director, or someone in the public relations office and ask them if they would be willing to sponsor a scholarship for you. Of course, you'll need to prepare yourself well for such a meeting because you're selling a priceless commodity—yourself. Don't be shy, and be confident. Tell them all about yourself, what you want to study and why, and let them know what you would be willing to do in exchange—volunteer at their favorite charity, write up reports on your progress in school, or work part time during school breaks and full time during the summer.

Explain why you're a wise investment. Bottom line: The sky's the limit.

One More Thing

We have not listed financial aid that is awarded to veterinary students in this section. Why? Because this is a book about what you can do now to prepare for a career, and to earn a veterinary science degree, you first need to earn a bachelor's degree. Many aspiring veterinary science students pursue undergraduate majors in pre-veterinary science, biology, or other fields. Many colleges and universities offer financial aid for pre-veterinary students and those pursuing other majors; check with your college for details on available programs. Additionally, you will find many general scholarship Web sites below that will provide you with information on financial aid in a variety of fields, including the aforementioned majors. Use these to help you locate funding sources for your undergraduate education. And when you're ready to attend veterinary school, contact the American Veterinary Medical Association and other veterinary science organizations for information on financial aid for veterinary students.

❏ THE LIST

American Kennel Club

Attn: Juniors
8051 Arco Corporate Drive,
  Suite 100
Raleigh, NC 27617-3390
919-816-3514
http://www.akc.org/kids_juniors/
  scholarships.cfm

The club offers the Junior Showmanship Scholarship Program for high school students who are interested in breeding purebred dogs. Scholarships are awarded based on the applicant's financial need and academic achievement and potential. Applicants must submit a completed application (available at the club's Web site), academic transcripts, and complete a 250- to 500-word essay. Recent essay questions included "How will you assist the sport of purebred dogs in your community as a breeder/dog exhibitor when mandatory spay/neuter legislation is proposed?" and "What is your intended future involvement in purebred dogs as a breeder/club member?"

CollegeBoard: Scholarship Search
http://apps.collegeboard.com/
    cbsearch_ss/welcome.jsp

This testing service (PSAT, SAT, etc.) also offers a scholarship search engine at its Web site. It features scholarships worth a total of nearly $3 billion. You can search by specific major (such as agribusiness, agriculture, animal sciences, veterinary medicine, wildlife/fisheries, or zoology) and a variety of other criteria.

CollegeNET: MACH 25-
Breaking the Tuition Barrier
http://www.collegenet.com/mach25/
    app

CollegeNET features 600,000 scholarships worth more than $1.6 billion. You can search by keyword (such as "animal science" or "zoology") or by creating a personality profile of your interests.

FastWeb
http://fastweb.monster.com

FastWeb is one of the best-known scholarship search engines around. It features 1.3 million scholarships worth more than $3 billion. To use this resource, you will need to register (free).

Foundation for the Carolinas
Attn: Scholarships
217 South Tryon Street
Charlotte, NC 28202-3201
704-973-4537
tcapers@fftc.org
http://www.fftc.org

The foundation administers more than 105 scholarship programs that offer awards to high school seniors and undergraduate and graduate students who plan to or who are currently pursuing study in a variety of disciplines. Visit its Web site for a list of awards.

GuaranteedScholarships.com
http://www.guaranteed-scholarships
    .com

This Web site offers lists (by college) of scholarships, grants, and financial aid that "require no interview, essay, portfolio, audition, competition, or other secondary requirement."

Hawaii Community Foundation
1164 Bishop Street, Suite 800
Honolulu, HI 96813-2817
888-731-3863
info@hcf-hawaii.org
http://www.hawaiicommunity
    foundation.org/scholar/scholar.php

The foundation offers a variety of scholarships for high school seniors and college students who plan to or who are currently studying a variety of majors in college. Applicants must be residents of Hawaii, demonstrate financial need, and attend a two- or four-year college. Visit the foundation's Web site for more information and to apply online.

Hispanic College Fund
1301 K Street, NW, Suite 450-A West
Washington, DC 20005-3317
800-644-4223
hcf-info@hispanicfund.org
http://www.hispanicfund.org

The Hispanic College Fund (HCF), in collaboration with several major corporations, offers many scholarships for high school seniors and college students who plan to or who are currently attending college. Applicants must be Hispanic, live in the United States or Puerto Rico, and have a GPA of at least 3.0 on a 4.0 scale. Contact the HCF for more information.

Illinois Career Resource Network
http://www.ilworkinfo.com/icrn.htm

Created by the Illinois Department of Employment Security, this useful site offers a scholarship search engine, as well as detailed information on careers (including animal-related jobs). You can search for animal- and environment-oriented scholarships based on major (such as animal grooming, animal husbandry, pre-veterinary, animal training, animal physiology, animal biology, business, etc.), and other criteria. This site is available to everyone, not just Illinois residents; you can get a password by simply visiting the site. The Illinois Career Resource Network is just one example of the type of sites created by state departments of employment security (or departments of labor) to assist students with financial- and career-related issues. After checking out this site, visit your state's department of labor Web site to see what it offers.

Imagine America Foundation
1101 Connecticut Avenue, NW,
  Suite 901
Washington, DC 20036-4303
202-336-6800
http://www.imagine-america.org/
  scholarship/a-about-scholarship.asp

The Imagine America Foundation (formerly the Career College Foundation) is a nonprofit organization that helps students pay for college. It offers three $1,000 scholarships each year to high school students or recent graduates. Applicants must have a GPA of at least 2.5 on a 4.0 scale, have financial need, and demonstrate voluntary community service during their senior year. The scholarships can be used at more than 500 career colleges in the United States. These colleges offer a variety of fields of study, including biology, business administration, equestrian/equine studies, farm and ranch management, horseshoeing, pre-veterinary studies, and veterinary technology. Visit the foundation's Web site for more information.

Marine Technology Society
Student Scholarship
5565 Sterrett Place, Suite 108
Columbia, MD 21044-2606
410-884-5330
https://www.mtsociety.org/education/
  scholarships.aspx

The society offers approximately $59,000 in scholarship funds annually to high school, undergraduate, graduate, and two-year college students who are interested in pursuing careers in a marine science/engineering/technology-related field. Visit its Web site for detailed information on available scholarships.

National Dairy Shrine (NDS)
PO Box 1
Maribel, WI 54227-0001
920-863-6333
info@dairyshrine.org
http://www.dairyshrine.org

The NDS offers a variety of scholarships to high school juniors and seniors and college students who are interested in pursuing careers in animal science, dairy or production agriculture and science, agricultural economics, agricultural communications, agricultural education, general education, and food and nutrition. Application requirements and award amounts vary by scholarship. Contact the NDS for more information. The application process for all scholarships spans from March 1 to May 1.

National FFA Organization
Scholarship Office
6060 FFA Drive
PO Box 68960
Indianapolis, IN 46268-0960
317-802-6060
https://scholarshipapp.ffa.org/
OnlineApps/Welcome.aspx

National FFA Organization awards approximately $2 million in scholarships via its Collegiate Scholarship Program. Several scholarships are available. Applicants must be high school seniors or college students, members of the organization for some scholarships, and satisfy other requirements. Eligibility requirements and award amounts vary by scholarship. Contact the National FFA Organization for more information on the scholarships.

National 4-H Council
7100 Connecticut Avenue
Chevy Chase, MD 20815-4934
301-961-2800
info@fourhcouncil.edu
http://4-h.org

4-H Clubs teach young people about science, engineering, and technology; healthy living; and citizenship via clubs, camps, competitions, and other activities. It has 6 million members in the United States. 4-H offers financial aid to high school and college students through its chapters, which are located throughout the United States. Visit the 4-H national organization's Web site for information on a chapter near you and the scholarship programs it offers.

Sallie Mae
http://www.collegeanswer.com/
paying/scholarship_search/pay_
scholarship_search.jsp

This Web site offers a scholarship database of more than 3 million awards worth more than $16 billion. You must register (free) to use the database.

Scholarship America
One Scholarship Way
PO Box 297
Saint Peter, MN 56082-0297
800-537-4180
http://www.scholarshipamerica.org

This organization works through its local Dollars for Scholars chapters throughout the United States. In 2008, it awarded more than $219 million in scholarships to students. Visit Scholarship America's Web site for more information.

Scholarships.com
http://www.scholarships.com

Scholarships.com offers a free college scholarship and grant search engine (although you must register to use it) and financial aid information. Its database of awards features 2.7 million listings worth more than $19 billion in aid.

United Negro College Fund (UNCF)
8260 Willow Oaks Corporate Drive
PO Box 10444
Fairfax, VA 22031-8044
800-331-2244
http://www.uncf.org/forstudents/
  scholarship.asp

Visitors to the UNCF Web site can search for information on thousands of scholarships and grants, many of which are administered by the UNCF. Its search engine allows you to search by major (such as animal science, biology, ecology, environmental science, pre-vet, and science), state, scholarship title, grade level, and achievement score. High school seniors and undergraduate and graduate students are eligible.

U.S. Department of Agriculture (USDA)
1400 Independence Avenue, SW,
  Mail Stop 9478
Washington, DC 20250-0002
202-205-5692
1890init@usda.gov
http://www.ascr.usda.gov/
  1890programs.html

The USDA offers the 1890 National Scholars Program to students who are seeking a bachelor's degree at one of the 17 historically black land-grant institutions and Tuskegee University. Applicants must be entering their freshmen year of college, have a high school GPA of at least 3.0, demonstrate leadership and community service, and be U.S. citizens. They also must plan to study agriculture; agricultural business/management; agricultural economics; agricultural engineering/mechanics, agricultural production and technology; agronomy or crop science; animal sciences; botany; farm and range management; fish, game, or wildlife management; food sciences/technology; forestry and related sciences; home economics/nutrition/human development; horticulture; natural resources management; soil conservation/soil science; and other related disciplines (e.g., biological sciences, pre-veterinary medicine, computer science). Contact the USDA for information on application instructions and deadlines.

U.S. Department of Education
Federal Student Aid
800-433-3243
http://www.federalstudentaid.ed.gov
http://studentaid.ed.gov/students/publi
  cations/student_guide/index.html

The U.S. government provides a wealth of financial aid in the form of grants, loans, and work-study programs. Each year, it publishes *Funding Education Beyond High School*, a guide to these funds. Visit the Web sites above for detailed information on federal financial aid.

Look to the Pros

The following professional organizations offer a variety of materials—from career resources, to lists of accredited schools, to information on membership. Many publish journals and newsletters that you should become familiar with. Some also have annual conferences that you might be able to attend. (While you may not be able to attend a conference as a participant, it may be possible to "cover" one for your school or even your local paper, especially if your school has a related club.)

When contacting professional organizations, keep in mind that they all exist primarily to serve their members, be it through continuing education, professional licensure, political lobbying, or just keeping up with the profession. While many are strongly interested in promoting their profession and sharing information with the general public, these busy professional organizations do not exist solely to provide you with information. Whether you call or write, be courteous, brief, and to the point. Know what you need and ask for it. If the organization has a Web site, check it out first: What you're looking for may be available there for downloading, or you may find a list of prices or instructions, such as sending a self-addressed stamped envelope with your request. Finally, be aware that organizations, like people, move. To save time when writing, first confirm the address, preferably with a quick phone call to the organization itself: "Hello, I'm calling to confirm your address. . . ."

❏ THE SOURCES

Academy of Rural Veterinarians
90 State Street, Suite 1009
Albany, NY 12207-1710
877-362-1150
arv@caphill.com
http://www.ruralvets.com

This is a professional association for rural veterinarians. Visit its Web site for information on membership and externships for veterinary students, school listings, and *The Rural Vet*. Veterinary students can also post their resumes online.

Academy of Veterinary Emergency and Critical Care Technicians
6335 Camp Bullis Road, Suite 23
San Antonio, TX 78257-9721
210-826-1488
http://www.avecct.org

Contact the academy for information on certification.

Alliance of Marine Mammal Parks and Aquariums
ammpa@aol.com
http://www.ammpa.org

Visit the alliance's Web site for information on marine mammals, internships, and publications.

American Animal Hospital Association

12575 West Bayaud Avenue
Lakewood, CO 80228-2021
303-986-2800
info@aahanet.org
http://www.aahanet.org

The association represents the professional interests of veterinarians who primarily treat companion animals. Visit its Web site for information on practice issues and publications.

American Association of Equine Practitioners

4075 Iron Works Parkway
Lexington, KY 40511-8483
859-233-0147
aaepoffice@aaep.org
http://www.aaep.org/index.php

Visit the association's Web site for job listings, information on careers, membership for veterinary students, internships/externships for veterinary students, and Shadow a Veterinarian, a program for students of all ages who would like to learn more about career opportunities in equine veterinary medicine.

American Association of Equine Veterinary Technicians and Assistants

http://www.aaevt.com

Visit the association's Web site for job listings and information on certification.

American Association of Wildlife Veterinarians

http://www.aawv.net

Visit the association's Web site for job listings and information about wildlife veterinarians.

American Association of Zoo Keepers

3601 SW 29th Street
Topeka, KS 66614-2054
785-273-9149
http://www.aazk.org

Visit the association's Web site to read "Zoo Keeping as a Career," participate in discussion boards about the career, access job listings, and learn more about *Animal Keepers' Forum*. The association also offers membership to college students and anyone who is interested in the profession.

American Association of Zoo Veterinarians

581705 White Oak Road
Yulee, FL 32097-2169
904-225-3275
http://www.aazv.org

Visit the association's Web site for job listings, news about zoos around the world, the *Journal of Zoo & Wildlife Medicine*, information on internships and externships and zoo and wildlife clubs for veterinary students, and discussion boards.

American Humane Association

63 Inverness Drive East
Englewood, CO 80112-5117
800-227-4645

info@americanhumane.org
http://www.americanhumane.org

The American Humane Association works to protect both children and animals. Its Web site lists current job opportunities in animal protection, offers information on publications, and provides links to other animal welfare organizations.

American Institute of Biological Sciences

1444 I Street, NW, Suite 200
Washington, DC 20005-6535
202-628-1500
http://www.aibs.org

The institute is a membership organization for biologists and professional societies and organizations. Visit its Web site for information on careers and publications.

American Kennel Club

8051 Arco Corporate Drive,
   Suite 100
Raleigh, NC 27617-3390
919-233-9767
http://www.akc.org

The club sponsors more than 15,000 dog competitions annually. Visit its Web site for information on becoming an animal breeder, including articles, publications, and podcasts. The club also offers scholarships for veterinary students and *Careers in Dogs*, an online publication that details a variety of careers for dog lovers—from handler and groomer, to animal behaviorist, veterinarian, and photographer.

American Society for the Prevention of Cruelty to Animals

424 East 92nd Street
New York, NY 10128-6804
212-876-7700
http://www.aspca.org

The society provides training programs for shelter workers and offers membership to people who support the humane treatment of animals. Visit its Web site for information on career options and volunteer opportunities, facts about animal shelters, membership, publications, blogs, and discussion boards.

American Society of Limnology and Oceanography

5400 Bosque Boulevard, Suite 680
Waco, TX 76710-4446
800-929-2756
business@aslo.org
http://www.aslo.org

The society offers information on careers, volunteer positions, publications, and internships and jobs for college students. It also offers diversity programs to encourage students of color to enter the field.

American Veterinary Medical Association (AVMA)

1931 North Meacham Road,
   Suite 100
Schaumburg, IL 60173-4360
800-248-2862
avmainfo@avma.org
http://www.avma.org

The AVMA is the leading veterinary professional association in the United States.

It "represents more than 78,000 veterinarians working in private and corporate practice, government, industry, academia, and uniformed services." Visit the association's Web site for information on careers, a list of accredited schools, publications such as the *Journal of the American Veterinary Medical Association*, job listings, and career advice.

Animal and Plant Health Inspection Service

U.S. Department of Agriculture
1400 Independence Avenue, SW
Washington, DC 20250-0002
APHIS.Web@aphis.usda.gov
http://www.aphis.usda.gov

Visit the service's Web site for information on veterinary opportunities in the federal government and scholarship, internship, and work programs for students in high school through graduate school.

Association of American Veterinary Medical Colleges

1101 Vermont Avenue, NW,
  Suite 301
Washington, DC 20005-3539
202-371-9195
http://www.aavmc.org

The association represents 32 veterinary medical colleges in the United States and Canada. Visit its Web site for information on applying to veterinary school, a list of veterinary programs, job listings, details on the *Journal of Veterinary Medical Education*, and information on externships and financial aid for veterinary students.

Association of Pet Dog Trainers (ADPT)

150 Executive Center Drive, Box 35
Greenville, SC 29615-4505
800-738-3647
information@apdt.com
http://www.apdt.com

Visit the association's Web site for dog training tips; career, education, and certification information; and to read a sample issue of *ADPT Chronicle of the Dog.*

Association of Zoos and Aquariums (AZA)

8403 Colesville Road, Suite 710
Silver Spring, MD 20910-3314
301-562-0777
http://www.aza.org

Visit the association's Web site for information on conservation programs and careers in aquatic and marine science, job listings, a list of accredited zoos throughout the world, and to read *CONNECT* magazine. It also offers an associate membership category "for zoo and aquarium professionals, as well as other interested parties, who want to support and forward the mission, vision, and goals of AZA."

Association of Zoo Veterinary Technicians

c/o Roger Williams Park Zoo
1000 Elmwood Avenue
Providence, RI 02907-3655
http://www.azvt.org

Visit the association's Web site for information on job listings; details on externships, internships, and preceptorships for college students and postgraduates;

and to participate in a discussion forum. The association also offers a membership option for "any technical or non-technical person interested in exotic or zoo veterinary technology."

Bureau of Land Management (BLM)

U.S. Department of the Interior
1849 C Street, Room 5665
Washington, DC 20240-0001
202-208-3801
http://www.blm.gov

This U.S. government agency employs environmental professionals, including zoologists. Visit the BLM's Web site for information on its land holdings and career and volunteer opportunities.

Certification Council for Professional Dog Trainers

Professional Testing Corporation
1350 Broadway, 17th Floor
New York, NY 10018-7702
212-356-0682
administrator@ccpdt.org
http://www.ccpdt.org

Contact the council for information on certification for dog trainers.

Delta Society

875 124th Avenue, NE, Suite 101
Bellevue, WA 98005-2531
425-679-5500
info@deltasociety.org
http://www.deltasociety.org

The Delta Society "is dedicated to improving human health through therapy and service animals." Visit its Web site for information on volunteer opportunities and publications. The society also offers membership to anyone who supports its goals.

Dogs for the Deaf

10175 Wheeler Road
Central Point, OR 97502-9360
541-826-9220
info@dogsforthedeaf.org
http://www.dogsforthedeaf.org

This organization rescues dogs and trains them to help people live better, more productive lives.

Earthwatch Institute

Three Clock Tower Place,
Suite 100
PO Box 75
Maynard, MA 01754-2549
800-776-0188
info@earthwatch.org
http://www.earthwatch.org

This organization offers international environmental expeditions that educate people about biodiversity, sustainability, habitat loss, coral reef health, indigenous cultures, climate change, and other environmental issues. Students can become members of the institute and participate in summer activities.

Ecological Society of America (ESA)

1990 M Street, NW, Suite 700
Washington, DC 20036-3415
202-833-8773
esahq@esa.org
http://esa.org

In addition to certification and membership for college students, the ESA offers a wide variety of publications, including *Issues in Ecology, Careers in Ecology*, and fact sheets about specific ecological concerns.

Friends of the Earth

1717 Massachusetts Avenue,
  Suite 600
Washington, DC 20036-2002
877-843-8687
http://www.foe.org

This group offers internships and fellowships for college and graduate students with an interest in environmental issues. Membership in the organization is also available.

Humane Society of the United States

2100 L Street, NW
Washington, DC 20037-1525
202-452-1100
http://www.hsus.org

The Humane Society of the United States advocates for animals, the earth, and the environment. Visit its Web site to read educational articles about animals and animal care and the work of the organization. Membership is available to anyone who supports the society's goals. Members receive *All Animals*, an attractive quarterly publication.

Intergroom

76 Carol Drive
Dedham, MA 02026-6635
781-326-3376
http://www.intergroom.com

Contact Intergroom for information on grooming competitions and conferences.

International Association of Canine Professionals

http://www.dogpro.org

The association offers membership options for walkers, groomers, kennel owners, veterinarians, pet sitters, and other professionals in the dog world—including a membership category for those who have "an active interest in making a career within the canine profession, but do not yet have the experience to qualify for acceptance" at professional membership levels. Visit its Web site for information on membership, certification, training, and other topics.

International Marine Animal Trainers' Association

1200 South Lake Shore Drive
Chicago, IL 60605-2490
312-692-3193
info@imata.org
http://www.imata.org

Visit the association's Web site for information on careers, endangered species, useful books and other publications, and student membership (for "anyone who is interested in the objectives of the association, and supports them").

International Society of Canine Cosmetologists

2702 Covington Drive
Garland, TX 75040-3822
http://www.petstylist.com/ISCC/
  ISCCMain.htm

Contact the society for information on certification and training programs and workshops.

Marine Technology Society
5565 Sterrett Place, Suite 108
Columbia, MD 21044-2606
410-884-5330
http://www.mtsociety.org

Visit the society's Web site for information on programs for students in grades six through 12, the publication *Education and Training Programs in Oceanography and Related Fields* (which is available for a small fee), and information on membership for college students and those with a general interest in the marine field.

National Animal Control Association
PO Box 480851
Kansas City, MO 64148-0851
913-768-1319
naca@nacanet.org
http://nacanet.org

The association "promotes professionalism in the animal protection care and humane law enforcement field." Visit its Web site for information on careers and publications.

National Association of Dog Obedience Instructors
PMB 369, 729 Grapevine Highway
Hurst, TX 76054-2085
http://www.nadoi.org

Visit the association's Web site for information on entering the field, schools, and publications.

National Association of Professional Pet Sitters
15000 Commerce Parkway, Suite C
Mt. Laurel, NJ 08054-2212
856-439-0324
napps@ahint.com
http://www.petsitters.org

The association offers information on pet care, pet sitting careers, certification, and more at its Web site. It also offers a membership category for "those who are interested in the pet sitting profession, but are not currently active in the industry."

National Association of Veterinary Technicians in America
50 South Pickett Street, Suite 110
Alexandria, VA 22304-7206
703-740-8737
info@navta.net
http://www.navta.net

Information on veterinary technician specialties, college student membership, college student chapters, *The NAVTA Journal,* and jobs is available at the association's Web site.

National Audubon Society
225 Varick Street, 7th Floor
New York, NY 10014-4396
212-979-3000
http://www.audubon.org

This is a membership organization for people and organizations that are committed to "conserving and restoring natural ecosystems, focusing on birds, other wildlife, and their habitats for the benefit of humanity and the earth's biological diversity." Visit its Web site for detailed information and illustrations of birds in the United States and an overview of its programs.

National Dairy Shrine (NDS)
PO Box 1
Maribel, WI 54227-0001
920-863-6333
info@dairyshrine.org
http://www.dairyshrine.org

The NDS is a membership organization for people in the dairy industry—from children and teens to college students and scientists. It offers scholarships for high school juniors and seniors and college students, publications, a list of internships available from other organizations, and other resources.

National Dog Groomers
Association of America Inc.
PO Box 101
Clark, PA 16113-0101
724-962-2711
http://www.nationaldoggroomers
   .com

Contact the association for information on shows, new grooming products and techniques, workshops, and certification.

National FFA Organization
6060 FFA Drive
PO Box 68960
Indianapolis, IN 46268-0960
317-802-6060
http://www.ffa.org

This organization is "dedicated to making a positive difference in the lives of students by developing their potential for premier leadership, personal growth, and career success through agricultural education." It offers more than $2 million in scholarships and a variety of programs for youth.

National 4-H Council
7100 Connecticut Avenue
Chevy Chase, MD 20815-4934
301-961-2800
info@fourhcouncil.edu
http://4-h.org

4-H Clubs teach young people about science, engineering, and technology; healthy living; and citizenship via clubs, camps, competitions, and other activities. It has 6 million members in the United States. 4-H offers financial aid to high school and college students through its chapters, which are located throughout the United States. Visit the 4-H national organization's Web site for information on a chapter near you and the scholarship programs it offers.

National Oceanic and
Atmospheric Administration
1401 Constitution Avenue, NW,
   Room 5128
Washington, DC 20230-0001
http://www.noaa.gov

The National Oceanic and Atmospheric Administration says that its reach "goes from the surface of the sun to the depths of the ocean floor." Visit its Web site for information on environmental topics such as climate monitoring, fisheries management, and coastal restoration, as well as details on careers, summer programs and paid internships for young people, and financial aid for college-level students.

National Parks Conservation Association

1300 19th Street, NW, Suite 300
Washington, DC 20036-1628
800-628-7275
npca@npca.org
http://www.npca.org

The association has a goal of protecting our national parks and historical sites. Visit its Web site for general information on national parks and to subscribe to *National Parks* magazine.

National Park Service (NPS)

U.S. Department of the Interior
1849 C Street, NW
Washington, DC 20240-0001
202-208-6843
http://www.nps.gov

Visit the NPS's Web site for information on national parks and other protected areas in the United States, careers, volunteer opportunities, internships, and youth programs.

National Wildlife Federation

11100 Wildlife Center Drive
Reston, VA 20190-5362
800-822-9919
http://www.nwf.org

Visit the federation's Web site for information on internships, volunteerships, job opportunities, and *National Wildlife* magazine.

The Nature Conservancy

4245 North Fairfax Drive, Suite 100
Arlington, VA 22203-1606
703-841-5300
comment@tnc.org
http://nature.org

The Nature Conservancy's "mission is to preserve the plants, animals and natural communities that represent the diversity of life on Earth by protecting the lands and waters they need to survive." It has protected more than 119 million acres of land and 5,000 miles of rivers throughout the world. Visit its Web site for information on conservation, careers, internships, membership, volunteerships, and more.

The Oceanography Society

PO Box 1931
Rockville, MD 20849-1931
301-251-7708
info@tos.org
http://www.tos.org

The society offers *Oceanography* magazine and membership for college students. Visit its Web site for more information.

Pet Care Services Association

1702 East Pikes Peak Avenue
Colorado Springs, CO 80909-5717
877-570-7788
http://www.petcareservices.org

This is a professional membership association for pet boarders, sitters, groomers, animal trainers, and pet suppliers. It offers a membership category for any "individual who is interested in the pet care industry, but who does not presently operate a non-veterinary pet care business." Visit the association's Web site for information on training opportunities, membership, certification, networking events, and pet health.

Pet Sitters International

201 East King Street
King, NC 27021-9161
336-983-9222
info@petsit.com
http://www.petsit.com

Visit this organization's Web site for information on certification, pet care, a general overview of pet sitting, and *The WORLD of Professional Pet Sitting.*

Society for Integrative and Comparative Biology

1313 Dolley Madison Boulevard,
    Suite 402
McLean, VA 22101-3926
800-955-1236
SICB@BurkInc.com
http://www.sicb.org

The society is a good source of information about all areas and aspects of zoology. Visit its Web site for information on careers, job listings, publications, and membership for college students.

Society of Animal Welfare Administrators

15508 West Bell Road,
    Suite 101- 613
Surprise, AZ 85374-3436
888-600-3648
SAWAconnect@ymail.com
http://www.sawanetwork.org

Visit the society's Web site for information on certification and job listings.

Student Conservation Association (SCA)

689 River Road
PO Box 550
Charlestown, NH 03603-0550
603-543-1700
http://www.thesca.org

The SCA is a nonprofit environmental organization that offers summer trail crew opportunities to high school students and conservation internships to those 18 years old and over. Visit its Web site for detailed information about these programs.

U.S. Department of Agriculture (USDA)

1400 Independence Avenue, SW
Washington, DC 20250-0002
http://www.usda.gov

Visit the USDA's Web site for information on careers, plant and animal safety, internships and employment opportunities, and financial aid.

U.S. Fish and Wildlife Service

U.S. Department of the Interior
Division of Human Resources
4401 North Fairfax Drive,
    Mailstop: 2000
Arlington, VA 22203-1610
800-344-WILD
http://www.fws.gov/jobs

The U.S. Fish and Wildlife Service manages the 96 million-acre National Wildlife Refuge System. This system includes

550 National Wildlife Refuges, thousands of smaller wetlands, and other special management areas. Visit its Web site for information on careers, conservation, the *Endangered Species Bulletin*, and volunteer opportunities.

Veterinary Business Management Association
http://www.vbma.biz

This organization is a "student-driven organization dedicated to advancing the profession through increasing business knowledge, creating networking opportunities, and empowering students to achieve their personal and professional goals." It has chapters on campuses across the United States and around the world. Visit its Web site to learn more chapters, externships, and suggested resources.

Wildlife Conservation Society
2300 Southern Boulevard
Bronx, NY 10460-1068
718-220-5100
http://www.wcs.org

The society seeks to save wildlife and wild places. Visit its Web site to learn more about programs for teens and to read sample articles from *Wildlife Conservation Magazine*.

The Wildlife Society
5410 Grosvenor Lane, Suite 200
Bethesda, MD 20814-2144
301-897-9770
http://www.wildlife.org

The Wildlife Society offers *Careers in Wildlife Conservation*, which details more than 10 careers in the field. The publication is available at its Web site, along with information on other publications, student chapters, certification, and membership for college students or anyone who is interested in wildlife conservation and management.

World Society for the Protection of Animals
Lincoln Plaza
89 South Street, Suite 201
Boston, MA 02111-2678
800-883-9772
http://www.wspa-americas.org

The society is the "world's largest alliance of animal welfare groups." Visit its Web site for information on animal welfare issues and society programs.

Zoological Association of America
PO Box 511275
Punta Gorda, FL 33951-1275
813-449-4356
info@zaa.org
http://www.zaa.org

The association "promotes conservation, preservation, and propagation of animals in both private and public domains." It offers a membership category for those who support its goals.

Index

Entries and page numbers in **bold** indicate major treatment of a topic.